THE STRUGGLE AND THE CONQUEST

by
Sir Novelle H. Richards, K.G.C.N.
1917 - 1986

2nd Edition
Volumes I, II & Appendices

Foreword by
Hon. Gaston A. Browne, M.P.

Editors:
Ivor B. Ford
Tyra Mason
Shawn M. Nicholas

SEABURN

New York ■ Athens

The Struggle And the Conquest
First Published by the Author,
Sir Novelle H. Richards, K.G.C.N.

1st Edition
(1963 & 1981)

2nd & Posthumous Edition
Researched, Edited and Compiled by
Ivor B. Ford, Tyra Mason, Shawn M. Nicholas

Published by Seaburn Publishers Group
PO Box 2085
Long Island City, NY 11102 USA
www.seaburn.com

ISBN: 1-59232-067-8

Acknowledgment

When I was invited by the Richards' Family to undertake the task of trying to put together a 2nd Edition of both the **Struggle and the Conquest** and the **Locusts' Years,** two literary works penned by the late Sir Novelle H. Richards, little did I conceive that the challenge would have been so demanding. However, despite the many temptations to abandon the project while in midstream, it was the continued encouragement of Sir Novelle's Grandson, the Hon. Gaston Browne, and the strong support and assistance of a personal friend and very talented Daughter of the Soil, Miss Shawn Nicholas, that provided that fortitude to complete this herculean mandate.

A project of this nature demands research, much time and energy. It would have been much easier to start from scratch to write the book rather than to have to try to improve upon another architect's masterpiece. Throughout the exercise, care had to be taken so as not to change the style and inmost thoughts of the author at the time that the two volumes were written. In this effort, I trust that we have succeeded.

After some two years' work on this project, I wish to take this opportunity to thank a number of persons who were in the forefront of the heavy task of preparing what you now hold in your hands.

Firstly, profound gratitude is due to the Hon. Gaston Browne who, after approaching me to take on the commitment, readily agreed to foreword this 2nd Edition. He was also available to reassure me and to give me a free hand to use my judgment and discretion whenever the situation demanded. The confidence of the Richards' Family is most valuable in such a difficult and challenging undertaking.

Secondly, after the initial typing of both volumes, words are inadequate to express appreciation and thanks for the tremendous amount of work and time expended by Miss Shawn Nicholas, who almost single-handedly edited the whole of Volume I. She was virtually pressured by the constraints of time to complete the exercise to fit into the vice-like schedule to meet the initial deadlines.

Then, too, there were two very dedicated individuals who have often felt the weight of my demanding pressure of getting back to me the portions of chapters they were assigned to proof. These two ladies, Mrs. Clair Willet-Tonge and Miss Consuela Parker, both worked untiringly and faithfully to meet the stipulated time slots. To these ladies, bushels of thanks.

The initial re-typing of the entire original two volumes presented a mountainous challenge which literally frightened me. However, this aspect of the project was skillfully and efficiently undertaken by Miss Chantian Kirwan who must be commended for even attempting the task. To Miss Kirwan, I offer warmest congratulations and heart-felt gratitude.

Cognizant of the valuable information contained in this Book, the Cabinet of Antigua and Barbuda decided firstly, to designate it as an official text for the schools in Antigua and Barbuda in the study of Political Science and Social Studies and, secondly, to acquire 3000 copies for distribution in the schools. These decisions by the Government of Antigua and Barbuda place a greater responsibility on us to ensure that the Book meets the required acceptable standard associated with official texts for our schools.

Next, our Publishers must be highly commended for undertaking the responsibility of publishing this Edition. Special thanks are due to both Tyra and her husband, Dr. Chekwas, owners of the **Seaburn Publishing Group** and the rest of their staff members for their personal interest in this project. Despite a number of inevitable hitches along the way, their support and guidance have been a source of strength to us in this National effort. Thanks to them all.

Finally, to any and everyone who played a role in the realization of the publication of this combined Posthumous Edition of the **Struggle and the Conquest**, a heartfelt thanks. We trust that your efforts will be justly rewarded by what you now hold in your hands.

To all I say Thank you most kindly.

Ivor B. Ford
Executive Editor

Foreword

Sir Novelle Hamilton Richards, K.G.C.N., appropriately was born in Liberty Village in the Parish of St. Paul, Antigua. This talented and versatile *Son of the Soil* never failed to express his love for his country and race. As well as an author of recognised repute, the man of whom I have the distinct honour of being his grandson, has penned several patriotic songs, each extolling the undiminished love he cultivated and fostered for his Native Antigua and Barbuda during his 69 years of life.

When my grandfather decided to record the events surrounding the birth and early growth of the trade union movement in Antigua and Barbuda, little did he envisage the void he would be filling by providing such an important reservoir of information relative to perhaps the most dynamic and active period in the social transformation and development in the life of the people of Antigua and Barbuda. This forty-two year period in the life of these two Islands, located at the gateway to the Caribbean Archipelago, was the most momentous and pivotal in this young Nation's existence. It was during this period too, that poverty was irrevocably toppled and the entire social order was reversed where the plantocrats, or ruling class, were challenged for leadership and management of the peoples' affairs.

Despite the rich and colourful history of the people of these two islands comprising the Nation of Antigua and Barbuda, much of it is regrettably un-recorded and accordingly is lost through the passage of time. Fortunately for us and in some smaller way the rest of the Caribbean, the events as recorded in this book, which have impacted so heavily on the overall development of the people of this country and our Region, were captured and preserved.

The contents of both volumes are not only relevant, but informative. The second volume in particular, outlines the circumstances surrounding the fracture of the Antigua Trades and Labour Union and the eventual birth of its splinter and rival organisation, the Antigua Workers Union. For the student of History, Political Science and Social Study, The Struggle and the Conquest offers an invaluable treasury of resource material which has been described by many as very enlightening and instructive. The decision of the Government of Antigua and Barbuda to designate The Struggle and the Conquest as an official text for schools throughout the country's education system in the study of History, Political Science and Social Study, is not only farsighted, but in the view of many historians, professors, teachers and students, well overdue.

Another important decision by the Family of the late author to combine both volumes into one concise book will, thankfully, eliminate the problems which prevented many individuals from having the complete work in a convenient edition. Editors of this 2nd Edition, with the approval of the Richards' Family, consciously decided to further enhance this new Edition with some relevant photographs. This addition will enable readers, especially young students, to see for themselves some of the individuals and places written about.

Preparation of this Edition was extensive, difficult and challenging, but I am confident that readers will appreciate the value of what has been published. With the publication of the 2nd combined Edition of <u>The Struggle and the Conquest</u>, it is hoped that the Caribbean Examinations Council (CXC) will eventually find it useful and necessary to include it as part of its resource and reference documents for use in the relevant subject areas of study for students throughout the Region as a whole.

And so, as you open the pages of this the 2nd and combined Edition of <u>The Struggle and the Conquest,</u> it is the hope and wish of the Richards' family that the efforts of the late Sir Novelle Hamilton Richards, K.G.C.N., will be cherished and appreciated. It is also our hope that the untiring, dedicated and invaluable contribution of the Editor of this Edition, Ivor B. Ford, and his able and efficient assistant, Miss Shawn M. Nicholas and the rest of the team, will surely achieve the original goals of my Grandfather, to provide accurate and invaluable information for students of History, Political Science and Social Study.

The 2nd Edition of <u>The Struggle and the Conquest</u> is published in memory of the life, work and time of the late Novelle Hamilton Richards, K.G.C.N., author, poet, journalist, trade unionist, legislator diplomat and statesman.

Gaston A. Browne
Grandson

National Anthem Antigua and Barbuda

Fair Antigua and Barbuda!

We, thy Sons and Daughters stand

Strong and firm in peace or danger

To safeguard our Native Land;

We commit ourselves to building

A true Nation, brave and free!

Ever striving, ever seeking

T'well in love and unity.

Raise the Standard! raise it boldly!

Answer now to duty's call:

To the service of your Country,

Sparing nothing, giving all!

Gird your loins and join the battle

'Gainst fear, hate and poverty,

Each endeavouring, all achieving:

Live in peace where man is free!

God of nations, let Thy blessing

Fall upon this Land of ours;

Rain and sunshine ever sending,

Fill Her fields with crops and flowers;

We, Her Children do implore Thee:

Give us strength, faith, loyalty;

Never failing, all enduring

To defend Her liberty.

Lyrics by
Sir Novelle H. Richards, K.G.C.N (1917-1986)

Melody & Musical Arrangement by
Walter P. Chambers O.M. (1908-2003)

Contents

APPENDIX 3 – Federate Now

APPENDIX 4

Author's Note

For sometime now, I have been seriously considering that it would be useful to get on record some of the things that have taken place during the eventful years of the Trade Union activities and political developments in Antigua and Barbuda.

While there are Minutes of the Legislative Council that may be referred to, and unfortunately, some of these Minutes were destroyed in the 1950 fire at the Federal Secretariat of the Leeward Islands, reference may be made to past editions of newspapers. These references would not throw a full light on many of the happenings of that period, some of which were never fully revealed to the public.

As one who was intimately involved with the activities of the Trade Union Movement almost from its inception and also with other aspects of public life in Antigua and Barbuda, I believe I am able to give as clear a picture as possible from my first-hand knowledge and experience of the growth and structure of the Antiguan and Barbadian society, and the events associated with it.

In this Book, I have tried to present an unbiased picture of a series of events, and if I have erred, I hope it is on the side of fairness. While the emphasis is on the Trade Union Movement and the struggles for its survival, it also touches on other aspects of the social, economic and political developments of the Twin-Island Territory. I make no pretensions to writing a history of Antigua and Barbuda, but many of the things I have outlined in this Book are now history and may be accepted as such. For no history of Antigua and Barbuda during this period could ignore the influence the Trade Union Movement had on the shaping of events. I might go so far as to say that the history of Antigua and Barbuda from 1939 to 1964 is the history of the Trade Union Movement in Antigua and Barbuda.

I therefore commend this Book to my readers and hope it gives the satisfaction it is intended to do.

Novelle H. Richards

Profile

The Island of Antigua has an area of 108 square miles, and is included in the Leeward Islands' group of the Lesser Antilles in the Caribbean. It has as its dependencies the islands of Barbuda with an area of 68 square miles and Redonda, approximately one half square mile, making a combined total area of 1776 ½ square miles.

The Island lies between 61° 40' and 61° 54' West Longitude and 17° 10' North Latitude; it is one of the most northerly of the chain of islands in the Eastern Caribbean.

Antigua was discovered by Christopher Columbus in 1493 on his second voyage and was named by him after a church in Seville Spain, Santa Maria de la Antigua. The Spaniards attempted to settle the Island in 1520, but it was too dry for them. There are no rivers in the Island, the highest hills are found in the southwest, where Boggy Peak, the highest point, reaches a height of 1,319 feet above sea level. In the north and east, the terrain is undulating and flat and is composed of calcareous marl and coarse sandstone, while the central portion is composed of sedimentary rocks and clay deposits. The average rainfall of Antigua is between 43 and 45 inches per annum and the Island is subject to severe droughts.

The coastline of Antigua is irregular in shape with many inlets and bays. These provide some very fine natural harbours but not sufficient depth to allow the entry of large ships, although they were excellent for the smaller vessels of the 18th and early 19th centuries. The Naval Dock Yard at English Harbour is of particular interest. It was the main base of the British Navy in the West Indies during Sir Horatio Nelson's command, and was closed as an operational base in 1854.

The Dockyard is associated with Prince William Henry, Duke of Clarence; afterwards, King William IV, who as a young man, was stationed at the Dockyard in charge of H.M.S. Pegasus. It was at the Dockyard that a deep friendship developed between the young Prince and Horatio Nelson, the Captain of the Boreas.

Antigua and Barbuda has a tropical climate, modified by oceanic influences. The mean annual temperature varies from 73°F to 83°F, whilst, the diurnal range is from 72°F to 83°F in winter, to 75°F to 87°F in summer. There is very little valuable forests cover; the original cover of logwood, mahogany, white cedar and acacia were removed in the early days of intensive sugar cultivation. Now what forest cover there is, comprises of thorn and scrub.

In 1629, the French, under d'Esnambuc, made an abortive attempt at settlement in Antigua, but abandoned it. Then in 1632, Thomas Warner coming from St. Kitts, succeeded in establishing a colony at Willoughby Bay. All through the Napoleonic Wars when colonies in the Caribbean changed hands between the Metropolitan countries, Antigua remained British. The French never captured Antigua, though they succeeded in making a landing on the Island. As a result, there is no trace of French influence on the Island.

In the early days, the chief crops of Antigua and Barbuda were tobacco and indigo. They gave way to sugar, which remained the most important crop in the Islands.

Antigua and Barbuda has an estimated population of 75,000, approximately 1,500 of whom lives in Barbuda. Redonda is uninhabited. The Chief Town is St. John's, the capital of the Islands, with a population estimated at 30,000. St. John's is also the main port, the centre of commerce and seat of Administration. There are 45 villages, the largest of which is Liberta with about 4,000 population. The Islands are supplied with a wide network of roads totalling some 160 miles. They are also served by one of the finest Airports in the Caribbean, the International Airport at Coolidge, where B.A.(British Airways), B.W.I.A. (British West Indian Airways), Air France, LIAT (Leeward Islands Air Transport), A.A. (American Airlines) and a host of other carriers support a thriving tourist trade. There are several first class hotels as well.

Antigua and Barbuda is a fully independent democracy which is governed by an elected Government operating under the Westminister Model of Parliamentary Democracy. Its constitution was negotiated with Great Britain in 1980 and on 1st November, 1981, the umbilical cord between Great Britain and the former Associated States was finally severed.

Antigua and Barbuda is served by a bi-cameral legislature comprising of a 17 member elected House of Representatives, each representing a defined constituency. The other chamber of the Legislature is the Senate which is composed of 18 nominated members: 10 by the ruling Party, 4 by the Official Opposition and the others representing special interests, including Barbuda. The 17 constituencies into which the Nation is divided are:

St. John's City West	All Saints East & St. Luke
St. John's City West	All Saints West
St. John's City South	St. George's
St. John's Rural West	St. Peter's
St. John's Rural East	St. Phillip's North
St. John's Rural South	St. Phillip's South
St. John's Rural North	St. Paul's
St. Mary's North	Barbuda
St. Mary's South	

The House of Representative is presided over by a Speaker whom may be elected from among the membership of the House, or the House may decide to elect any other individual from outside the House to be its Chief Presiding Officer. This presiding officer is known as the Speaker. The Senate is presided over by a President who is chosen from among them.

The chief source of day-to-day authority of administration of affairs of state in Antigua and Barbuda is the Cabinet which forms the executive arm of the three-pronged parliamentary democracy. The other two main arms are the Legislature, Elected House of Representatives and the Senate which is responsible for making the laws governing the society. Finally, the Judiciary is responsible for interpreting the laws enacted by the Legislature. The Judiciary cannot and does not make laws; it can only pass judgment on the enacted laws of the Legislature.

The Ceremonial Head of State is a Governor-General, who represents Her Majesty, Queen Elizabeth II. As a member of the Commonwealth of Nations and as required by the Westminister Model by which Antigua and Barbuda is administered, the British Monarch is the tutular Head of State of Antigua and Barbuda. Constitutionally, Antigua and Barbuda chooses its Governments by way of a general election every five years.

List of Photographs

Photo No. 1   H.E. Sir Kenneth D. Blackburne, G.C.M.G., O.B.E.

Photo No. 2   Mr. Clement Silston, Founder of Silston's Library

Photo No. 3   H.E. Sir Wilfred E. Jacobs, G.C.M.G., K.C.V.O., M.B.E., Q.C.
Associated States Governor, First Governor-General of Antigua
and Barbuda

Photo No. 4   Lord Oliver Baldwin, 2nd Earl of Bewdley
The man who broke the social barrier in Antigua and Barbuda
Governor of the Leeward Islands (1947 – 1949)

Photo No. 5   Wattle and Daub House, typical home of the working class

Photo No. 6   Industrial Park at Cassada Gardens, highlighting Cotton
Ginnery and an Edible Oil Factory

Photo No. 7   The new St. John's Post Office, circa 1950

Photo No. 8   Comrade Reginald St. Claire Stevens
First Elected President of the Antigua Trades & Labour Union

Photo No. 9   First Associated States Cabinet of Antigua and Barbuda, (1967)
Hon. Premier V.C. Bird, Deputy Premier Lionel A. Hurst,
Hon Ernest E. Williams, Hon. E.H. Lake, Hon. McChesney
George

Photo No. 10   H.R.H. Princess Margaret, Sister of H.M. Queen Elizabeth, II,
presents Instruments of Independence to Prime Minister, V.C.
Bird, 1st November, 1981

Photo No. 11   Hon, Vere Cornwall Bird,
Foundation Member, 2nd President of AT& LU
1st Premier and 1st Prime Minister of Antigua and Barbuda

Photo No. 12   The historic Anglican Cathedral Schoolroom, Birthplace of the
Antigua Trades & Labour Union, January 6th, 1939

Photo No. 13   The Hellsgate Steel-band, 1945
The longest surviving steel band in the world

Photo No. 14   The Sugar Mill is a symbol of the bygone era when sugar was
King

Photo No. 15   Slaves cutting cane on a Sugar Estate

PART 1
THE BIRTH AND GROWING PAINS
1939 - 1963

CHAPTER 1
THE SEEDS ARE SOWN

It was the bad thirties. Britain had recently gone off the Gold Standard. In the United States of America, Franklin Delano Roosevelt defeated President Herbert Hoover in the Presidential Elections; the people of the United States looked forward to the New Deal that would take millions of Americans from the bread line to a new era of prosperity.

The West Indies seethed with unrest. From Jamaica to Trinidad and Tobago, it was POVERTY and POVERTY and POVERTY. In the islands where sugar was the staple and only industry, mass unemployment was the order of the day as sugar suffered severely from bad prices and, as would be expected, wages were abysmally low. Several Estates went broke and out of production. Men with families walked for days to find work - any kind of work - without success. They saw their children hungry, sick and ragged, and were unable to help.

Of all the islands in the West Indies, Antigua was possibly the hardest hit. The Island had staked everything on sugar, and it was not only bad prices that had to be faced, but also the inevitable drought that resulted in disastrous crops. Ruin stared many people in the face. Some saw their cherished land holdings sold for taxes they could not pay. Some who were accustomed to receiving help in money and clothing from relatives who migrated to the U.S.A., found that source of help cut off, for their benefactors might have gone on the Bread Line. Antigua was a land of misery and depression, an island of slums and hovels, of barefooted, unkempt people.

The bankrupt Government sought help from the United Kingdom. which brought about a limited amount of relief work with some men securing about two or three days work weekly, or fortnightly, according to the funds available, at the lordly wages of one shilling (EC24 cents) a day. To see men from all parts of the Island lined up in hope of being picked for the windfall and to witness the expression of anxiety on their faces before they were selected was sufficient to move the hardest heart.

While the economic position improved in the United States of America and in Britain, there was hardly any change in Antigua and in the West Indies as a whole. Sugar prices improved slightly and, in Antigua, there were better crops due to good rainfall; the conditions of the workers in the Sugar Industry of the West Indies remained unchanged; Management absorbed the improved prices wholly in an effort to liquidate previous losses.

The unrest that began earlier, developed into a flame, which quickly spread like a bush fire from Jamaica to Trinidad. Riots broke out in Jamaica, St. Vincent, St. Kitts and Trinidad. Antigua and the other Islands were also on the brink of rioting. Law and order throughout the West Indies were severely threatened and reached a point where the British Government became concerned; in an effort to prevent their position from deteriorating yet further, a Royal Commission was appointed under Lord Moyne, to investigate the cause of the unrest and make recommendations.

The appointment of the Royal Commission was a wise step by the then British Government and its recommendations proved to be the turning point in the fortunes and history of the West Indies. Among those selected to serve on the Commission was Sir Walter, afterwards, Lord Citrine who was a great trade union leader in Britain and General Secretary of the powerful Trade Union congress.

In Antigua as in other Islands, the Commission got down to work and investigated the entire structure of the society with emphasis on the social and economic aspects. They found the society completely disorganised and the large numbers of unemployed and under-employed provided a proper breeding ground for the exploitation of labour. They found men with the capacity for leadership from the quality of the evidence given during the Inquiry, but unwilling to lead. It was Sir Walter Citrine who saw and advocated that one of the most pressing needs of the era, was for labour to be organised into the trade union movement.

In Antigua, Sir Walter Citrine undertook to address a meeting of people to explain about trade unionism and the benefits it brought to workers in other countries, and to encourage the workers of Antigua to form a trade union of their own. This meeting was held at the Anglican Cathedral Schoolroom in Church Street and the house was packed to overflowing. The chairman of the meeting was Harold Thomas Wilson, Editor of The Magnet, a daily newspaper, and a prominent public figure, and among those on the platform were Mr. M. D. Leonard Benjamin, a tailor and peasant farmer, who in those days was recommended for his gift of oratory, and Reginald St. Clair Stevens, a Legislator and jeweller.

Sir Walter Citrine was introduced to the audience after welcome remarks by the Chairman, and in a flowing eloquent address, he gripped the full attention of his listeners with his description of the working class movement in Great Britain, and moved then, to resolve that every effort be made to start such a movement in Antigua. It was from that meeting at the Cathedral School Room on the evening of January 1st, 1939, that THE SEEDS WERE SOWN, which eventually germinated, and gave birth to the Antigua Trades & Labour Union.

CHAPTER 2
THE LODGES

The Friendly Societies, or Lodges, were powerful social forces in Antigua. The Free Mason Lodge was created almost entirely for the plantocracy and the upper middle class, while the Odd Fellows and Household of Ruth, the Ulotrichan Friendly Society and others, were created to the lower middle class and the working class. The powerful Lodges, in terms of members, were Odd Fellows with the Household of Ruth as affiliate.

To be a member of the Lodge was one of the greatest ambitions of the Working Class man and woman. Apart from the distinction that it gave them in society and the benefits received, small as they were, during sickness and in times of death, the secrecy surrounding the ritual initiation into membership had a strong and fascinating appeal to people, not only from the superstitious, but because of the curiosity in finding out what really happened behind those closed doors, for the Initiated Lodge Member is bound to secrecy about his Initiation and the Business of the Lodge. Sometimes, persons applying for membership were black-balled as undesirable by a member who would have grievances against them.

The Lodge gave birth to many erstwhile orators, who depended most often on their ability to speak and 'make points' to capture support for their election to high office. The most talkative men found in many villages and in the City were usually office holders in the Lodges. Some of these men considered themselves the patriarchs of the communities. They were all knowing and would be prepared to give advice on everything under the sun.

The highest official post in the Odd Fellows was that of Grand Master. To reach that position depended a great deal on the ability and influence of the individual over the members and officers of the Lodge, for a lot of canvassing goes on at election times and a person has to be very influential to hold an high office as Grand Master for any period after his first election.

The Lodges also had their special banquets for members, and their thanksgiving services when all their members would turn out on parade were led by brass bands bearing their symbols of office. These parades were usually a picturesque sight and drew large crowds. The thanksgiving parade was, to some extent, the crowing glory for Lodge members. At death, the Lodge member is paid the final tribute by a 'turn out' of his Lodge which lead the procession to the church and to the burial place, where members performed their own funeral rites over the grave of their departed brother or sister.

The Antigua Trades & Labour Union was born during the influential period of the Lodges, and in looking for leadership for the Trade Union, it was to the Lodges that all eyes were turned; for it was realised from early that the Trade Union had to be a people's Organization, and therefore, could only draw its membership from the Working Class people who comprised the membership of the several Lodges. It was therefore that the majority of the Trade Union leaders were Lodge Men, a factor which contributed positively to the decline of the Lodges, but saw the rise to greatness of the Trade Union Movement. However, the Lodges began to make a recovery, which was an indication that the Lodge and the Trade Union could live side by side and prosper in a free society.

CHAPTER 3
THE TRADE UNION IS FORMED

Among those who attended the historic meeting at the Cathedral Schoolroom on that New Year's Night, 1939, were to mention a few, N.R. Allen, an Antiguan who resided for a number of years in the United States of America, but had returned to Antigua on vacation to establish a small local business; F.O. Benjamin, a businessman who lived in the U.S.A for a long time; R.H. Lockhart, a prominent lawyer who hailed from Dominica, but had set up practice in Antigua; Berkley A. Richards, a businessman and former accountant at S.R. Mendes, Ltd.; V.C. Bird, one-time Salvation Army Captain and businessman and Samuel A. Henry of Dickinson Bay Street.

These men and others were stirred by the message of trade unionism brought to them by Sir Walter Citrine and immediately after the meeting, got together in discussions to see if action could be taken to form a trade union. It must be remembered however, that an abortive effort was made sometime before by Harold T. Wilson and others to establish a workingman's association that was short-lived. That organization was limited to only certain categories of workers with emphasis on the waterfront and did not include agricultural workers. Internal dissension, (money matters it is believed) was the cause of the failure. Wilson still had hopes of resurrecting the organization and did not take part in the early development of the Antigua Trades & Labour Union, seeing in this new movement a threat to his hopes. He was prepared to have the new Movement come as a bolster to his previous efforts, but others thought differently, for they were afraid that since the people had already lost confidence in the first organization, it would be associated with it.

The Jewellery shop of Reginald St. Clair Stevens located at High and Thames

Streets at the same site of O'Neal's Drug Store, became the meting place for these early discussions. Paradoxically, the Union was to have one of its strongest fights with O'NealS Drug Store. The men concerned were looking for a leader who could rally island wide support for the new movement and in their opinion, Reginald Stevens came close to that choice of leader.

Reginald Stevens was a short man, about five feet four inches in shoes, brown skinned with bushy eye brows and medium size inclining to be fat, quiet looking, but a great fighter. Stevens was Grand Master of the St. John's Lodge, the largest Odd Fellow branch in the Island and so commanded a great deal of influence among the members at any rate. He was at first reluctant to take on the leadership because he felt it would affect his business and his activities in the Lodge and because of the time he would have to devote to the trade union movement. But by persuasion, he decided to give it a try.

N.R. Allen, one of the biggest live wires in the discussions, felt it was time that a meeting should be called, so invitations were sent out to a number of people to attend a meeting on 16th January, 1939. The proposals for forming the trade union were put to the meeting by Allen, who served as Chairman, and the meeting went about appointing provisional officers.

Reginald Stevens was selected first President; B.A. Richards, General Secretary; F.O. Benjamin, Treasurer; V.C. Bird, Griffith Matthew, Randolph H. Lockhart, Thomas Martin, James Jarvis, Stanley R. Walter, C.A. Perry and Thomas Brookes, were elected members of the first executive. Those officers were eventually ratified at the first conference on 26th February, 1940, just after the Antigua Trades and Labour Union was one year old. On 3rd March, 1940, the union was officially registered under the Trade Union Act (1939), with the Registrar of Friendly Societies, the late Roland E. Henry.

The job of organising the trade union was not an easy one. Meetings had to be convened in the city of St. John's and in the villages to explain to the people the reasons for forming the new movement. Thereafter, follow-up meeting were held by the Executive Officers and others, to select leaders in the several areas where it was desirous to have trade union sections.

Eager crowds attended the meetings all over the Island, but the great

22

difficulty was in finding the type of individuals in the various villages that were prepared to undertake the job of running the Sections. Some who were ready to lead did not have the ability, and many who had the ability, were afraid or reluctant, because they did not want to contend with Management. The Estates had great influence over village life and many villagers depended on the willingness of Estate Management to rent small plots of lands for cultivation to augment the low wages received on the Estates. A few leading villages would be able to secure as much as five acres of land to rent, but there was no security of tenure, and they had to keep on the good side of management if they were to be left undisturbed. It was difficult to get these people who rented lands on the Estates to take part officially in the Union, for they saw before them the loss of their land; management went as far as to threaten workers with eviction if they joined the Union. Many of them who defied the threat were given short notice, with little or no compensation for their crops. The Agricultural Small Holdings Act (1938), a Statute of the Leeward Islands Federal Legislature, was more in favour of the landlord than the tenant, and the majority of the tenants did not have the means of going to court to protect their interest, and, with the security of land, chose rather to take matters easily, with the hope of getting back at a later date in the favour of the management, to have their land restored.

Despite these difficulties however, the drive for membership of the Trade Union continued and the ranks began to swell. Men from St. John's travelled far and wide throughout the Island - Sunday after Sunday - and weeknights, taking the message of Trade Unionism to the people. The backbone of resistance to the Trade Union Movement was broken, and many who were at first reluctant, offered their services as Section Officers. The stage was now being set for action. During those early months of organising the Trade Union, there was regular correspondence between Reginald Stevens and Sir Walter Citrine, whose willing help and guidance were sought by the Union. A Letter to Sir Walter Citrine dated 18th March, 1939 and signed by Stevens and B.A. Richards is re-produced below.

St. John, Antigua,

18th March, 1939

Sir Walter Citrine

Port of Spain,

Trinidad

Dear Sir,

We, the undersigned beg to acknowledge receipt of your letter dated 27th January addressed to Mr. S.A. Henry who at one time affiliated himself with us has resigned on account of his religious convictions.

The copies of the model rules and other documents sent to us have been received for which kindly accept our hearty thanks and appreciation.

Again we must say thanks for the very advice given to us in regard to the Charter and Trade Union Laws here. We feel perfectly sure that you will do your best to recommend that this law be changed so as to enable us to be registered under the proper and suitable law.

For your information; please note that we have started to form this organization about seven weeks ago and are pleased to state that we have now on record 750 members and 78 pounds on the Bank. It has entailed quite a lot of work on the shoulders especially to traverse the country districts where most of the labouring class live and who have the worst financial difficulties to exist, we however hope that in a short time these poor people will be greatly relieved from their present conditions.

We are just preparing to form our rules and shall appreciate any useful advice you may think fit.

Yours faithfully,

The Antigua Trade & Labour Union,

R. St. Clair Stevens, President

B.A. Richards, Secretary

Other letters followed the same pattern. On 20th April, 1939, Stevens was able to report to Sir Walter Citrine who had then arrived back in London that the membership had reached 2860 and that there was £360 on the Bank. An extract from the same letter is of significance. The letter referred to the encouraging response of the people and went on to say: "Despite the obstacles that are placed in our way by those who feel themselves rulers of our country by their financial positions, and are trying all they can to debar our progress, we are bound to succeed, so that we are now asking you to be our instructor and director for all times and for which we shall be thankful."

"From our feelings as stated before and for our better protection, if it is possible, we will like to be affiliated with your Unions and be under your supervision and be given the Charter which you thought could be fixed up by your officers as mentioned in your letter of a previous date, as we feel if that could be done, we would be safe against the laws they may feel to legislate and more so you felt that the present laws are not good enough for a Union."

It its important to note the fears that existed at that time among the leaders and the feeling of paternalism they sought to encourage and develop between the British movement and the new organisation.

It was this fear and paternal, negative approach that eventually led to Stevens' downfall in 1944, when it was felt that greater initiative and bolder imaginative effort was needed in the leadership, rather than looking outside for guidance.

During 1939, very little was achieved by the Union in improving the lot of the workers. Attempts by Union officers in some areas to get better conditions of work were spurned by management, and in some instances, union officers were arrested as causing a breach of the peace.

During the 1939 sugar season, Stevens reported to Sir Walter Citrine as follows: - "Conditions here are still the same as you left them, although the sugar cane crop is in operation and as far as we understand, it is to be closed at the end of June, if not sooner. So you see at that rate the working classes will still be hard put for finance, and moreover, will be back on the grounds of starvation."

It is evident that during 1939, the Union was powerless to act and the efforts of the leaders were concentrated on organising the people and building up their strength for the fights that lay ahead.

CHAPTER 4
SYSTEM OF LAND TENURE

Land holding in Antigua was based mainly on resident European family estate holdings, with some families owning two or three estates, and on Company ownership by absentee landlords, such as the Gunthorpes Estates. Many of these estates were in the hands of the same families for generations. There were very few large holdings by coloured natives and what they held were the lands of least importance, being either marginal or sub-marginal, as the family estates and absentee landlords, owned the valuable lands.

The Estates were geared mainly to the production of sugar. This followed the tradition of the 18th century when the ownership of Sugar Estates in the West Indies was the main source of wealth of many British families. Scattered all over Antigua today are the remains of many walled towers used as a base for the wind-driven shafts that operated the numerous sugar mills, an indication of the intensive cultivation of sugar cane in the past.

Sugar however, underwent a change of fortunes towards the end of the 18th and beginning of the 19th centuries, when following the Free Trade Movement in Europe, the protection that Colonial sugar enjoyed in the British Market was gradually removed, and West Indian sugar had to compete without preferential assistance with cheaper sugar from suppliers including Santo Domingo. Later came the threat from the Beet Sugar Industry of Europe, which generated great expansion at the end of the 19th and early part of the 20th centuries. This expansion of beet sugar production in Europe was stimulated for political and economic purposes, as a means of providing a home-based supply of this important commodity, to safeguard European countries from having their supplies cut off from overseas, in the event of war. As a result, the beet sugar industry received strong protection at home by increasing import duties on colonial and other overseas sugar, and the provision of export bounties to exporters. Although the export bounties were short-lived, it had a damaging effect on Colonial sugar.

Faced with the challenge of stiff competition from beet sugar, the price of West Indian sugar had to be considerably reduced to penetrate the British and European markets. West Indian sugar, unable to effectively cope with the decline in production, hit the doldrums, and resulted in the bankruptcy of many Estates.

While other islands sought to diversify their crops in an effort to offset the shock caused by the decline in the Sugar Industry, very little attempt was made to diversify in Antigua. Sea Island Cotton was introduced, but production was half-hearted, as the planters' only love was sugar. They understood it and did not relish a change, especially as cotton production was a more risky business.

Some Estates eventually changed hands after they became unprofitable to operate, and in 1901, a Central Sugar Factory was built on Gunthorpes Estate by private interest with a substantial Government Grant, in an effort to institute economical production and greater efficiency. The Central Sugar Factory displaced most of the old Estate Mills. One of the conditions of Government's assistance to the new Factory was that it should receive and process cane from the peasant producers in the Island. Until late in the 30s however, there was one small sugar factory at Bendals Estate, a Muscovado Factory at Montpeliers and a molasses factory at Clairmont. A small Muscovado factory at Brooks in Liberta survived up to the late 1920s or early 1930s. During the early years of World War II, the Bendals Factory went out of operation and its parts were taken over by the Antigua Sugar Factory, which became the only factory, producing sugar in the Island.

The centralisation of the Sugar Factory, while displacing workers who were employed in the small sugar mills helped to keep the Sugar Industry alive during times of fluctuating fortunes. Indeed, it was said at one time that the Antigua Sugar Factory was one of the most profitable factories in the colonies, paying the highest dividends to shareholders.

Because of its special and privileged position, the Antigua Sugar Factory wielded great power in the community. It dictated the price for cane and held great influence over the sugar Estates. Its management were also close advisers to the

Colonial Governors and Government on economic matters of the day. The peasants were unrepresented at the Factory and had wholly to depend on the figures supplied by the Factory for cane received. This system caused great dissatisfaction as peasants felt they did not receive their true figures, and very often, the cane supplied was heavily penalized, according to the Factory, for being stale, thereby bringing little return to them. The peasants felt they should have someone to check on the weight of cane delivered to the Factory and to have the condition of the canes verified on arrival at the Factory. Regrettably, they achieved very little from their dissatisfaction and from representation made on their behalf to Government.

Another grievance of the peasants was the wide gap in the price received by the Estates for the supply of cane to the Factory as against that received by the peasants. The Factory argued that the Estates contracted to supply cane, while there was no such guarantee by the peasants; therefore, the contractors had to be given a better price so as to maintain production. This agreement, however, did not go down well with the majority of peasants who had to market their own cane through the Estates, whose lands they rented, and in most instances, the peasants were compelled by the Estates to plant cane, and this entitled the Estates to secure their rent, plus commission for marketing and other hidden charges.

It was felt by the Government and others that the peasants were only making unfair accusations; that the Factory and Estates could never think of doing anything unsavoury; so no investigations were launched to see if the peasants really had a case that needed remedial attention.

A few resourceful small farmers and influential persons organised an association of peasants for the purpose of marketing cane on a contractual basis. The movement was organized by a Moravian Minister named Charles Franklin Francis, who lived at Grace Hill in Liberta for a number of years. Before that, Rev. Francis, or the Parson, as he was called, was responsible for the death of the Donkey Tax, when he drew up a petition and canvassed the length and breadth of the Island, getting signatures of thousands of peasants and others who owned donkeys, for submission to the Governor and the Secretary of State for the Colonies. This petition demanded the removal of the tax, which was a burden to the people.

In those days, the donkey was the chief means of transport for the peasants to haul their crops and to ride long distances through difficult terrain to get to work, or to cultivate their plots. The majority of the people could not afford to pay tax on their animals and some had to sell their donkeys because of default in meeting the payment of the tax; in some cases, this resulted in some owners losing their animals altogether by having them impounded by Government, and in some cases, the animal was shot if the tax was not paid. The Petition was successful and the Donkey Tax Ordinance was repealed. It must be noted that to own a donkey was the ambition of many people in those days; a man's standing in the rural community was based to some extent on how many donkeys, horses or cattle he owned. A man who owned a horse and buggy was regarded as a Country Squire, and if he went as high as an extension, the local name given a coach, he would be regarded as a prince.

The peasant organisation mentioned above had as its Secretary, T.T. Henry from Sweetes, and Rev. Francis as its first President. It was registered as the Antigua Agricultural Association Ltd. The Organisation had to guarantee the Factory an annual minimum of 100 tons of cane in order to get contractors' prices. The organisation purchased its own truck for hauling cane and subsequently went into business.

There was however, a lot of dissention and mistrust among the leaders of the organisation. Rev. Francis resigned from the post of President and was succeeded by others, including Harrold T. Wilson and Walter (Barclay) Davis, who held the post for short periods. T.T. Henry was never changed as Secretary. Eventually, the organisation faded out of existence.

CHAPTER 5
CONSTITUTIONAL CHANGES

Before the passage of the Trade Union Act on 5th December 1939, in the Federal Legislature of the Leeward Islands, and thereafter the assent by the Governor, Sir Gordon Lethem, on 20th December 1939, there were several legal obstacles in the way of successfully forming trade unions in Antigua. These obstacles were referred to in Stevens' letter to Sir Walter Citrine and were quite evident in the Trade Union Act of (1931); they were repealed on the passage of the new Act of 1939.

Previous legislation restricted the actions of trade unions by making a union liable for loss or damage caused to employers as a result of strikes. This completely made futile any effort of a trade union to operate successfully, because the employers could always plead loss or injury, and a sympathetic court would always give judgment in favour of the employers. In fact, the inerrant rights of a worker to refuse wages and to seek better conditions of work, long accepted in Britain and elsewhere, were not considered rights of the Colonial worker in Antigua. Peaceful picketing was illegal and a criminal offence.

Besides these, vested interests such as the Sugar Factory and the sugar planters who had the sympathetic ear of the Government, saw to it that no effort was made to encourage the development of a trade union in Antigua. These obstacles were extremely formidable and caused the workers - despite their grievances and unrest - to remain fettered to a condition of economic and industrial slavery. No effort was made by the Government of the Leeward Islands to remove the hostile clauses in the Trade Union Act that were inimical to the interest of the workers. As a result, very few workers cared to brave the law by exposing themselves to conditions that might cause their imprisonment.

It was evident that suggestions and recommendations by the British Government through Secretaries of State for the Colonies to encourage the development of trade unions were ignored, or turned down, on the advice of the Executive Council, which comprised of business owners on the unofficial side. The official representatives considered it in their best interest to support the unofficial view.

Sir Gordon Lethem was a liberally minded Governor, a slight departure from the customary Colonial Vice-Regent, whose only duty was to see that law and order prevailed in the Colonies. He was a Scotsman and most likely from the understanding that the Scots were considered the under-dogs in association with the Englishman, felt a certain amount of sympathy for the welfare of the people. He decided to take action on the suggestions of the Colonial Office and the Royal Commission; and issued instructions for the drafting of a new Trade Union Act. This made it possible for the new Labour Movement, which was recently created to get an unrestricted start, hence, the Trade Union Act of 1939 was accordingly enacted.

One aspect of this quick action that should not go unnoticed was the Constitutional changes that had taken place in the Leeward Islands; these changes started with the elections in 1937. The Crown Colony System of Government in which the Unofficial Members of the Islands' Legislatures were all nominated by the Governor was repeated by a slightly improved Constitution Ordinance of 1936; this provided for a limited number of Elected Seats in the Legislatures, based on a limited adult franchise of property and income qualifications. A few new faces were able to slip into the Legislative Seats of the Leeward Islands, and although the Nominated and Official element still outnumbered the Elected Members, there were the occasional liberal sounds that had to be repeated from time to time, even though not accepted.

Among those from Antigua who contributed at that time to bringing about the more liberal Trade Union Legislation were Reginald Stevens, who was then President of the Antigua Trades & Labour Union; John Lushington Jeffrey, a merchant of Scot Row in St. John's and a popular cricketer who was elected to the

Legislature of Antigua, and afterwards served on the local and Federal Executive Councils; Major Hugh Hole, an Englishman of influence who lived on Guiana Island and paid periodic visits to his home in England, he was also very interested in the workers' cause, and did quite a lot of work behind the scenes. Major Hole was elected to the Antigua Legislature as the people's champion and First Elected Member. Harold T. Wilson cannot be forgotten, who in his daily newspaper, The Magnet, never ceased to criticise Government and to awaken public opinion to the wrongs that were perpetuated against the people. Similar changes took place in St. Kitts and Montserrat.

Faced with the Constitutional changes and the out-cry from the Press and people, the plantocracy and businessmen who dominated the Councils of Antigua and the Leeward Islands, felt it discreet to give way. Perhaps too, they feared the disturbances that took place in British Guiana, St. Kitts, Barbados, Jamaica, Trinidad and Tobago and St. Vincent, would spread to Antigua. But in giving way, there were feelings that like previous organisations, the new Workers' Movement would be short-lived; so there was no harm in allowing the workers to enjoy themselves for a time, provided they did not interfere with the power and influence that Management still wielded. Future events however, proved that perception to be mistaken, because, the workers and their newfound leaders were determined to make the Labour Movement succeed. To them, the Trade Union was the long awaited Promise Land and the President, Reginald Stevens, was the Moses sent to deliver them from the bondage of Pharaoh. Indeed, in many meetings, Reginald Stevens was introduced to the huge audiences as the Moses of Antigua, and was recognised as such.

CHAPTER 6
WAGE STRUCTURE
AND SOCIAL CONDITIONS

At the time of the Royal Commission and before the Trade Union was formed, the wage structure of Antigua while not substantially different from the other Islands and Barbados, was the lowest of them all.

On the large Estates, rates varied from one shilling (EC24 cents) to one shilling and sixpence (EC36 cents) per day for a male worker, the majority being paid the lowest rate; and from seven pence (EC14 cents) to eight pence (EC16 cents) per day for women. On the smaller Estates, a male worker would receive 10 pence (EC20 cents) per day and a woman six pence (EC12 cents) per day. There was also child labour, or the small gangs as they were termed, with children earning from two pence (EC4 cents) to four pence (EC8 cents) per day.

These wages could not touch the fringes of the needs of the average worker and with employment on the estates a seasonal occupation, a worker might be left for months without the opportunity to earn a livelihood. Unemployment and under-employment, together with the low wages obtained while employed, were the basis of the low standards that existed among the workers and the cause of frustration and unrest among the people.

Another serious condition was the long hours that constituted a day's work. This was usually from 6.00 a.m. to 6.00 p.m., with a few minutes off for a meal - if any; at the end of the week, it was sometimes at midnight on Saturdays that workers received their wages from the overseers on the Estates. Of course this meant that workers were only able to make their purchase of goods on Sunday mornings in the

Village shops, which tried to accommodate them - sometimes illegally - because the law prescribed the shops' opening and closing hours, and Sunday sales were illegal.

The villages where the majority of the agricultural workers lived greatly reflected the bad conditions of the Working Class people in Antigua. Crude Wattle and Daub huts with thatched roofs and earth floors provided shelter for many workers, some of whom did not have beds but slept on straw covered with crocus bags - most often in their working clothes. The calabash served as a utensil for eating and drinking. Cooking was done in the open with firewood in crude clay pots made at Sea View Farm. There was scarcity of water, especially when the ponds near the villages were dry. There were very few pit latrines and excreta was thrown in the nearest bush. The village roads were like ravines.

Over-crowding in the wattle and daub huts was the order of the day, and sex was the only source of pleasure. This resulted in a number of children being born in these conditions. Many times, mothers and daughters were having children under the same roof, at the same time, in the same unsanitary and primitive conditions; naturally, in such squalid conditions, infant mortality was extremely high.

Although Primary Education was free, the economic conditions of the worker were a deterrent to many children reaching a high standard of education. Some did not attend school because of lack of clothing, and many who went to school had to leave at an early age to join the small gangs on the Estates in order to contribute to the family income. The result was a high rate of semi-literacy and a regrettable tide of associated superstitions and other social ills resulted in large-scale juvenile delinquency. One other handicap in the hindrance of children benefiting from the available free primary education in those days was the long distances some children had to walk daily to attend school - more often than not with hungry bellies, as many villages were without schools. It was not surprising therefore, that many children played truant, because as they perceived it then, school held no hope nor joy for them. A swim in a nearby stream and a prowl in the cane fields or in an orchard belonging to a known or unknown owner, provided greater fun and satisfaction for them, rather than listening to a teacher, who, for all that mattered, might have been talking Dutch to them.

When these urchins were caught in their raids on private property, they sometimes had to suffer the indignity of being reluctantly led to a nearby police station, where it was usually Skerrit to which they were sent by a Magistrate (Skerrit being a reform school for boys, - a juvenile prison -) or the parents had to pay their last few pennies to the owner, the family going without food as a result. But although these urchins' buttocks would resound to the tune of the whip and sometimes after being whipped at home, would have to prepare for another round from the teacher for being absent from school; dodging school still remained a regular routine and some did not reach beyond the first three letters of the Alphabet and could not write their own names.

Chigoes and Yaws were plentiful in the villages and the unsanitary conditions provided a breeding ground for these two parasites. It was customary to see children and grown-ups in the villages with deformed feet and toes, some with Chigoes bulging out of their feet, as the majority of the villagers were bear-footed, they did not have shoes. Pulling Chigoes out of the toe or heel was a regular past-time for those who couldn't stand the discomfort and wanted the fleas out. Some got accustomed to having Chigoes in their feet, and could not bother with removing them. Children infected with Chigoes and Yaws hardly attended school; they were teased by healthy schoolmates and called "Chigoes foot" John or Mary, as the gender might be.

The schools were generally in very poor sanitary conditions, and over-crowding was a regular feature. Most of the schools were old buildings owned by the churches, particularly the Moravian Church; this was from the days of slavery when the Churches undertook responsibility for the education of the children of slaves. They continued with the voluntary Education Programme for some years after slavery was abolished. After the Government undertook to provide Primary Education, these buildings were rented from the churches and very little effort was made by the Government to build school buildings, or to assist in improving those in use.

A look into the position of education in the British Caribbean, showed that apart from Montserrat and the Virgin Islands, Antigua spent the least amount of money on education. In 1928, Antigua spent approximately 6,000 pounds

36

(EC$28,800.00) on Education as against St. Kitts/Nevis' and Anguilla's 10,000 pounds (EC$48,000.00), Grenada's 17,000 pounds (EC$81,600) and Barbados' 66,000 pounds (EC$316,800.00). But despite this disparity, Antigua was able to produce some men and women of sound mind and great ability who were capable of holding their own against the best of the other territories, despite the obvious gap which existed in the educational opportunities provided in the other islands. For instance, there had been Government-owned secondary schools in most of the other islands with low school fees, while in Antigua, secondary school fees were high and prohibitive; also, the additionally high cost of text books which had to be purchased by the students, placed Secondary Education beyond the reach of many parents who could not profit from it. Government scholarships to Secondary Schools were negligible.

The Antigua Grammar School founded by the late Archdeacon, The Rt. Rev. James Branch in 1884, and the Antigua Girls' High School, were the chief secondary schools in the Island. The Antigua Grammar School has a most colourful history; over the years, it produced several outstanding and prominent students, many of whom have distinguished themselves in many fields in public and private life and Religion, both at home and overseas. Its roll included students from many parts of the Caribbean and further afield. What the Antigua Grammar School did for the boys, the Antigua Girls' High School did for the girls. Both Schools were administered by the Anglican Diocese of Antigua (now North-Eastern Caribbean & Aruba).

Later, the Roman Catholic Church started a secondary convent school, which was co-educational at first. The separation took place afterwards, when the St. Joseph's Academy for boys was formed. These Schools, while catering mostly for Roman Catholic children, have, generally in policy, been non-sectarian.

In the midst of the other problems that existed on the Island, very little philanthropic work was done in education. There were however, a few persons who devoted their time and energies to providing Secondary Education at very low cost to children of low-income persons who could not afford to pay the high school fees at both the Grammar and the Girls' High Schools. Prominent among these were Miss Nellie Robinson, then Principal of the T.O.R. Memorial High School and Mrs.

37

Agatha Goodwin, the Founder and past Principal of the Faith and Hope High School. The Antigua Trades & Labour Union was instrumental in the late 40s in securing a number of scholarships from Labour Welfare Funds to assist in keeping the Faith and Hope High School alive, when because of the low school fees, it became difficult to meet its operating expenses. At one time, Mrs. Goodwin considered turning over the school to the Union.

Samuel Lushington Athill, a famous magistrate of Antigua, organised a Christmas treat at his own expense annually for a large number of children of poor parents. After enjoying their refreshments, the children would also receive toys and other gifts. Even after his retirement from civil service, the Ex-Magistrate still continued his Christmas tradition with donations and contributions from friends.

A landowner who was very kind to poor people and may be considered a philanthropist, was Colonel Stapleton Cotton, a member of the British Nobility, who owned Delaps, Gambles and Villa Estates. He lived at Gambles Bluff. The poor were always welcomed at his home, and when he died at Gambles, instructions were that his body should be borne on a cart driven by oxen to the place of burial. His chief mourners were the workers on his Estates who lamented his death because of his kindness to them.

Nor could be forgotten the most popular Governor of the Leeward Islands, Sir Eustace Fiennes Bart, who was the poor man's friend. He was the man of action who did what he felt was right, then consulted the Colonial Office. He was instrumental in the development of the Fiennes Wells at Body Pond and was the moving force in the introduction of pipe-borne water to several villages. He was also directly involved in seeing that funds for relief work to the poor people were made available from time to time. The Fiennes Institute at the entrance to Holberton Hospital, stands as a memorial to his efforts on behalf of the poor of Antigua.

Governor, Sir Reginald St. Johnson, who succeeded Sir Eustace Fiennes, also made a significant contribution to the development of a housing scheme at St. Johnson's Village, just on the eastern fringes of the City of St. John's.

CHAPTER 7
UNION RECOGNITION

September 1939, was the outbreak of war between Germany and Great Britain. Automatically, the colonies became involved and Antigua, like other Colonies, got ready to contribute to the war effort. The demand for sugar and sea island cotton increased, and prices for these commodities rose. Wages in the Sugar Industry remained at a standstill however, and the workers and the Union resented the attempt of Management to keep wages down; the Union then decided to approach management to negotiate agreements for improved wages and conditions for workers in the sugar industry.

The Antigua Sugar Factory, which was under the management of L.I. Henzell -considered the most powerful man in the Island, had a new manager in Mr. J.O. McMichael, who succeeded Henzell on his retirement. Mr. Alexander Moody-Stuart, who married Mr. Henzell's daughter, was attorney for the Gonthorpes Estate and also had connections with the Sugar Factory, owning a large number of shares between himself and his brother, Mark Moody-Stuart. Other influential planters were Messrs. R.S.D. (Bob) Goodwin and his brother, Frank, the Maginley Brothers, Ernest and Robert, Bennett Bryson & Co. Ltd., Joseph Dew & Son and Mrs. John J. Camacho, whose wealthy husband died and left several estates to her.

There was at that time a planters' association which had very little binding office on its members, but would occasionally meet to discuss broad policies on matters affecting the Sugar Industry; these included wages and prices of sugar and varieties of cane and so on. They would have a gentleman's agreement between them to accept decisions when they were made. The usual haunt of these planters was the exclusively white New Club west of Government House at the top of Newgate

Street. There, not only was sugar discussed, but the policies governing the economic and political life of the Island were formulated, because many of the Club Members were Representatives of the Legislative and Executive Dynasty that was the pattern of society in Antigua. Mr. A. Moody-Stuart was the Secretary of the Planters' Association and Mr. R.S.D. Goodwin, President. The Estates generally made the Planters Association their negotiating agency with the Union.

In January 1940, even before the Union was recognised, about 90% of the workers at the Antigua Sugar Factory were members of the Union. Enthusiasm was high among these workers and they felt that, at long last, they would be able to make demands on management.

The Sugar Crop was scheduled to start early that season, but the factory workers decided among themselves that they would not start the Crop until agreement was reached to pay increased wages. Management took no notice of them, because until then, the Union was in the formation process and accordingly, it was not sufficiently strong to make firm demands of Management, because it was yet to be recognised by Management.

With their efforts spurned, the Factory Workers decided to call a strike at the Factory. The strike lasted for seven weeks. The Crop was delayed and the strike spread to the Water Front, where the Water Front Workers refused to work unless their claims for increased wages were recognised by Management.

The strikes were unauthorised by the Union but were a struggle by workers to force the hands of Management, until the Union was strong enough to fight their case. The Factory and Water Front workers had island-wide support for the strikes, and many people joined the Union as a result of this demonstration of workers' solidarity.

James Dondas Harford was at the time Administrator of Antigua. He was later Knighted, and became Governor of the Seychelles. Upon instructions of Sir Gordon Lethem, the Governor of the Leeward Islands, Mr. Harford, undertook the responsibility for bringing the Trade Union, the Factory and the Planters together to negotiating agreements within the Sugar Industry. This measure became more imperative because of the War Effort and because every ounce of sugar was needed by Britain.

On 2nd February, 1940, Mr. Harford, as Administrator, wrote the following letter to the General Secretary of the Antigua Trades & Labour Union:

"Dear Sir,

At a recent discussion, through the Governor's brief visit here from St. Kitts, attended by His Excellency, Mr. Stevens, Mr. Lockhart and myself, it was agreed that an informal round-table conference at which both employers and employed should be represented, to discuss conditions of employment during the coming crop, would be very desirable before the opening of the present reaping season.

First, I am desirous of holding such a conference between representatives of the management and the employees of the Antigua Sugar Factory, and I write to enquire whether your Union is in a position to arrange for representation of the employees at such a discussion, and, if so, to invite them to attend. I am not completely aware of the precise stage of negotiations, which the Union has reached; I believe it would not be fully organised for a little time yet; but, in view of the proximity of the crop, you will, I feel sure, agree that it is desirable to take steps on the lines proposed at the earliest opportunity.

I have ascertained that the Manager of the Factory is prepared to attend such a conference under my chairmanship. I would propose that the Acting Treasurer and the Superintendent of Public Works, who, at my request, are at present engaged on a very close examination of the position of the local sugar industry this year, should also attend.

The Government feels that the War Conditions and the response of this community to the most generous priority of Colonial Development which has just been announced by His Majesty's Government, make it imperatively necessary for all those concerned to do all in their power to ensure a smooth opening and a smooth working of the Crop this year.

Yours very truly,

J.D. Harford

Administrator"

It must be noticed that the War Effort was conceivably the main motive that prompted Government's action in getting the Union recognised by the employers. The inherent loyalty by Antiguans to the British Crown had the most sobering effect on the Union - despite past neglect of the people. The promise of Colonial Development Aid was tantalizing bait to bring about speedy agreements, and as much compromise as possible for all parties concerned.

Despite Mr. Harford's efforts however, the negotiations did not run smoothly. They started on 3rd February, and on 7th March, a letter from Mr. Harford to the General Secretary of the Union stated: *"As a deadlock appears to have been reached in the negotiations regarding conditions of employment at the Factory, I am anxious to have a further meeting of representatives of the Union and of the Factory's Management as early as possible."*

On 18th March, Stevens informed Sir Walter Citrine about the result of the negotiations with the Antigua Sugar Factory. He said: *"We were able to secure 50% increase on all normal daily wages, payable at the end of each week, and a further increase on a sliding scale from 1% to 10% on wages payable to the workers at the end of Crop, providing the Sugar Crop yields more than 14,000 tons as alleged by Management. This arrangement runs up to 17,000 tons of sugar.*

Although the actual price of cutting by the line is not more than last year's, the workers will in fact have more to gain, due to the thinness of the line; that is to say, the canes have not borne as well as last year. The price per ton for cutting has increased by 20%, thus making 1 shilling (EC24 cents) per ton as compared with 10 pence (EC20 cents) paid last year."

These early gains by the Union, although almost negligible today in terms of cash, represented the first successful effort of getting union recognition from employers; most of the credit had to go to the Factory Workers who held out, despite much suffering and many hardships. A 5% increase on a shilling (EC24 cents) a day added up to very little when the needs of the workers were considered, but the important thing was that the movement of wages had started, and with strength and resourcefulness by the Union, it would be difficult afterwards to arrest that upward movement.

It must also be noted that Stevens and his colleagues felt themselves obliged to help the War Effort and did not adhere to anything that would impede that effort.

Early in 1940 and during the period of negotiations in the Sugar Industry, the Government proposed to set up advisory boards to advise on matters affecting wages and conditions of employment in the Sugar Manufacturing Industry, the Cane Producing Industry and the employment of labour on the Waterfront. The Union was asked to select representatives who could be considered for appointment to the Boards and the same request was made of Management. After some delay, the Advisory Boards were set up and the Union's representatives were Reginald Stevens, F.O. Benjamin, Samuel James and B.A. Richards. The Boards however, did not function until 1941.

During this period, efforts were made by the Union to get wage increases and better conditions for workers on the Waterfront. George W. Bennett Bryson & Co., Ltd., and Steven R. Mendes, Ltd., were the two main shipping agencies employing stevedores and lightermen. Mr. Keithley Heath was in charge of the Stevedoring Department for Bennett Bryson; the general responsibility for the Waterfront was Mr. A.F.A. Turner, a Director of the firm.

The Firm of Bennett Bryson & Co. placed the onus of negotiations on Mr. T.F. Burrows, a prominent barrister and solicitor. These negotiations were long, drawn out affairs, and a certain amount of unrest developed among Waterfront Workers, who had an accumulation of grievances.

One of the main points of disagreement was the payment for overtime work. The proposals of the Union were that overtime should be paid after normal working hours of 7.00 a.m. to 4.00 p.m. Bryson contended that overtime should be paid from 6.00 p.m. as provided in the law regulating the hours of work for porters and Watermen workers - from 7.00 a.m. to 6.00 p.m. Union leaders and the workers were not concerned with the law, as they felt the law was onerous and outdated; accordingly, they threatened to strike on the Waterfront if concessions were not given to overtime payment among other things. While Mr. Burrows and the Firm were prepared to argue on the basis of the law, the Union felt a more humanitarian approach was necessary.

Eventually, the workers on the Waterfront refused to work on some boats in the Harbour, causing the second strike on the Waterfront in the same year. This strike was unsuccessful in that outside workers were taken onboard to unload the ships in port, thereby making the strike ineffective. That was a serious setback for the Union, and what made things worst, some of the men who were considered ring-leaders in calling the strike were not re-employed by the Firm.

Despite strong Union representation and requests, the Firm took the stand that the Executive of the Union was fully to be blamed for instructing the men not to work; but while the Directors were prepared to re-employ as many of the men as possible, they were not prepared to be dictated to by the Executive of the Union as to whom they should employ.

CHAPTER 8
BAN ON STRIKES

As was mentioned earlier on, constitutional changes took place in 1937 with elections that provided for five Elected Seats to the Legislative Council. To be a voter, one had to own property to the value of at least100 pounds (EC$480.00) or have an income of 30 pound (EC$144.00) per annum. Persons offering themselves for election must own property to the value of 500 pounds (EC$2,400.00) or have an income of 200 pounds (EC$960.00) per annum. These amounts would appear small today, but in 1937, very few people could have boasted of these qualifications, because with wages at 1 shilling (EC24 cents) per day or less, the average agricultural worker had an annual income of less than half that qualification to vote. Antigua was declared one constituency.

The composition of the Legislative Council in 1936 previous to the Elections and the changed Constitution of 1937, were eight ex officio members and nine unofficial members, all nominated. Those who served on the Legislative Council were: the Governor, the Council Secretary, the Attorney General, the Treasurer, Dr. W. McDonald, Chief Medical Officer, Mr. J.P. Purnell-Edwards, Superintendent of Public Works, F.H.S. Warneford, Superintendent of Agriculture, S.L. Athill, Magistrate - these were the officials. The unofficial members were: Major J.T. Dew, planter and merchant, Frank Goodwin, planter, W.M. Howell, Manager of Barclays Bank, A. Moody-Stuart, planter, R.S.D. Goodwin, planter, Joseph E. James, Retired Inspector of Schools, J.L.E. Jeffrey, merchant, E. Scot Johnson, Company Director, L.I. Henzell, Manager of the Antigua Sugar Factory.

From the make-up of the Council, it was not difficult to see whose interest was represented. The ordinary beggar had not a chance. In 1937, the new

Constitution reduced the size of the Legislative Council and provided for the Administrator as President, the Attorney-General and the Treasurer, as the three official members. Those nominated were R.S.D. Goodwin, L.I. Henzell and J.E. James. The Elected Members were Major Hugh Hole, First Elected, John L. Jeffrey 2nd Elected, Reginald St. Clair Stevens 3rd Elected, A. Moody-Stuart 4th Elected and Captain L. Edward Scot Johnson 5th Elected Members.

It was felt that Stevens owed his election to Major Hole, whom he supported before and during the Election Campaign, much to the annoyance of men like Harold T. Wilson, who for some reason, could not get along with Major Hole. Wilson in his newspaper The Magnet, questioned Stevens' qualifications to be elected to the Legislative Council.

On 18th October, 1937, a motion was moved by J.L.E. Jeffrey on behalf of the Unofficial Members, asking for an inquiry into the qualifications of the 3rd Elected Member, Reginald Stevens, as there was doubt in the public's mind, of Stevens' qualifications to be a Member of the Council. The Motion was passed with one dissenting vote, that of Stevens. An inquiry was later held by Mr. Clement Malone of St. Kitts, a barrister-at-law; afterwards becoming Sir Clement Malone, Chief Justice of the Windward and Leeward Islands. He found against Stevens who promptly resigned from the Legislative Council.

Stevens was nominated for election on a qualification of property ownership of £500 (EC$2,400.00.). A survey of the value declared his property at less than £500. This survey was felt to be biased against Stevens.

However, Stevens was otherwise qualified, for he had paid income tax on a return of £200 (EC$960.00) per annum income, and in the by-election that followed, he ran again and won. It is believed that Stevens was not considered of the social standard to be a member of the Council at that time.

In the following elections in 1940, Stevens as President of the Antigua Trades & Labour Union, was at the peak of his popularity. The Union was not fully organised to play an important part in politics, and of the several leaders, Stevens was among the few who had the qualification to be a member of the Council. However, a large number of people who were not registered but were eligible to vote, registered as voters, and when the votes were counted, Stevens received the largest number of votes and so had the honour of becoming 1st Elected Member of the Legislative Council. Major Hugh Hole did not run in that election, and those elected were Stevens, Jeffrey and Moody Stuart, with two newcomers, Sydney T. Christian, a Barrister-at-law, and Harold T. Wilson.

The responsibility for the Union and being 1st Elected Member of the Legislative Council seemed to have a sobering effect on Stevens, for he seemed to have lost much of his early fire. He also came up against very stiff opposition from men like Moody-Stuart, who had great influence with the official and nominated members of the Council. As a result, Stevens suffered some very frustrating encounters, in seeing many of his views rejected by the Council.

World War II had taken a bad turn for the British and French. France had fallen, and the Nazis occupied the smaller countries of Western Europe. Britain was preparing for an invasion of her shores as she fought alone for her life. Many of Antigua's youths had already enlisted in the Canadian and British Armed Forces, and were seeing service in Europe and elsewhere. The Trade Union was also expected to play its part in this serious challenge that faced Western Civilisation, hence Stevens was so persuaded by the Governor, Sir Gordon Lethem, and the Administrator, Mr. Harford, to play his part too. Reginald St. Clair Stevens was a profoundly loyal subject to the British cause, as was every Antiguan and Barbudan; he wanted to help as much as possible.

In January 1941, at the request of the Governor of the Leeward Islands, the Antigua Trades & Labour Union adopted a resolution, renouncing the weapon of strike for the duration of the War. The same action was instituted by the St. Kitts-Nevis trade union. While this was understood by the more intelligent leaders as an effort to assist in the struggle and to provide Britain with the vital supplies of sugar and cotton, the ordinary members of the Union did not fully appreciate the position, and considered it as a "sell-out" by the Union Leaders. The Union was organised in the midst of a strike, and the workers considered that this - their only weapon, was taken away from them. Difficulties in getting some workers at the factory and the waterfront reinstated after the strikes also caused dissatisfaction and frustration among the workers who lost their jobs. They felt the Union did not do as much as it could for them.

The result was that between 1941 and early 1943, membership of the Union fell off, and the Union suffered its leanest period since its inception. The coming of the Americans, while placing money into circulation, did not do much to promote trade unionism. The American Base had to be completed in a hurry, in an effort to subdue the German submarine menace in the Atlantic and the Caribbean. In as much as the rates paid by the American contractors to the various categories of workers were higher than local wages, there was little left for the Union to do. Also, the Bases were constituted military zones under the Base Arrangement, and workers had to receive passes to enter. Unionists and non-Unionists were employed alike without any effective effort by the union at organising the Base workers, because the contractors refused to enter into any agreements with the Union and the Government did nothing to help, indicating that this would be outside its jurisdiction.

With the demand for labour on the Military Bases at higher wages than those paid in the Sugar Industry, many sugar workers rushed for jobs at the Bases, thereby reducing the ranks of those employed in reaping the Crop. The Sugar Crop suffered as a result of the shortage of cutters and loaders in the fields. The employers appealed to the Union to provide workers to reap the Crop, and a similar appeal was made by the Administrator, Mr. Hartford Boon of St. Kitts, who succeeded Mr. Harford as Administrator of Antigua.

At a meeting of the Labour Advisory Board, Agricultural Section, presided over by Mr. Boon on the 28th May 1941, the Administrator explained to the meeting that there was a serious hold up in the reaping of the Crop, and asked the Labour Representatives why the labourers were unwilling to work. Mr. Stevens explained that among other things, the labourers had many grievances on account of actions by the employers, and they were not making sufficient money. To this, the Administrator replied that the financial side was not of such great importance, as the obligation on the Island to deliver every ounce of sugar that could be produced to the Mother Country, then fighting in a life and death struggle.

Whatever actions Stevens might have been taken with respect to the Union, was dogged on all sides by the advice *"do nothing to impede the war effort! Give all you can to the War."* He gave, and as a result, the Union became almost ineffectual, a condition which suited the employers and nerved them for the greater fights which were to later come.

In January, 1943, Mr. D.L.B. Wickham was appointed Federal Labour Officer and was stationed in Antigua. He was later appointed Chairman of the Advisory Board and took over the duties of Labour Affairs, hitherto undertaken by the Administrator; he later became the Crown Attorney. There was a deadlock in the sugar negotiations between the Union and the Antigua Sugar Planters' Association, and during that time, there was cessation of work on several estates. According to agreement, the workers went back to work and the dispute was placed before an Arbitrator, who eventually made an award in slight favour of the workers.

The workers were however, dissatisfied with the award and several stoppages of work ensued during the Crop. The Union's hands were tied; having submitted their dispute to arbitration, they were legally bound to respect the award of the Arbitrator, so the officers could do nothing more than persuade the workers to reap the Crop to the resentment and dissatisfaction of many workers.

With the completion of the construction of the Bases, large numbers of the Base Workers became redundant and were laid off. Unemployment once more began to raise its head, and the position became more aggravated; for the workers who had become accustomed to working for good wages on the Bases and for the first time enjoyed some free spending, were not prepared to go back to the low wages on the Estates. Moreover, many of these workers who went to the Bases as unskilled workers, had acquired some experience in technical jobs, and could now be considered as skilled or semi-skilled workers. They had no further interest in the cane fields; other avenues of employment would have to be found to absorb these workers.

One important development took place in the Sugar Industry at that time. In August 1943, the company known as Gonthropes Estates, Ltd., of which Mr. Moody-Stuart was attorney, acquired a number of other Estates, including the Tudway Estates, which comprised of Parham Hill, Parham New Work, Parham Old Work and Vernons. The Estates formerly owned by George W. Bennett Bryson & Co., Ltd., namely, Long Lane Lavingtons, Hoyes, Burkes, Willis Freemans, Sandersons, Mercers Creek, Cochranes, Thomas and the Jolly Hill Estates plus the Estates known as The Syndicate Estates, namely, Parry's, the Diamond, Morris

Looby's, Bodkins and Delapse Estate were also purchased. This merger brought under one ownership almost all of the prominent sugar estates in the Island, and the name was changed to The Antigua Syndicate Estates, Ltd. Later, other Estates joined the group.

Mr. R.S.D. Goodwin became Chairman of the Board of Directors of the new Company and Mr. Moody-Stuart a Director and General Manager. Earlier, Mr. Moody-Stuart had given up the post of Secretary of the Antigua Sugar Planters' Association and was succeeded in that post by Mr. Ronald Cadman, a Director and General Manager of Joseph Dew & Son, Ltd.

This new company however, gave the Union the understanding that the company's change of name did not alter the relationship between the Company and the Antigua Planters' Association and the Antigua Trades and Labour Union; the Company still retained membership of the Association and would be bound by all agreements entered into by the Association.

The amalgamation of the estates came about in an effort to introduce economy in operation, and to bring about greater efficiency in sugar production. Despite the higher wartime price for sugar than what was obtained earlier on, the cultivation of cane by many estates still left much to be desired with the uncertainty of labour, the cessation of work and the reluctance of former sugar workers to go back to the estates. Mr. Moody-Stuart and others felt that a more tightly knit and controlled productive unit would be better than individual estates operating on their own.

An amalgamation of policy was also desirable if the Estates were to stand up to the demands of the workers, and a powerful group of estates like the Antigua Syndicate Estate Ltd., could more easily take on a challenge by the Union, and take a lead in determining the planter's position. It was realised that to cope with the Union, it must be from a position of strength.

While there could be no argument against the need to bring about greater efficiency on the estates, the amalgamation was not well received by the workers and many overseers. They saw in it a threat to their security and prospects of finding ready work. Many times, a worker, if dissatisfied with work on one estate, could secure similar work on another estate, as they were under different management. The same thing could be said of overseers and some junior managers. The amalgamation denied that opportunity, for if a worker fell out with management of one estate, it was to the same management he would have to apply for work on another Estate, therefore, he had no freedom of choice. He must stick to his present job and give satisfaction, or expect to be refused employment wherever he went. Many workers did suffer in that respect. The Trade Union was in no position to prevent the amalgamation but had to make the best of it. However, the amalgamation made things easier for the Union in future years, as the Union could muster its forces in one direction, rather than dissipating its energies in various directions.

The St. Kitts-Nevis Trade Union experienced similar troubles with the planters and the St. Kitts Sugar Factory during the 1943 Sugar Crop. The trouble in Antigua hinged on the payment of an after-crop bonus, to which the workers were accustomed, but which management both in St. Kitts and Antigua wanted to stop, in view of the increases given for reaping the Crop. In St. Kitts, the dispute was placed before a Board of Inquiry, and the Board recommended that the bonus should be continued. The planters however felt they were not obliged to accept the recommendation of the Board and decided not to pay.

As a consequence, the St. Kitts Trade Union which, as mentioned before, adopted a resolution in January 1941, to abstain from calling strikes for the duration of the War. But by a subsequent resolution, on the 2nd July 1943, rescinded the resolution of January, 1941, as it felt that the Union had no further obligation in the matter, if management was not prepared to agree to the recommendation of the Board of Inquiry.

Eventually, the planters and the factories both in St. Kitts and Antigua decided they would pay the bonus, as they realised that there would be serious trouble ahead in the forthcoming negotiations for the 1944 Sugar Crop. Antigua did not rescind the resolution as did St. Kitts, although it appeared at times necessary to do so, in an effort to restore the worker's morale. Sequentially, matters followed their own course, and when the workers found it necessary to strike, resolution or no resolution - they went on strike.

CHAPTER 9
CHANGE IN LEADERSHIP

The Union itself had its ups and downs during these early years. There was very little money available to undertake the big task of organising the whole Island and to pay satisfactory salaries to full-time Officers. Transportation consumed most of the money, but the work had to be done.

B.A. Richards, the first General Secretary resigned late in 1941 to work at the U.S. Army Base, and the post was filled by David Nelson, a young man about 23 years old. He did not last very long, for in May, 1942, the Executive of the Union decided to relieve him of his responsibilities as General Secretary of the Union and gave him one month's notice in the process. After that Harold B. Llewellyn acted as General Secretary for a short period and was eventually succeeded by Adolphus W. Williams, a former teacher who - after some travel abroad, later resigned to take up employment at the Antigua Sugar Factory. He was in turn succeeded by Samuel J. James as General Secretary of the Antigua Trades & Labour Union.

There was also dissatisfaction among members of the Executive with some of Stevens' policies. Stevens was a very stubborn and quick-tempered individual who, when he held on to a point, would not easily let go, and became annoyed whenever he was opposed. In September, 1939, Stevens resigned as President of the Antigua Trades & Labour Union, but the Executive of the Union did not accept his resignation; so he decided to withdraw it. The Executive was continually divided on policies, some supporting Stevens while a younger group, with V.C. Bird as leader, thought more forceful and enterprising actions were needed by the Union. The strength of the Union was also dwindling because of war time pressures and the efforts of Stevens and others to pacify the workers as a means of honouring the resolution not to call strikes for the duration of the War. Many heated debates would take place at Executive Meetings, with Stevens at times threatening to resign, but changing his mind after he calmed down.

Eventually, at the Annual Conference of the Antigua Trades & Labour Union in September, 1943, Vere Cornwall Bird was nominated and elected by an overwhelming majority of votes as the President of the Union against Stevens, who conceding defeat, walked out of the conference, and gradually faded out of the picture and out of active trade union work. Stevens felt that he would have been the Union's President for life, but the Trade Union Rules provided for an Annual Election for a President.

Stevens took his defeat hard and never got over it. He was a sick man believed to have suffered from high blood pressure, which most likely was the cause of his irritability and quick-temper under strain. The Trade Union had actually outgrown Stevens at that time, and younger, bolder leadership was needed, if the Union were to rise out of the morass into which it had fallen. While not discrediting Stevens, the Conference was satisfied a change was necessary.

Despite everything, much credit must be given to Stevens and those who pioneered the Trade Union Movement through most difficult times; for it was they who laid the foundation through great sacrifice and with high purpose that helped to make the Union the powerful force it is in Antigua and Barbuda today. About 18 months after his defeat, on 21st March 1945, Stevens passed away. The Union, his Lodge and the Legislative Council paid their final tribute to a man who did his best to serve his country and its people.

Before Stevens' defeat as President of the Union and his death in 1945, new elections for the Legislative Council had taken place in 1943. Stevens had by then begun to lose his popularity, and the results of the elections relegated him to the position of 4th Elected Member, as against his previous position of 1st Elected Member Harold T. Wilson succeeded Stevens as First Elected Member. Others elected were: J.L. Jeffrey, A. Moody-Stuart and Luther George.

Stevens' death in 1945 resulted in a by-election, and V.C. Bird the new President of the Antigua Trades & Labour Union, was nominated for the seat held by Stevens, and was elected unopposed. Soon after, Luther George fell ill, and after a prolonged illness which necessitated his being away for a long time at hospital in Jamaica, he resigned his seat, which was filled by J. Oliver Davis, an ex-head teacher, who was elected First Vice-President of the Trade Union.

Around that time, Sir Gordon Lethem was promoted to the position of Governor of British Guiana, and was succeeded by Sir Brian Freeston as Governor of the Leeward Islands; Herbert Boon was in turn succeeded by F.H. Harcourt, as Administrator. One thing, Sir Brian Freeston might be remembered for, is his encouragement for the establishment of the Mill Reef Club in Antigua, which eventually contributed so much to the economic and social life of the Island.

CHAPTER 10
THE STRUGGLE STARTS

The Trade Union Movement received a new lease of life after V.C. Bird became President. Stevens' defeat brought into prominence younger and more energetic men who eventually replaced the Old Guard in the Executive of the Union. J. Oliver Davis became Vice-President of the Union, and the Executive comprised such men like Lionel Hurst Sr., Edward Mathurin, Bradley Carrott, William Kirwan, Emanuel DeSouza and Douglas (Kem) Roberts, with Samuel T. James as General Secretary and Hugh O. Pratt, Treasurer.

Emphasis was placed on re-organising the sections and restoring the morale of the workers, which had fallen very low. It was most important to improve the Union's finances, to enable the Officers to successfully carry out their duties of organising, which required considerable travelling to meet their commitments.

Britain and the Allies were winning the War in Europe and Africa. The taste of victory was also welcomed in Antigua. Spirits became more buoyant and everybody looked forward to an early end of the War. Pearl Harbour was to come later, with the Japanese surprise attack on the USA fleet, while talking peace. The Union was also gathering strength for its greatest challenge on the Waterfront, while the planters under the leadership of Alexander Moody-Stuart and Ronald Cadman were preparing to do battle on wage increases and fringe benefits for workers. The Sugar Factory was much more co-operative. Its Manager, Mr. J.C. McMichael, was a man of few words and shunned trouble. All he wanted was to get along with the job of producing sugar, and leave the fighting to the others.

The Waterfront was a problem to the Union and much effort had to be concentrated to keep it properly organised. There was strong rivalry between Keithly

Heath who did not welcome Union intrusion in his province, and was able to organise strong support among certain waterfront men, who in turn would work on the Union members to get them to disregard Union leaders or ignore union instructions.

This rivalry developed into a feud, and the Waterfront for years was like a tinder box, ready to spark at the first scratch of a match. The Union assigned one of its young and energetic leaders, Douglas (Kem) Roberts, to organise and lead the Waterfront Workers. It was a big task, for Heath's supremacy was evident, and he had the support of the Directors of Bennett Bryson & Co. If the Union called a strike on ships assigned to the Firm of Bennett Bryson & Co., Ltd., Heath would be able to organise his own gang of workers who were non-unionists, or strike-breakers, to unload the ships, very often to the deterrent of regular workers who would not be picked again to work on several ships, because they supported the Union.

This situation fuelled strong bitterness among the Waterfront Workers, and industrial peace was in jeopardy, for a strike on the waterfront would eventually affect the factory and the sugar plantations. Bennett Bryson as the shippers of sugar for the Antigua Sugar Factory also provided storage for sugar at the Point Wharf. If work came to a halt at Point Wharf during the Crop, the Factory would soon run out of storage space on its premises, and with the porters at the Point Wharf refusing to handle the cargo, the Sugar Factory would have to cease grinding operations; consequently, the plantations would have to cease cutting cane also.

The war on the waterfront went on with an uncertain truce from month to month. Heath and Bryson sometimes scored gains, but the Union gradually built its strength, and the Firm's influence began to erode. However, what might be considered a last-ditch stand by Bennett Bryson & Co. against the Union, saw both combatants locked in a struggle in 1946, which lasted very close to ten weeks. The case of the strike was not only for increases of waterfront rates and fringe benefits, but on the question of rotation of workers.

The Union workers complained that there were certain workers, mostly non-unionists, considered henchmen of the Firm, who would be picked to work on every ship that brought or took cargo, while other stevedores might only get a chance to work once in a while. The staunch Union members felt they were discriminated against, and so the Union proposed to Management to rotate the workers. Management would not agree, stating that the men in question were key men, of whom they could not do without. The complaining stevedores and the Union refused to accept the statement that the stevedores concerned were key men, and insisted they be rotated with other workers, so that all the men who worked on the Waterfront would get equal opportunity for work.

The strike caused many hardships to the Waterfront workers, and as it dragged on for weeks without any signs of settlement, many families began to despair. The Union did not have sufficient funds to maintain all the striking workmen with strike benefits, and had to hold regular meetings in the Point Area to bolster the strikers' morale. Strict watch also had to be kept on workers who were weakening and planning to break the strike. In the meantime, a number of Union sympathisers donated money and food to assist the strikers and their families.

As the strike began to affect the whole island, the Government, through the Labour Commissioner, Mr. F. Payne, tried to get both sides together. The Firm of Bennett Bryson & Co., maintained the right to hire whom it pleased, and as often as it pleased. It must be said of Payne that he was scared stiff of the employers and the Union, neither side having any confidence in him. By that time, the Labour Office had become ineffective. The Waterfront workers grew hostile, and two expensive launches owned by Bryson & Co. were blown up while lying at anchor in the Harbour. There was fear of further acts of destruction against the Firm.

T.W. Greening had succeeded Harcourt as Administrator. The new Administrator was an able man and a man of action, and undertook to arrange a practical solution to the dispute that was disrupting the island's economy. He persuaded the Directors of Bennett Bryson & Co. to accept the proposals of the Union and to introduce a roster in which all the names of working stevedores would be included, and that a committee of the Union, the Firm and the Labour Department should select the stevedores to work on each ship, aiming as far as practicable to have an equal division of earnings among the stevedores. The roster system is still in use today, although the Labour Department no longer serves on the committee. The selection is carried out by a team, representing the Firm and the Union.

This decision was important because it brought an end to a system of discrimination on the Waterfront. For the Union, it was a great victory, having removed the sole power of workers selection from Heath and Bryson & Co, thereby preventing them from using one set of workers against another. The peace on the Waterfront, which apart from minor incidents has existed over the years, had its origins in the 1946 strike and its settlement.

CHAPTER 11
DAYS OF TRIAL

The period between 1944 and 1951 was one of great trials for the Union. There was never much money available in the Union's treasury, for the majority of members only paid dues when there was trouble and at negotiation times. After which, they ran themselves non-financial. Sometimes money was not available to pay the staff, several of whom might have to wait months, before their full wages were finally paid. However, the union struggled on.

In the midst of these financial difficulties, there were a series of strikes not only in the sugar industry and on the waterfront, but with business firms also. No year could go by without a strike or threats of strikes by the Union. The workers relished these fights and their response was always sound and dependable, but their contributions improved very little. Each strike caused further drain on the Union's dwindling finances, but strikes had become an accepted fact and a part of life. There were many workers who hated to see a settlement without a strike being called.

One of the ironies of fate was a strike called at Bennett Bryson, not against the firm, but against a contractor, Walter (Barclay) Davis, who was in charge of re-building the head office and business department of the firm, which were destroyed by fire in 1944, and resulted in heavy losses to the firm.

During the construction of the new building in 1946, Davis had about 26 men working with him, including a carpenter with a Dominican accent, who was destined to play a very important role later on in the Union. This carpenter was Davis' chief assistant. A labourer by the name of Abraham Allen who was assigned a certain task by Davis, was instructed by the chief assistant to do something else, which he did. Davis on his return, warned Allen that in the future, when he gave him instructions and he did otherwise, he would be dismissed.

Some days later, Allen who was given duties by Davis, was again called by the carpenter to assist in lifting a form. When Allen refused, the carpenter thereupon reported the matter to Davis who dismissed Allen forthwith. All the other workers walked off the job in sympathy with Allen.

The Union requested that Allen be re-instated, but Davis refused, and a long strike ensued. The chief assistant, Levy Joseph, also a Union member, decided to go on strike with the other workers. Pickets were placed in the vicinity of the job. Eventually, the matter was placed before a Board of Arbitrators with Charlesworth Ross, at the time, a Magistrate appointed as sole Arbitrator. The Union was represented by Randall Lockhart and Davis by Sydney T. Christian.

The Arbitrator found that Allen was unfairly dismissed and Davis acted in exasperation and haste. The matter was amicably settled.

In January 1948, Douglas Roberts who was then a clerk at Joseph Dew & Sons, Ltd., was dismissed by the Firm, without the Directors giving reason for the dismissal. Campbell Barrow, a Chief Clerk at Dews, said he was instructed by one of the Directors, Mr. Mees, to dismiss Mr .Roberts on the grounds that Roberts, who was then serving on a jury for a trial, spent time elsewhere when he was not needed at the court and while he should be working. This Roberts denied.

As previously mentioned, the Executive of the Union assigned Roberts to organise and deal with Waterfront matters, and in the process of his activities, he came up against certain employers as well as against the Firm of Bennett Bryson & Co. It was felt by tbe Directors of Joseph Dew & Sons that Roberts was dangerous to their business, and as a clerk with their company might cause estrangement between them and other Firms; so the best thing was to get rid of him.

The Union requested Robert's re-instatement, but the Firm refused. Pickets appeared before the doors of the firm the next day, and Porters were called out for a strike that lasted for weeks. An agreement was eventually reached whereby Roberts would receive compensation for loss of work, and the dispute was settled after an award was made by J.C. Wooding, who was appointed Arbitrator by the Governor.

The greatest test of the Union's strength however, was to be displayed in the Sugar Industry, particularly with the Antigua Syndicate Estates, Ltd., upon the retirement of Mr. L.I. Henzell from the Antigua Sugar Factory and the gradual decline due to age, of Mr. R.S.D. Goodwin. Moody-Stuart's star that was in ascendancy for some time burst in all its glory, as he became the recognised leader of the Plantocracy and the Ruling Class. Stuart as Managing Director of the Syndicate Estates was in virtual control of most of the arable lands in the island. He was a large shareholder of the Antigua Sugar Factory, representative of the Pan American Airways and other interests, and member of the Legislative and Executive Councils of both the Presidential and Federal Legislatures. In short, he was rich and powerful.

Moody-Stuart was also highly respected by the entire community, and was known to be kind-hearted and generous to people who sought his assistance. This increased his popularity, and at one time, he was the most popular man in Antigua, highly respected and most feared. The latter because of the influence and power he wielded or could wield, in private or public. The economic and social structure of the island also provided the atmosphere for men like Moody-Stuart to thrive.

The Crown Colony System of Government was still in strong evidence, despite the revised constitution of 1936; the dominant voice in the Executive Council of the Territory was Moody-Stuart's. The entire population was conditioned to accept the superior status of White Plantocracy, and any member of that group who stood out especially for ability and paternalism, would be accepted as a god or hero. The acclamation and support of the masses of Major Hugh Hole when he came on the political scene in 1937, was indication of how the populace still looked up to the white man for leadership and guidance. Even when the Union was organised, Stevens and others also looked up to the British Trade Union Congress and Sir Walter Citrine for direction; as Stevens put it, Sir Walter should be their 'instructor and director at all times'.

It is necessary to understand Moody-Stuart and the role he filled. He sprang from the Managerial and Employing Class. As a young man he came to Antigua and met a feudalistic type of condition, in which the white planter was the Lord of the Manor. Chattel slavery was the order of the day - men and women could be fired or imprisoned for not turning out to work on the estates according to their bond. At the Antigua Sugar Factory, men who showed dissatisfaction or were found breaking regulations could be whipped, and gladly received the whip if they wanted to keep their jobs. Although these conditions gradually changed, the power of the planter remained, and Stuart became the embodiment of that power. However, he was not the tyrannical type; very few people if any, doubted his integrity, nor questioned his benevolence. Apart from his struggle to maintain what he held and the means he employed to do so, he must be recognised as a straight forward man of character.

The growth of the Trade Union Movement under the new leadership of Vere Bird, Sr. was a threat to Moody Stuart's power. Bird had by this time won the confidence of the working class people, and was fast becoming the symbol of the Labour Movement in Antigua and Barbuda. He had a quiet dignity and respectful approach to people, but underlying that was a strong and determined will to fight for what he considered was the best for the workers. He never deviated from this role, and even when faced with making important national decisions, it was the workers who had his first loyalty.

In organisations such as the Trade Union Movement in under-developed countries, personalities play an important part in keeping things together and in attracting loyalties. Bird who was a wide reader, knew that and had trusted lieutenants who were prepared to support him through and through. Apart from his Sense of Mission, there was also a certain amount of mysticism about Bird; perhaps this was from his religious training in the Salvation Army. He drew people to him and the workers were prepared to sacrifice anything to follow him. They called him "Papa Bird".

The Plantocracy led by Moody-Stuart, recognised in Bird a different metal from that of Stevens. They saw in him the rising threat to their edifice of power and influence, and therefore, everything had to be done to arrest Bird's growth in stature. Bird on the other hand, realised that only a strong, organised and powerful Trade Union could break the power of the Plantocracy, and provided he had the people on his side, the struggle could be waged from a position of strength. Bird also saw that there could be no real freedom for the people, until the Plantocracy's power was broken.

While the basic challenge was the Plantocracy against the Trade Union

Movement, it became a personal struggle between Moody-Stuart for the Old Guard, and Bird for the New Order. It was a struggle between two giants, which lasted for about a decade, and eventually brought full victory to the Union, and made Bird the most popular man in Antigua.

The aim of the Trade Union Movement was that the workers in the Sugar Industry should be accepted as partners, whereby they could share in the wealth created by the Industry, rather than being tools employed to do a job. This the planters resisted and every increase in wages and fringe benefits had to be fought for and skilfully negotiated. It must be realised too, that every increase given to the workers reduced the margin of profit for the sugar producers, unless there was improved production efficiency. The Trade Union Movement threw out a challenge to the producers of sugar who could no longer allow production to be carried on in the haphazard manner as previously, and although men like Moody-Stuart and others were willing to accept the challenge and saw the necessity for higher efficiency, there were others who did not relish the additional exertion and planning necessitated by this challenge.

In 1945, Samuel T. James took over the post of General Secretary and Hugh O. Pratt, that of Treasurer. J. Oliver Davis became 1st Vice President of the Movement. However, he did not serve long in that position, because he fell out with the Executive of the Union on a political issue, in the selection of candidates for the Legislative Council in1946, and ceased from then to take an active part in the union. He was succeeded by Lionel Hurst as 1st Vice President of the Union and Douglas (Kem) Roberts became 2nd Vice President.

Early in 1943, the Union started to set up a co-operative store and bank. A number of shares were sold to members and a small business was established. The co-operative store was still in existence up to the time of publication of Part I of this Book. Although its life had been one of financial struggle, it was able to come to the assistance of the Union many times during the hard and bitter fights over the years. The bank however, had a short and merry life. Many people borrowed money on the strength of their shares and some people were loaned more money than the value of their shares. The majority of borrowers never repaid these loans, despite strenuous efforts to recover the outstanding debts. At an Annual Conference, the union made a decision to close the bank.

Negotiations in the Sugar Industry became an annual affair, and several months before the Crop, the workers from their Trade Union Sections would send their requests for increases to the Union's Head Office. These requests would be corroborated and condensed, then submitted to the employers for consideration before the negotiations started. The employers on the other hand could be expected to counter by asking for a reduction in wages. Whether this was really intended or not was another matter, but it set the stage for negotiations. Without the union, this tactic could have had an adverse effect on the psychology of the workers, who would have had to start arguing at first to preserve the status quo.

This move by the employers did not succeed with the Union's negotiating team, who by then had become well skilled in negotiating, and attempts to reduce wages were brushed aside as not worthy of consideration. Many times, for weeks, the Union and Planters' Association would be locked in struggles over the negotiations, and it was very seldom that talks did not reach a deadlock, when the Planters' Association would refuse to concede certain demands. Afterwards, it would be the inevitable strike before both sides got together again and worked out a compromise.

By 1951, the 12th Anniversary of the birth of the Antigua Trades & Labour Union, wages on the Sugar Estates increased from EC20 cents and EC24 cents per day in 1939 to EC$1.92 per day for men; and from EC12 cents per day to EC72 cents per day for women. In the Factory, unskilled workers received from EC48 cents per day to EC$1.72 per day; semi-skilled workers moved from EC72 cents to EC$3.00 per day and foremen moved from EC$1.00 per day to EC$22.50 per week. On the Waterfront, Stevedores moved from an average of EC$1.68 per day to EC$5.00 per day and carpenters from EC60 cents and EC72 cents per day to EC$2.00 and EC$3.46 per day.

These were the substantial gains made by the workers within the short period of 12 years; but wages were still inadequate and the Union's objectives were to press on further, to obtain as reasonable and fair a return as possible, for all workers throughout Antigua and Barbuda.

For many years, the workers were dissatisfied with cutting cane by the ton, as they claimed that they were not in a position to check on the weight of the cane cut, and felt they were paid less for the work they did, than what they should have received. The Union appealed to the employers to change the system of measuring cane by the ton, to measuring cane by the line, but the employers insisted that it was not profitable, because it entailed additional work. A line consisted of 100 linear ft. and it was felt by the Union that a field could be calculated on the number of lines to the bank and correspondingly to an acre. If the field averaged, 20 tons per acre and the acre had so many lines, the price per ton for cutting cane could then be broken down according to lines. This the Union advised would satisfy the workers, because they would be able to calculate for themselves how much work they had done.

This proposal was put before the Planters' Association at several negotiations, but it was persistently turned down. The workers became adamant that they would not continue to cut cane by the ton, and because the planters did not agree and no amicable settlement could be reached, the workers were called out on strike. This strike lasted for several weeks. One Union Leader in the Eastern Districts, Daniel Skepple, could be remembered for his activity during the strike. He went from Village to Village and from field to field ringing a small bell and calling out to workers, "KILL TON" - this became the slogan of the striking workers.

All efforts by the employers to get the workers to reap the Crop failed, and the good reaping weeks went by with the cane still standing in the fields. Eventually, the employers gave in and agreed to co-operate in working out a system, whereby cane cutters would be paid by the line, instead of the ton. It was a great victory for the workers, and for months throughout the villages, all that could be heard was "TON DEAD". Since then, cane cutters were paid by the line to reap cane.

CHAPTER 12
THE PRESS

As in most organisations, there are times when a shake-up of officials takes place, and so in the process of time, the Union had to dispose of certain leaders. Hugh Pratt, the Treasurer, left his office because of some misunderstanding on his part, and his refusal to adhere to Executive instruction. Lionel Hurst who was succeeded by Douglas Roberts as first Vice President succeeded Pratt, who probably felt the Union would have asked him to return to his post, as he thought he was indispensable to his office. He was mistaken, Hurst took over and made a good job of it.

Shortly afterwards, there was a feeling among certain leaders that Samuel James, the General Secretary and a few other officers of the Union, were not pulling their weight as they ought. There was definite dissatisfaction among some section leaders and members of the organization with the service they were receiving, and internal dissension threatened the union's stability. Bird moved swiftly in this matter, and a clean sweep was made to officers who were deemed to be associated with the dissident faction.

This move also affected Douglas Roberts, who was considered to be sympathetic to the James' faction. Although he was not removed from office by the Executive, he seemed to have fallen into disfavour, and was defeated in the following conference for First Vice President by Ernest Williams, and just barely made the Executive. He soon disassociated himself altogether from the Union and became one of the leaders in an abortive rival movement against the Union.

Lionel Hurst succeeded Samuel James as General Secretary, and the Conference also decided that the post of Treasurer should become an honorary post. This was filled by Novelle Richards, at that time an accountant at Stephen R. Mendes, Ltd., Edmund Lake and Bradley Carrott were elected 2nd and 3rd Vice Presidents respectively. McChesney George, a Civil Servant, was also elected to the Executive, until General Orders ruled that he could not serve.

This period saw the real development of the trade union movement. The Executive became more composite and comprised men who brought a fresh approach to the problems of the day. It was also a period of greater challenge for the Union, for the storm was gathering for the more significant fights, the results of which have changed the entire social, economic and political picture of the island.

One important aspect of the struggle was the part played by the Workers' Voice Newspaper, in bringing the issues to the public and fighting the issues on behalf of the Workers.

It was early in 1943 that Edward Mathurin, a printer and at one time a Vice President of the trade union in its early days, pioneered the publication of a newspaper for the trade union. This first came out in pamphlet form and was later to develop into the Workers Voice as a daily newspaper.

On 7th August, 1943, Mathurin wrote the Executive of the Union, imploring them to start a journal to disseminate news of the Working Class and advancement of the Union, and suggested the Union either enter into a contract with him to publish the journal, or stand bond for him to do so. He also mentioned the coming elections campaign, in which certain officers of the Union might participate, and the usefulness of a journal in the elections.

The Executive, while accepting the suggestion of Mathurin to publish a newspaper, decided to do so on their own, and the Worker's Voice was established in 1944, with Musgrave Edwards a former Editor of the Antigua Star as its first Editor.

At that time, The Antigua Star, founded some years previously, was well established as the leading daily newspaper of the island, representing the conservative view. It was owned by businessmen and catered to business. The Magnet, published by Harold T. Wilson was on the decline, but still found time to attack the Government. The Workers Voice had to win its spurs.

Musgrave Edwards was quick to get the newspaper started, but he was a difficult man. Self willed and self opinionated, he soon found himself quarrelling with the Union Executive. Within a year of the newspaper's founding, Musgrave Edwards left. This placed the Executive in a quandary, but Novelle Richards stepped in to fill the breach in writing editorials and supervising the paper until an Editor was found. After looking around for a suitable person, the Executive decided to appoint Rolston Williams of Parham to the post of Editor.

During this period, there burst upon the public a series of articles in the Workers Voice, "Ringside by By-stander" and "A View from the Amphitheatre by Onlooker," touching on all the problems of the day in Antigua. The Workers Voice from simple beginnings, began to dominate the scene as a journal of thought and opinion. The writers were Novelle Richards and McChesney George, and much interest was taken far and wide from these contributions. Correspondents from various London Dailies, would be sent from England, to discuss the problems and issues of the island, with the article's writers.

During the 1948 shake-up of the Union Executive, Ralston Williams was removed from the post of Editor as one of the James' faction and the job was taken part time by Novelle Richards, until the following year when he broke association with Stephen R. Mendes Ltd., and so became full time Manager and Editor of the paper.

Throughout the bitter struggles of the Union, the Workers Voice served as the refreshing tonic to the workers, by bolstering morale and challenging all the issues that tended to break the organisation. It never dodged an issue, and carried the fight fearlessly until victory was won.

In 1958, George Walter succeeded Novelle Richards as Editor, after the latter was selected to serve on the Federal Parliament and Council of State of the West Indies. In 1960, Milton Benjamin was appointed Editor after Walter became General Secretary, succeeding Lionel Hurst, who was appointed to a Ministry in the Antigua Government.

During the early life of the Workers' Voice, The Magnet went out of production. Wilson had diverted his attention from attacking the Government to attacking the Union. In a straight fight between both newspapers, Wilson was unable to sustain readership. Circulation fell, and the newspaper ceased production.

This left only the Star and the Workers Voice in the field. The Star held to the past and supported the plantocracy's interest, while the Worker's Voice advocated freedom and democracy for the workers in every respect.

In 1956, an opposition group started a new newspaper called The Anvil, to bolster a new political party called the Antigua National Party. This paper was short lived and might only be remembered for its virulent and scurrilous attacks on certain labour readers. It came to be recognised as a scandal sheet and its readership fell rapidly without recovery.

CHAPTER 13
LORD BALDWIN'S APPOINTMENT

Sir Brian Freeston was transferred in 1946 on promotion to the post of Governor of the Fiji Islands and was succeeded by Sir Douglas Jardine. The new Governor was an able administrator with wide experience, but in poor health, his wife was also ill. She died within a year of their coming to Antigua after an abdominal operation and was buried in the St. John's Cemetery. Shortly thereafter, Sir Douglas resigned and returned to England. He died within two years after his wife, and his instruction were that his body should be cremated and his ashes returned to Antigua to be buried in the same grave with his wife. A tombstone in their memory now stands near the entrance to the St. John's Cemetery.

The Labour Party under the leadership of Clement Attlee won the National Elections in Great Britain and had formed the Government, defeating Winston Churchill's Conservative Party, in the first elections after World War II was declared.

The new Labour Government as one of its colonial policies, decided to experiment with a few non-careerist Colonial Governors. Among the three new Governors outside of Colonial Service who were appointed was Oliver Baldwin, the Second Earl of Baldwin of Bewdley and son of Stanley Baldwin, the pre-war Conservative Prime Minister, to be Commander-in-Chief and Governor of the Leeward Islands.

Lord Baldwin unlike his father was a socialist peer, and sat in the House of Lords on the Labour Benches, while his father was head of the Conservative Government. Lord Baldwin was kind and sympathetic to the under-dog and labour. He was somewhat of a recluse, but had vision and ability. He disliked protocol and red tape. The Trade Union welcomed his appointment, for at long last, the workers

70

felt they had a man who from his record, identified himself with the working class people of Britain, with the programmes and policies for the betterment of their welfare, despite being an aristocrat and of the nobility.

At the time of Lord Baldwin's arrival in Antigua, there was an open and undisguised struggle between Moody-Stuart and Bird for economic supremacy in the island. The plantocracy's power was gradually eroding, but Moody-Stuart was still powerful. Bird, who was in the Legislative Council, was the only Labour representative on the Executive Council, which was the centre of power; in the Executive Council, Moody-Stuart had all the influence. Bird did not disguise his resentment of the Executive policies, and the frustration of liberal legislative actions.

In the meantime, the Antigua Syndicate Estates, Ltd., was extending their stranglehold on the economy, by acquiring many more estates, until there was very little of the island's valuable productive lands, not owned by the Company. This resulted in many small farmers with no security of tenure, who were displaced as the Syndicate Estates began to expand its production, and adopted a policy whereby certain areas of the land that was cultivated by the former owners and peasants would be left in reserve. The Trade Union feared the Syndicate Estates expansion programme would leave the majority of peasants and workers at the mercy of one employer.

The struggle between the Union and the Syndicate Estates developed into deep feelings of bitterness. There was no sign of a return to industrial peace and the dark clouds of labour unrest threatened the economic and social stability of the Country. Antigua had become an unhappy island, as there could be no settlement of disputes without strikes. Personal relationship between Moody-Stuart and his colleagues and Bird and his colleagues was so strained, that both sides avoided each other. The Business section and the Chamber of Commerce sided with the planters' group, and there was a distinct battle line drawn between the Union and the employing class.

Lord Baldwin who was sympathetic to the Labour Movement, appreciated the Union's struggle, and persuaded the employers to compromise on certain issues. The employers considered that he was taking sides with labour, and made strong representation against him to the Colonial Office. It was alleged that Moody-Stuart and others requested Baldwin's removal from Office.

Both the planters in Antigua and St. Kitts decided they would yield no more to Labour demands for increases, and as the two Unions would not be satisfied with a freezing of wages in the Sugar Industry, Lord Baldwin agreed with Labour Leaders that in the best interest of all concerned and of industrial peace, a Commission of Inquiry should be appointed for the Sugar Industry of the Leeward Islands. And so in 1948, an Inquiry was set up under Lord Soulsbury, to examine the Sugar Industry's operations, including means of production, profits and their distribution, wages and working conditions, utilisation and distribution of lands. It was also decided that V.C. Bird would serve as a member of the Commission from Antigua, and Robert Bradshaw, President of the St. Kitts Trade Union, as a member from St. Kitts.

While the Commission did not recommend many sweeping changes, Bird and Bradshaw wrote a Minority Report, recommending that the Antigua Syndicate Estates, Ltd., should not acquire any more properties, but that the continuance of the commercial operations of the Syndicate Estates, were essential to the island's economy.

The Report also recommended that The Antigua Syndicate Estates, Ltd., should, where possible, make lands available to the Government for land settlement for the peasants. This was eventually agreed to by the Syndicate Estates, but it took another big struggle in 1951 and another Commissioner of Inquiry under Sir Clement Malone, a former Chief Justice of the Windward and Leeward Islands, to settle once and for all the system of land tenure and land ownership in Antigua.

CHAPTER 14
UNION ENTERS POLITICS

In 1946, there were General Elections to the Legislative Council of Antigua. The Union at that time felt it was capable of contesting all the elected seats. This was considered a necessary aspect of development, to ensure that the Legislature was not used to check the organisation's growth, by introducing hostile labour laws and other repressive measures.

During the course of the selection of candidates by the Union, Joseph Oliver Davis, the 1st Vice President and Member of the Legislative Council, disagreed with the names of certain candidates who were nominated by the Union's Executive. He felt that the Union should have considered more experienced persons, who though not union members, would have been sympathetic to the Union. He did not feel that some of the candidates selected had the educational qualification nor the experience to serve in Council. On this point, he and the rest of the Executive disagreed, and he decided he would not be associated with the election of those candidates and gave the Executive an ultimatum on the matter.

The Union's Executive, undaunted by the ultimatum, decided to drop Davis and went on to select such candidates who were in their estimation, capable of serving on the council. The men selected by the Union were V.C. Bird, D. Leonard Benjamin, Edmund Hawkins Lake, Hugh O. Pratt and Ernest E. Williams. All these men were able to produce the necessary property qualifications for the Council, and all five were elected.

Davis contested a seat in the elections as an independent candidate and was badly defeated. He ceased from then on to take an active part in politics, and devoted his time to business. One thing that must be mentioned in his favour, he refused all invitations to join any other organisation opposed to the Union. He later served for two terms as President of the Senior Chamber of Commerce.

Having won all Elected Seats to the Council, the Union started soon after to plan for Constitutional reform, which would provide for greater Executive powers among the elected members. Despite the fact that the Union had won all of the elected seats, only one union member, V.C. Bird, was again selected to serve on the Executive Council. While his views were respected, very few of his suggestions were upheld or implemented.

The Labour Party in Britain had gone ahead with its nationalisation programme of basic industries and public utilities. There was much talk in Antigua about nationalising the Syndicate Estates lands and the Sugar Factory. But although the question was raised several times, the Union never seriously considered that the Syndicate lands and the Sugar Factory would be nationalised. The first major legislation moved by the Labour Union representatives in Council, was the Nationalisation of the Antigua Electricity Service, a private company. This measure was passed with the assenting Vote of Sydney T. Christian, a nominated member, opposed by two other nominated members, Alexander Moody-Stuart and Ronald Cadman, with the officials abstaining.

Sydney Christian supported the Union's views, that the electricity service was a public utility, and as such would better serve the public as a government-owned project than a private enterprise. This support paved the way for his becoming the first Chairman of the new Statutory Board, which was appointed to operate the electricity.

Electrical Service was the first private enterprise to be nationalised by the Government of Antigua. Although the owners first appeared reluctant to part with the business, they were well treated by the Government and received very fair and favourable compensation. Not long after its acquisition, the former D.C. System and accessories were dismantled to make way for a modern A.C. System, at a cost which might have been beyond the means of the private company. It was difficult too, to contemplate the company sustaining the cost of extending electricity to the rural areas of the island, with possible loss and minimal yield of income from that source.

CHAPTER 15
LORD BALDWINS DILEMMA

In the meantime, Lord Baldwin was earning a reputation for kindness to the poor and destitute, and for his interest in the promotion and development of local art. He was determined to break what he considered class and colour snobbery in the island.

His first action in this respect was to invite people from various segments of society to Government House which was a departure from the policy that only high Government Officials, the white plantocracy, important businessmen and a few coloured folk were invited. For the first time, Government House parties saw as many coloured as white or more coloured than white persons. He went further and entertained inmates of the paupers institute to a party on the Government House Gardens. The colonial whites and upper middle class coloured resented this encroachment of ordinary people on their preserve; some even threatened to boycott Government House parties in the future. This only amused the Governor, who seemed to have found pleasure in crossing swords with the local white and coloured aristocrats.

The steel bands had just begun to emerge. At first they were a riot of sound, with the bandsmen beating pieces of iron accompanied by a bugle or other wind instrument, and they did make a din wherever they went. Many citizens in St. John's wanted the steel bands to be out-lawed as a nuisance. Lord Baldwin and the Labour Union Leaders saw in these bands the beginning of something cultural, and opposed all attempts to interfere with them, provided they kept within legal bounds.

Very soon after, Lord Baldwin offered his services to be the patron of one of the band "The Hells Gate" steel band, and encouraged persons interested in music to come forward and assist in training the bandsmen in the art of music. Mrs. Bertha Higgins was quick to respond to the Governor's appeal, and very soon out of the rabble and medley, came the provocative melodies that soon brought fame to the Antigua Steel bands. Hells Gate and Brute Force becoming the most popular bands owed much to Mr. Vere Griffith, a retired civil servant, who became the music instructor.

Mrs. Bertha Higgins also with Lord Baldwin's support, began to organise displays of local paintings and photography, and very soon, local art groups began to develop and take their place in the cultural life of the island. There were several art exhibitions by the group after its formation.

It was during this period that the first serious attempt was made to solve the water problem of Antigua. A half hearted effort was made in the past, but very little was achieved and each new dry period brought with it the inevitable shortage of water for domestic purposes and livestock.

Lord Baldwin discussed the water problem at length with Bird and his colleagues, and suggested to them that he should invite a water diviner or dowser he heard of from Jamaica, to see if he could help. Bird was willing to try anything, for the greatest interest of the trade union was to ameliorate the hardship caused to the people by the periodical droughts. Lord Baldwin then at some expense to himself, invited Claude Bell, a Jamaican Civil Servant, who won recognition as a Water Diviner in that island, to come and help. Several persons jeered at the proposal in a debate of the Legislative Council, when the matter was raised on the approval of funds to meet some of the diviner's expenses. Even a progressive individual as Sydney Christian, condemned the idea as mumbo jumbo.

Claude Bell found water and lots of it. Many of the wells which provided water for the island's growing demand were located by him, with his tamarind rod. Incidentally, the exercise had its ironic side, for very soon after, the new Administrator, Richard St. J.O. Wayne and the Superintendent of Prisons, Alfred Peters, a sportsman and brother-in-law of the same Christian who ridiculed the idea, were seen with the Divining Rod, looking for underground water, when it was realised that they too had certain divining powers. By then, Christian was convinced that a dowser can find water.

The relationship between Lord Baldwin and the employers did not improve. They prayed for his recall to London or transfer, and maintained a continuous stream of complaints into the Colonial Office. The dignity of the Office of Governor, his accusers claimed, had been lowered, and he bowed to the Labour Union rather than exhibiting firmness. Labour on the other hand appreciated his liberal approach to the problems that existed, and hoped he would use his influence to bring about general political liberties to the island. There was an urgency for constitutional changes, that would give elected Council Members a greater voice in governmental affairs than they enjoyed. Bird and his colleagues impressed to the Governor, the necessity for such changes.

Jamaica at that time had already received an advanced system of internal self-government with the introduction of a Ministerial System of Government, and appointment of a Chief Minister. The 'Bushe" experiment proved successful in Barbados, and that island was also moving on to full Ministerial responsibility, under Grantley Adams. The Antigua Labour leaders felt that the Ministerial system should be introduced in Antigua.

While these discussions were going on, Lord Baldwin received a summons from the Colonial Office to return to London for discussions. He was however "tipped off" by friends in England that it was not routine discussions, but a recall, and a successor was being considered to take his place as Governor of the Leeward Islands. Baldwin intimated this to Bird, who realised that the plantocracy was again gaining the upper hand by influencing the actions of the Colonial Office.

Bird immediately got in touch with the other Leeward Islands Labour Leaders, - Robert Bradshaw of St. Kitts and Robert Griffith of Montserrat, to strongly protest against any attempt by the Colonial Office to remove or transfer Lord Baldwin from the Leeward Islands. Petitions were drawn up in the islands bearing thousands of signatures, requesting that the Governor remain. In the meantime, Lord Baldwin relaxed on a French Banana Ship on his way to England via France, while anticipating the wrath of the Colonial Office. The petitions reached London by air, before his arrival.

The Colonial Office expressed their dissatisfaction to Lord Baldwin, and would have removed him for what it termed incensing the wrath of the leading citizens of the islands. They were however faced with the hostility of the vast majority of the people of the islands against Baldwin's removal, as was borne out by the petitions received and reports reaching London. Lord Baldwin also had friends in high places.

Bird was summoned to London to discuss the matter, and the Colonial Office officials pointed out to him that they had more useful persons to send out. Bird himself would not be moved, and threatened non-cooperation. In light of Bird's sentiments, it was agreed that Lord Baldwin would be sent back, but he should cooperate as much as possible with the leading citizens. Had it been a Conservative Government, things may have been different. But the Labour Government did not want to go down on record as sacrificing a colleague for reactionary matters.

There was great rejoicing in Antigua and the entire Leeward Islands at the news that the Governor was to return. The day of his arrival could be compared to New Year's Day in Antigua. Thousands upon thousands of people from country and town, packed High and East Streets (now Independence Avenue), on the route leading to Government House. Correspondents and photographers from leading newspapers in Great Britain, the United States and Canada, converged upon the island, to cover this important event. Steel bands paraded the city streets, drawing yet more crowds to the scene of the Governor's arrival. As the Governor stepped onto the pier from the launch, a great shout of welcome filled the air, and his car had to be pushed through the thick crowd that mobbed him.

One unfortunate incident took place that day. Alexander Moody-Stuart who was among the welcoming party of dignitaries was assaulted by a young man named Lazarus, who felt that Moody-Stuart was behind the move to recall the Governor, took off his shoe and struck Moody-Stuart in the face with it. Lazarus was convicted for the offence. The majority of the people were incensed at this behaviour, but some thought Lazarus was carried away by the crowd's emotions, not realising what he did was wrong. The Magistrate thought otherwise.

CHAPTER 16
LORD BALDWIN RESIGNS

There was an anti-climax after Lord Baldwin returned. He tried to reform his ways in order to satisfy the Colonial Office, but in doing so he disappointed labour leaders, who, though they realised he was doing his best to be a Colonial Governor and a diplomat, became suspicious and went on their guard.

The Governor was still very popular and beloved by the masses, but he made one serious error; to try to hold in check the rise to power of Bird and the Labour Union by not proposing or pushing as fast as was hoped for the constitutional changes that the Union was advocating. Instead he proposed a type of constitution that would leave himself as sole arbiter, holding the balance of power to the way decisions should swing.

The Governor felt he had the confidence of the people and that Bird knowing his sympathies to the labour movement, would trust him to see that the rights of labour were safeguarded. In short, Baldwin's proposals for constitutional reform were somewhat akin to a sovereignty with him as the benevolent ruler. This was a direct departure from the constitutional changes that had been taking place in the Colonial Empire and Bird was astounded at such proposals. Not that Bird doubted Baldwin's genuine sympathies for the poor; he realised a constitution of that type would place too much power in Baldwin's hand – a power that could easily pass on to his successors, unless there was an immediate Constitutional change to head off this inevitability.

Baldwin might have had other views, but he never disclosed them. It was however obvious to Bird that Baldwin wanted it understood that he was the man in charge, and as such, he could keep Moody-Stuart and Bird under control. Under the epidermis of kindness and sympathy was the true character of the Englishman, whose ambition and work were always to be in command, or as expediency might dictate, to be the Benevolent Patron.

The result of this was coldness between Baldwin and Bird, which also reflected in the relationship between Baldwin and the Union. Gone was the ardour of the past, and it became necessary for the Union through its mouthpiece, the Workers' Voice, to expose Baldwin. It must be realised too, that Bird and his colleagues could not sit idle and allow the Governor to build popularity at the Union's expense. The Union's achievements were through the efforts of its leaders and members, therefore, any erosion of the plantocracy's and Moody-Stuart's power, should rebound to the Union and Bird as the leader.

The plantocracy was happy at this change in relationship between Baldwin and the Union. "We warned you about those Labour leaders," they told Baldwin; however, they did not trust him nor he them. Baldwin soon found himself alone - unwanted by the Colonial Office, disliked by the local aristocracy and middle class, under suspicion by Labour leaders. Though well loved by the masses, his position became almost untenable. He however stuck to his guns for a while, then with almost dramatic suddenness, announced his resignation on the grounds of ill health.

Despite their differences on the constitutional matter, Labour Leaders were sorry to see him go. In his own way, he helped to bring about social change throughout the island, and left his post still in the people's high regard. Though never to see him again in the flesh, ten years after he said goodbye to Antigua, its citizens mourned Baldwin's death, and followed his ashes to its final resting place, among the pagan dead on top of Green Castle Hill.

W.A. MacKinie the Colonial Secretary, was appointed to act as governor until a new appointment was made. Soon after, a dispute arose between the Union and Clarence Johnson, an American contractor, who was responsible for the construction of the club and dwelling houses at the Mill Reef Properties, on the matter of union recognition for the workers employed in the construction work.

Before the dispute was settled, MacKinie was transferred and his successor, Colonial Secretary P.D. MacDonald, acted as Governor. Although Johnson denied it, the Union was convinced that he was encouraged by the other employers not to recognise the union as representative of the workers. Johnson substantiated his independence of the Union, by insisting that while he employed Union members, he had no intention of discussing causes for dismissal with Union representatives; and more so, the majority of workers he employed were non-unionist. The Union disputed that statement, by producing the workers' contribution books for inspection.

A strike was called at Mill Reef which lasted for several weeks. In the meantime, some workers who were not union members because of their religious denomination as Seventh Day Adventists were encouraged to break the strike. This incensed the striking workmen, some of whom resorted to violence.

Government was forced to intervene, and eventually, Johnson decided to recognise the Union as the bargaining agent for the workers. Relationships between Johnson and the Union were flawless from that time onwards.

CHAPTER 17
HURRICANES

In 1950, Antigua experienced several disasters. Fire destroyed the Globe Hotel in St. Mary's Street, and a week or two afterwards, the Leeward Islands Secretariat building in Church Street adjacent to Government House was completely destroyed by fire; all records and documents stored there were lost. Later that year, fire also destroyed a large portion of the Public Works building with loss of material and records.

In August of the same year, two hurricanes struck Antigua and Barbuda within ten days of each other. The first was not very severe, but the second caused considerable damage. Thousands of houses were destroyed or damaged, crops and livestock perished. The second hurricane was accompanied by a tidal wave, which swamped the Government's warehouse, and drove small boats into the streets of St. John's. Thousands became homeless, without food and clothing, and experienced much suffering.

The Red Cross on neighbouring islands and the British Government were quick to assist the stricken island, and soon relief in food and clothing was available. Schools and churches became temporary shelter for many who were homeless, and tents provided by the Red Cross and others helped to ease the serious congestion in the schools. Available homes which withstood the storm assisted in sheltering the victims. The government was quick to organise a hurricane relief committee and soon matters were under control.

The new Governor, Sir Kenneth Blackburne, successor to Lord Baldwin, arrived just after the hurricanes, and he immediately threw himself into the task of providing relief and planning for a comprehensive reconstruction. His services were invaluable to the people, and he used this abundant energy to see that the relief work was carried out with the utmost efficiency.

The hurricanes had destroyed almost all the Wattle and Daub houses in Antigua and the other sub-standard houses as well. To the Labour leaders, this provided a unique opportunity to be rid once and for all of the unsuitable houses and to introduce a progressive re-housing scheme. The Governor supported the views of the Labour leaders, but there were influential persons in the community who suggested that the wattle and daub houses be rebuilt. Labour leaders raised a hue and cry against any attempt to go back to the wattle and daub houses, and enlisted the support of Bustamante in Jamaica and other influential persons. With the Governor's assistance, the Colonial Office eventually decided to support a proper hurricane re-housing programme, to be financed by an Imperial Grant and Loan.

The Antigua Syndicate Estates also fell in line with the scheme and offered free of charge to the Government certain portions of their land adjacent to several villages which could be used as village extensions. These extensions may be seen all over the island. In other places the land was purchased by Government from private owners or might have been land originally owned by Government. The re-housing programme also enabled the Government to secure a large grant for a slum clearance scheme on Garlings Land between South Street and New Street and for purchase of certain portions of land at Ottos as an extension of the scheme. The responsibility for the implementation of the hurricane re-housing and slum clearance scheme was given to the Central Housing and Planning Authority (CHAPA).

The Central Housing and Planning Authority was set up as a Statutory Board in 1948, and had the Senior Medical Officer, Dr. Norman Griffin, as its first Chairman. In 1953, after the death of Alfred Peters, then acting Chairman, Novelle Richards was appointed as the first unofficial Chairman. He was eventually succeeded by Donald Sheppard in 1958 as Chairman. The Secretary of the Authority was Clarence Simon, who held the post for a number of years.

Under the auspices of the Governor and more or less at his suggestion, a Committee was set up to promote village improvement and an annual festival was later launched in 1951, known as the Homes, Families and Gardens Festival. The Festival was highly supported by the trade union and other institutions, and had become an annual feature of community life in Antigua. The Villages that enter the competition were judged by standards of village appearance during the year, and at the time of the festival, school attendance record, criminal record, repayment of Government Loans, and other community functions were also judged. There were also prizes to individuals for best gardens in the village. Community concerts and other entertainment were also presented during the festival week.

One other important effort of the Governor was the organising of the restoration of Nelson's Dockyard at English Harbour, which included as patron, Her Royal Highness, Princess Margaret, Countess of Snowdon, and as members, many influential people in Britain, the U.S.A., Canada and the West Indies. The restoration work was completed and the Dockyard became a yachting centre, and an important tourist attraction for the island.

Efforts were also made by the Governor to salvage the archives of Antigua, which were allowed to deteriorate considerably from age and disuse, and had nearly reached a stage of decay. An archivist from the United Kingdom was loaned to the Antigua Government for a short time, during which he was able to save many of the important documents, some having been sent to Britain for photographic reproduction, or treatment against further deterioration.

CHAPTER 18
DARK DAYS

Life had returned to normal after the hurricanes, and the island looked green with prospects of a good sugar crop. The first sign of trouble in 1951, began with the dismissal of a domestic worker by Quinn Ferrara, a merchant of St. John's, who refused to re-instate the worker after a request from the Union of which she was a member.

The Union decided to picket Quinn Ferrara's place of business, as an extension of the trade dispute. Quinn Ferrara on the advice of his lawyer, took the matter to Court. The Court decided in his favour, that there was no trade dispute and the Union was ordered to remove the pickets and to pay cost and damages. Although his business suffered considerably, Quinn Ferrara did not claim damages, and only settled for costs. He said he wanted the matter closed and forgotten.

During the Ferrara dispute, the question of the Syndicate lands cropped up with angry suddenness. The Soulsbury Commission previously recommended that the Syndicate Estates should turn over some of their land to the Government for peasant cultivation. The Company, although agreeing in principle to the recommendations, was hesitant to turn over the lands, despite repeated requests by the Trade Union. The Department of Agriculture had already earmarked lands in certain areas belonging to the Company, which could be used for land settlement purposes while not disturbing the commercial activities of the Company.

Besides that, the workers in the field and factory had a number of grievances, which were due for settlement; the result was numerous stoppages of work on the Estates. A further development arose when the Syndicate Estates, through their solicitor prohibited Union Field Officers Jonathan Ireland and Levi Joseph, from entering the Syndicate's lands, a matter which greatly impeded the work of the Union in handling disputes in the sugar industry.

The Union decided that the question of the Syndicate Estates tenant lands should be settled once and for all, even if it meant a general strike in the island. The Government was requested to see that the Syndicate Estates implement the agreement, whereby tenancy lands would be turned over to the Government.

* * *

For some years, the idea of the workers celebrating Labour Day on the 1st of May was supported by the Union, and management was requested to co-operate, so that workers could have the day off for celebrations. Management refused, pointing out that taking off the day would interfere with reaping the Crop. The Union responded that it would be like any other holiday, and the workers were not seeking payment for the day, but like other workers, afforded the opportunity to also celebrate Labour Day.

Disregarding management's resistance, the Union went along with its programme for Labour Day, and the majority of the workers turned out to celebrate the event. Following this activity, the management of the Syndicate Estates and the Factory published a notice that the reaping of the Crop would stop indefinitely. However, the Trade Union protested to management and requested that good relationship be restored and all outstanding matters be settled in the interest of industrial peace.

On 8th May, 1952, the Antigua Employers' Federation, successor to the Antigua Planters' Association, in a letter to the Trade Union, listed certain actions of the workers which they considered a breach of the 1951 Agreement, and argued that the breaches were deliberately made by the Union's Executive, or that the workers acting on their own initiative, were beyond the control of their own leaders. In either case it continued, the 1951 Sugar Agreement became a useless instrument in the cause of industrial peace and prosperity in Antigua, and the Federation regretted that they had no alternative but to consider it null and void from the time of receipt of the letter. Further, that the Antigua Trades & Labour Union, could not be recognised as the only organised body representing workers in the Sugar Industry.

The Union replied in a manner explaining its side of the story, which went as follows:

> "...We would like to say that for some time we have been aware of the fact that your Federation was little more than a farce created for the specific purpose of insuring the ganging up of capital on the Union and the engineering of its destruction. In spite of this, we have gone out of our way not only to recognise and co-operate with your Federation, but also to turn a soft answer to many insults and rebuffs in which members of your Federation notably the Syndicate Estates and the Factory have hurled at us from time to time. Your design to destroy rather than co-operate with the Union was often manifested...when it comes to non-recognition of the organisation, this you must realise strikes at the very root of trade unionism, and we shall take the necessary steps to see that it does not occur."

The "pot was on the fire", and the coming days saw a general strike in the island with the waterfront and even workers at the Antigua Printiery out on strike. The whole island was plunged into an atmosphere of gloom, as the workers insisted that this was a fight for their survival, while management was prepared to strike the final blow to put the trade union on its knees.

As the strike continued, relations between management and labour deteriorated yet further, and the business community, the majority of whom were also members of the Employers' Federation, were all on the side of the Syndicate Estates and the Factory, in condemning the labour leaders for bringing about the serious situation that existed. "The Star", the employers' newspaper, viciously attacked the Labour leaders, and the Workers Voice retaliated just as viciously.

While the wild verbal attacks went on, mysterious fires broke out in St. John's, and damage to property was reported. Without evidence to support their allegations, management blamed the workers for the fires. The atmosphere was tense and volcanic, and as the days went by without signs of settlement of the disputes that by then were numerous, workers became restless and were almost hostile.

In the midst of this, the Governor, Sir Kenneth Blackburne, appealed to both sides to settle matters. While the Union was willing to come to terms, the Employers Association felt this was the opportunity to force the Union to a point of surrender. Moody-Stuart it was alleged, informed the Governor that his company had sufficient money, and only needed time to break the Union. To this the Governor replied, Moody-Stuart was mistaken, and would only be hitting his head against a wall.

As there were no signs of settlement and matters seemed likely to grow worse, the Governor, contrary to Bird's advice representing the Union, but on the advice of the rest of the Executive Council declared a State of Emergency, and called for a detachment of British soldiers from Jamaica to maintain order. This was considered one of Blackburne's few mistakes, for local opinion felt that the situation did not occasion such measures, the cost of which had to be borne by the Country.

The Soldiers, the Welsh Fusiliers, came to Antigua and enjoyed themselves for a few weeks, then returned to Jamaica without being called upon, for there was nothing to do. The people remained calm and there was no incident.

It was evident however, that the situation had to be taken in hand. The Governor in an effort to restore peace, appealed to both sides in a broadcast - to do everything to reconcile the position in the Country and for industrial peace. The broadcast seemed to have had an effect on the employers and the Union, because within a few days after it was put on air, both sides wrote to the Governor agreeing to meet to discuss all outstanding matters and to submit all disputes that took place during the year to a Board of Enquiry.

One paragraph from a letter to the Governor by the Employers' Association on his broadcast read as follows:

"I have to inform you that my Federation shares Your Excellency's view that improved relations among all sections of the community are much to be desired, and that, so far from seeking the destruction of the Trades Union in Antigua, it is our desire to see the day when agreement can be made and kept between the Federation and the Union. We hope that as a result of Your Excellency's broadcast, that day has been brought nearer, and we desire to place on record the fact that we shall encourage our members at all times to abstain from any avoidable step which may tend to injure

good relations. Your remark on the subject of the part the Press can play was particularly noted and we ourselves shall endeavour to see that our Member who operates a newspaper does not in fact by undue provocation at any time tend to worsen human relations in this island."

With this and similar expressions by the Union, the way was clear to bring about the long-hoped-for reconciliation which was to evolve after the Board of Enquiry was set up under the chairmanship of Sir Clement Malone and which touched on all vital questions affecting both the employers and the Union.

Apart from the Royal Commission under Lord Moyne, the Malone Enquiry could be considered the most important of its kind to be held in Antigua, since the Trade Union Movement came into existence.

The Inquiry was convened at the Legislative Council Chamber on 11th June, 1951. The Trade Union was represented by A. Richard Hart, a solicitor from Jamaica who was Secretary of the now defunct Caribbean Labour Congress, and who was assisted by Claude Earl Francis, a Barrister-at-Law from Antigua. The Employers' Federation was represented by Sydney T. Christian, assisted by E.E. Harney, both Barristers-at-Law from Antigua. The late Quintin O'Connor, Secretary of the Trade Union Council in Trinidad, also attended in an advisory capacity to the Union.

The Commission comprised Sir Clement Malone, Chairman, and Frank Walcott of Barbados who was Secretary General of the Barbados Labour Union, and Richard Buswell Allnutt, Director for Antigua. The Secretary was Henry J. Elwin, an Antigua Civil Servant.

V.C. Bird as President of the Antigua Trades & Labour Union and other Union Officials attended the Enquiry. Also, A. Moody-Stuart as Chairman of the Employers' Federation, several other employers, the Manager and several staff members of the Antigua Sugar Factory, also attended the Enquiry.

During the Enquiry, the Welsh Fusiliers were brought to Antigua, and the Trade Union refused to take further part in the Enquiry until the troops were withdrawn. The Hearing at the Enquiry resumed after the Troops' withdrawal.

The Board of Enquiry covered all the causes of dispute between the Trade Union and the Employers, and strongly recommended the removal of fear and suspicion by both. It also recommended that the Syndicate Estates should take steps to implement the sale of lands rented by tenants to the Government for establishment of Land Settlement, as the Enquiry felt that the land issue was the main source of the trouble that existed. The Syndicate Estates agreed, and very shortly afterwards, the change over of tenancy lands took place, with the Government becoming the sole owner of large tracks of land in various districts.

The Board also recommended that a day should be agreed upon between the Union, Employers and Government for Labour Day, and if necessary, it be made a public holiday. This was also implemented as were other recommendations.

It is necessary however, to pay a well-deserved tribute to Sir Kenneth Blackburne, a former Governor of the Leeward Islands, for his great assistance and encouragement to the Labour Movement and, in particular, to its leaders during his term of office, and, also for the example he set in promoting the economic and social advancement of the territory of Antigua and Barbuda. Much less could have been achieved under a different Governor but, Sir Kenneth exerted admirable skill and energy into the work of developing this Country as though he had a vested interest in it. For this the Territory has been most grateful and will ever hold him and his wife in the highest esteem.

In 1957, Sir Kenneth Blackburne, after getting an extension of his term of appointment retired, and was afterwards appointed Governor of Jamaica. He was succeeded by Sir Alexander Williams who became the last Governor of the Leeward Islands.

CHAPTER 19
POLITICAL DEMOCRACY

After long negotiations, sweeping constitutional changes came about in 1951. For the first time there was full adult suffrage without qualifications of income or literacy test, and the individual had the right to vote or to stand for election provided he was a British subject, 21 years old, was not a lunatic and registered as a voter. The person nominated for election was required to pay a deposit of EC$100.00 to the Elections Officer on the day of his nomination.

The new Constitution also provided for an increase in the Elected Members from five to eight, for three nominated members, and for the introduction of a Committee System of Government as a preliminary to the Ministerial system. There were to be three Elected Chairmen of Committees, who in time would become Ministers of the Crown, once further arrangements came into effect and other members of Council were to associate themselves with the work of the Committees in order that they could get some insight into the functions of Government.

Instead of having an all-Island constituency, Antigua was to be divided into eight separate constituencies. The Chairmen of Committees were to be members of the Executive Council, which then provided for three elected members and one nominated member, together with the Governor, the Administrator, the Attorney General and the Financial Secretary.

Similar constitutional changes were to take place in St. Kitts and Montserrat, and the Federal Legislative Council was to be re-constituted with five Elected Members from both St. Kitts and Antigua and Barbuda, two Elected Members from Montserrat, one from the British Virgin Islands and a nominated member from each of the four territories; the Colonial Secretary, the Federal Financial Adviser, the Attorney General and the Governor being the Official Members.

The eight Constituencies in Antigua and Barbuda were as follow:

> St. John City North
>
> St. John City South, which included Barbuda
>
> St. John Rural North, with St. George
>
> St. John Rural West
>
> St. John Rural South
>
> St. Paul
>
> St. Peter with St. Philip
>
> St. Mary

The Union selected eight candidates to contest the eight seats and all were successful. The three Chairmen of Committees were:

> V. C. Bird
>
> E. H. Lake
>
> E. E. Williams

The candidates elected were:

> Bradley T. Carrott
>
> Lionel Hurst
>
> Novelle Richards
>
> Denfield W. Hurst
>
> Donald Sheppard

The Nominated Members were:

> Alexander Moody-Stuart (re-appointed to the Executive Council)
>
> Sydney T. Christian
>
> Ronald Cadman

The Committee system was so successful in Antigua, that there was no hesitation in the Governor recommending an advanced Constitution for the Territory. This did not take place however until 1956, with the new elections and a revised constitution, which then provided for the Ministerial System of Government. There were to be three full-time ministers and another elected member to serve on the Executive Council, who could act as Minister during the absence from the Colony or illness of any Minister.

The Union again contested all eight elected seats with the same candidates as the previous election, and all were successful.

V. C. Bird was appointed Minister of Trade & Production; E. H. Lake, Minister of Social Services; E.E. Williams, Minister of Public Works & Communications. Bradley T. Carrott was appointed as the Fourth Elected Member to the Elective Council, while A. Moody-Stuart was again re-appointed to the Executive Council as a Nominated Member. Dr. Luther Reginald Wynter and Stephen Roy Mendes replaced Sydney T. Christian and Ronald Cadman respectively, as Nominated Members of the Legislative Council.

During 1956, the 81 year old Federation of the Leeward Islands was dissolved and Antigua and the other Islands became separate Colonies. The dissolution of the federation was the stepping stone to the proposed Federation of the West Indies, which was inaugurated in 1958.

The Union contested the two elected seats allocated to Antigua in the Federal Parliament of the West Indies, and the two candidates, Novelle H. Richards and Bradley T. Carrott were successful in the Federal Elections. These two resigned from the Antigua Legislative Council and were succeeded by George Sheppard and Edgar Turner. Carlton Moore, a retired Civil Servant, and Mrs. Bertha Higgins were recommended to the Governor-General for appointment to the Federal Senate, and were duly appointed.

In1961, further constitutional changes came about, when the elected membership of the Legislative Council was increased from eight to ten, and a Chief Minister was appointed. There was also an increase in the Ministries with the appointment of an additional Minister and a Minister without portfolio.

The nominated membership was reduced from three to two, and the Chief Minister was responsible for choosing his Ministers.

The post of Governor of the Leeward Islands was abolished and the Administrator became the Queen's Representative. Provision was also made for the appointment of a Speaker for the Legislative Council.

With the increase of elected seats, the constituencies had to be revised. Barbuda was made a separate constituency, and a new constituency was carved out of the rural areas of St. John's Rural East, with some adjustment of boundaries. This new constituency became St. George.

The Union again contested all the elected seats and won. This brought three newcomers to the Legislative Council on the elected side - McChesney George representing Barbuda, Joseph Lawrence representing St. George and Christian Simon replacing Edgar Turner in the Constituency of St. Mary. Alexander Moody-Stuart declined further nomination to the Legislative Council and was succeeded by James Watson, Manager of the Antigua Sugar Factory; Stephen Roy Mendes was again appointed as a Nominated Member. Shortly after the elections, A. Moody-Stuart was commissioned a Knight, in the Queen's New Years Honours, for services to Antigua, and so became Sir Alexander Moody-Stuart.

V. C. Bird as leader of the Union Party, was requested by the Administrator, Ian Turbott, who succeeded Alec Lovelace, the former Administrator, who at that time was Defence Officer of the Federal Government, to form a Government. Bird selected as his Department Ministers: Lionel Hurst who was then General Secretary of the Antigua Trades & Labour Union; E.H. Lake, E.E. Williams, McChesney George as Minister without Portfolio. The Legislative Council selected Denfield Hurst as Speaker and Joseph Lawrence as Deputy Speaker

CHAPTER 20
PICKETING AND THE COURTS

The period between 1951 to the present was one of comparative industrial peace in the island. The settlement of the tenancy lands of the Syndicate Estates and the application of the roster system on the waterfront removed the basic causes of the former grievances and the way was made clear for free negotiations on specific industrial matters, without having extraneous matters introduced.

One other significant factor that cleared the air, was the agreement reached by the Union, the Employers Federation and the Government to have Labour Day recognised as a public holiday, on the first Monday in May of each year. The workers were jubilant at that decision, for at last they could celebrate on a day of their own without interference.

Gradually, relationship between the Union, the Sugar Factory and Syndicate Estates improved, everyone concerned saw the fruits of co-operation. The workers still demanded increases and management was still reluctant to concede. But negotiations were entered into with a spirit of goodwill, which eventually saw both sides making compromises in the interest of industrial peace.

The guaranteed price for sugar provided for in the Commonwealth Sugar Agreement also enabled both Management and the Union to reach agreement on increases to the workers, who made substantial gains over the years, in sharing the wealth the Sugar Industry created.

There were however, minor incidents and misunderstandings in the Sugar Industry, which resulted in further inquiries and investigations into the operations, profits and losses of the Sugar Factory and Syndicate Estates. Payment to peasants for the supply of cane to the Industry also came under scrutiny of the inquiries and investigations. Professor Simon Rottenberg of the University of Puerto Rico among others, made investigations, and recommended the course to be followed by the Union and Management. Many of the recommendations were implemented.

It was however clear to the Union, that the Sugar Industry was becoming a cause for concern. Three consecutive years of drought between 1959 and 1961 resulted in very poor crops, and the Syndicate Estates with an accumulation of heavy losses contemplated liquidation, because the Banks refused to extend additional credit to the Company. The Union and the Government realised that any such action would be disastrous to the economy of the island, dependent as it was on the sugar industry. The Government was compelled to go to the assistance of the Sugar Industry, by providing financial aid through loans and guarantees to the Banks. Management made recovery efforts, with Government keeping a watchful eye on operations.

In 1955, the Union was to have one of its greatest challenges in a legal tussle with O'Neal's Drug Store, when a dispute arose between O'Neal's and the Union on the dismissal of a clerk. The Union felt that the clerk was wrongfully dismissed and asked for re-instatement. When the employers refused, the matter was taken before the Labour Commissioner, who met both parties and gave his opinion that the dismissal was unjustified.

The employers felt they had a legal right to dismiss any worker in their employ, and refused to consider the matter further. The Union then asked the Government to carry out an inquiry into the matter, as it threatened industrial peace. The employers refused to take part in the Inquiry, giving as their reason that there was no trade dispute. However, the Board of Inquiry sat and took evidence, including the summary of the meeting held between the employers and the union with the Labour Commissioner. After examining the facts, the Board of Inquiry subsequently supported the Union in its claim that the worker was wrongfully dismissed. Accordingly, the Board made its recommendations to the Government, which were also submitted to the employers for their information and implementation. The employers again ignored the recommendations. As a consequence of the employers' action, the Union by Executive Resolution, caused the Drug Store to be picketed.

O'Neal's Drug Store took the matter to Court, charging the Union with conspiracy to do damage, and claimed for losses sustained by the business as a result of the conspiracy. V. C. Bird and other Executive members together with two picketers, were accused by the Drug Store to have committed unlawful acts, by molesting people who went to the Store to buy and creating a nuisance.

The Union engaged as its Counsel Errol Barrow, a barrister-at-law and politician from Barbados, who later became Premier of Barbados; the Drug Store had as its Counsel E. E. Harney assisted by his brother Harold Harney.

Justice Date in his decision found there was a trade dispute, and the Union had used unlawful means of furthering the dispute thereby conspiring against the Drug Store. The Union was ordered to pay costs and damages and to remove the pickets.

The Union appealed the decision to the West Indies Court of Appeal, comprising Chief Justice Joseph Mathieu-Perez of Trinidad as President, Donald Jackson and Frank Holder, Chief Justices of the Windward and Leeward Islands and British Guiana, respectively. In his submission to the Court, Mr. Harney contended that the dismissed clerk was not a workman within the terms of the Trade Union Act, Trade Dispute and Arbitration Act. The definition of workman includes labourers, and as such, was restricted to that category of workers. Justice Date's decision was upheld by the Appeals Court, which ruled there was no Trade Dispute, dismissed the Union's appeal and increased the damages.

In the course of the legal submissions by Counsel, the President of the Court, Chief Justice Mathieu-Perez, on hearing the name Levi Joseph, who was said to be the picket organiser, remarked that Joseph should be bound hand and feet and thrown overboard. From that moment, Joseph absented himself from the Court's proceedings until the case ended. The hearing lasted for several days.

The Union dissatisfied with the Court of Appeal's decision, which did not disguise its hostility towards the Union during the hearings, decided after discussions with Errol Barrow, to appeal to the Privy Council. The Appeal was allowed and the decision of the Privy Council was noteworthy; it settled the question of a Trade Dispute and altered the decision of the West Indian Court of Appeal. The interest and importance of this case, makes it worthwhile to publish the judgment rendered.

PRIVY COUNCIL APPEAL No. 22 OF 1958

Vere Cornwall Bird and others   -   -   -   Appellants

v.

Joseph Reynolds O'Neal and another   -   -   Respondents

FROM

THE WEST INDIAN COURT OF APPEAL

JUDGMENT OF THE LORDS OF THE JUDICIAL COMMITTEE OF THE PRIVY

COUNCIL

Delivered 26th July, 1960

PRESENT AT THE HEARING:

Lord Radcliffe

Lord Tucker

Lord Cohen

(Delivered by Lord Tucker)

This Appeal by special leave from a judgment of the West Indian Court of Appeal arises out of an action claiming damages and an injunction brought by the respondents against the appellants as a result of events which followed a resolution of the Executive Committee of the Antigua Trades and Labour Union authorising the General Secretary to take necessary steps to picket the business premises of the respondents. The circumstances leading up to the passing of this resolution are conveniently set out in the judgment of the trial Judge, Date, J., as follows:-

In May 1949, one Averyl Winter was employed as a clerk at the Drug Store on a weekly basis. She continued working there until Saturday, 11th June, 1955, when she was summarily dismissed by the Plaintiff, Gertrude O'Neal, and paid one week's wages in lieu of notice; no reason was given for the dismissal.

Sunday, 12th June was, of course, *a dies non.*

On Monday, 13th June, the Defendant, Ireland, a Field Officer of the Antigua Trades and Labour Union, of which Miss Winter is a member, went to Miss O'Neal and asked for the reasons for Miss Winter's dismissal. Miss O'Neal refused to give any. Thereupon, according to Miss O'Neal, Mr. Ireland demanded one year's pay for Miss Winter, and this was also refused.

Representations were then made by the Union to the Labour Commissioner of Antigua and Barbuda about Miss Winter's dismissal, and conciliation meetings under his Chairmanship were held at the Labour Department between representatives of the Drug Store and representatives of the Union on 23rd June and 7th July. At both meetings, the Union representatives asked for the reinstatement of Miss Winter. The representatives of the Drug Store said that in dismissing Miss Winter without giving reasons and paying her a week's wages in lieu of notice, they were acting within their legal rights, and that they were not prepared to consider the claim for reinstatement. At the second meeting, a written undertaking was signed by Miss Winter to the effect that nothing said there would be used by her in any case of slander or libel; the representatives of the Drug Store persisted in their refusal to reinstate Miss Winter. The Chairman inquired whether they would be prepared to consider settling the matter on a basis other than reinstatement, to which they replied in the negative.

The voluntary negotiations having broken down, the Union approached Government for the appointment of a Board of' Inquiry under the Trade Disputes (Arbitration and Inquiry) Act, 1939, Section 8 (1) of which reads:

"8 (1) Where any Trade Dispute exists or is apprehended the Governor may, whether or not the dispute is reported to him under this Act, inquire into the causes and circumstances of the dispute, and, if he thinks fit, refer any matter appearing to him to be connected with or relevant to the dispute to a Board of Inquiry (hereinafter referred to as the Board) appointed by him for the purpose of such reference, and the Board shall inquire into the matters referred to it and report thereon to the Governor."

By instrument dated 16th August 1955, the then Acting Governor of the Leeward Islands appointed a Board of Inquiry to inquire into the causes of the dispute that arose over the dismissal of Miss Averyl Winter by the Proprietors of O'Neal's Drug Store, St. John's, and to report thereon to the Governor and to submit to him such conclusions, recommendations and observations as the Board sees fit.

At the Inquiry, which was held on the 24th August, Mr. E. E. Harney, representing the Plaintiffs, submitted in inter alia that there was no Trade Dispute between Miss Winter and the Drug Store and that the appointment of the Board was, consequently, invalid. The gist of his contention was that the relationship of employer and employee had been legally terminated by the giving of a week's wages to Miss Winter in lieu of notice, and that there could therefore be no Trade Dispute within the meaning of the Act under which the Board was operating. The Board ruled that 'the terms of reference contained in the instrument dated 16th August, 1955, which gave the Board its validity showed *prima facie* that there was a Trade Dispute existing between the proprietors of O'Neal's Drug Store and Miss Averyl Winter and therefore the Board had full power and authority to inquire into the dispute'. At this stage Mr. Harney sought and was granted permission to withdraw from the Inquiry, and the Plaintiffs took no further part in the proceedings, but the minutes at the Labour Department, which contained *inter alia* the reasons given by Miss O'Neal for the dismissal of Miss Winter, were produced in evidence and closely examined.

In its report submitted to the Acting Governor on 31st August 1955, the Board, after setting out its findings, expressed the opinion that there was no moral justification for the dismissal of Miss Winter and, using as a norm one of the accepted principles of mutual respect and tolerance of human rights between employer and workman, recommended the proprietors of the Drug Store be asked to pay her a sum equivalent to thirteen weeks' wages 'as a compensation for her dismissal.'

Under cover of a letter from the Administrator of Antigua dated 6th September 1956, a copy of the report was sent to Mr. Harney for the information of his clients and himself 'and such action with the view to a settlement of the dispute as may be deemed advisable'. In a letter, the Administrator also informed Mr. Harney and his clients that the Acting Governor agreed generally with the recommendations of the Board. The Plaintiffs ignored this communication, and on the 26th September the Administrator caused the Report to be published in the local press. The following day the Plaintiff's business premises were picketed.

The picketing took place pursuant to the resolution referred to above of the Executive Committee of the Antigua Trades and Labour Union on the 9th September 1955, which read as follows:-

> "Be it resolved that provided up to the time of the publication of the Board's award the dispute between Miss O'Neal and the Trade Union is not settled and the General Secretary should take the necessary steps to picket the business premises."

After the meeting, the appellants Joseph (No. 7) and Hurst the General Secretary (No. 8) engaged six paid pickets to picket the respondent's business premises.

The appellants numbers Nos. 1 to 7 and number 9 were all members of the Executive Committee of the Union. Samuel (No. 8) was not a member, but was described as the chief picket. Nos. 4 and 6 (Williams and Ireland) were not present at the meeting of the Executive Committee when the resolution was passed. Hurst in his evidence at the trial stated that he gave the pickets instructions to conduct themselves in an orderly manner and told them that their duty was to pass on information to members of the public with regard to the dispute and not to molest anyone.

Paragraphs 5 -10 of the respondents' Statement of Claim are as follows:

> 5. The first seven named and the last named Defendants and each of them wrongfully and maliciously conspired and combined amongst themselves (with intent to injure the Plaintiffs and thereby compel them to submit to the demand of the Antigua Trades and Labour Union to pay compensation to one Averyl Winter a former clerk in O'Neal's Drug Store who had recently been lawfully dismissed from her employment by the Plaintiffs) wrongfully and without legal authority to watch and beset or cause or procure to be watched and beset the said business places of the Plaintiffs and the approaches and entrances thereto in such manner as was calculated to intimidate customers and prospective purchasers.

> 6. In furtherance and execution of their said conspiracy and combination the first said seven named and the last named Defendants

and each of them wrongfully and without legal authority caused or procured the Defendant Joseph Samuel and other persons to the number of 12 or thereabout (hereinafter referred to as the pickets) wrongfully and without legal authority to watch and beset the said business places of the Plaintiffs daily from the 17th day of September 1955, in such a manner as is calculated to intimidate customers and prospective purchasers and to obstruct the approaches thereto. The first seven named and the last named Defendants and each of them in acting as in this paragraph stated acted for the purpose of intimidating and preventing customers and prospective purchasers from entering the said business place and purchasing therein.

7. The first seven named and the last named Defendants on several occasions on the 17th day of September 1955, and on diverse other occasions thereafter attended outside the said business places of the Plaintiffs or in the vicinity thereof and gave encouragement to the said pickets.

8. The Defendant, Levi Joseph and the pickets have by threats and acts of violence and intimidation and coercion prevented diverse customers and prospective purchasers from entering the said business places and purchasing therein."

PARTICULARS

1. On the 17th day of September 1955, the Defendant, Levi Joseph led a Steel band and a number of pickets carrying placards to the said business places of the Plaintiffs and surrounded same blocking the approaches and entrances thereto and shouting in a threatening manner to persons who attempted to enter the said business places "Don't buy from O'Neal's Drug Store, a Strike is on.

2. On the said 17th day of September 1955, and on several days thereafter the Defendant, Joseph Samuel, who is well known to the general public as a local constable paraded up and down outside the said business

places ringing a bell shouting "Don't buy from O'Neal's Drug Store people. "You no hear you no foo buy from this Drug Store". And when people asked why not? Defendant Samuel told them that the police will lock them up.

3.   The said Defendant, Joseph Samuel, on the 19th day of September 1955, assaulted a person whose name is unknown who was attempting to enter one of the business places for the purpose of purchasing therein.

4.   The said pickets carrying flags and placards with slogans such as "Hold the line. The workers security is challenged" written thereon attend daily around the said business places and in a menacing and threatening manner surround and obstruct persons, especially old men and women and children, who attempt to enter the said business places shouting at them "Hold the line".

5.   The Defendant, Levi Joseph, on the morning of the 24th September 1955, and other pickets conducted themselves in a boisterous and disorderly manner, marching up and down in front of the said business places shouting "Hold the line" ___ "Don't buy from this Drug Store, workers must be respected".

6.   In the alternative, the Defendants and each of them wrongfully and maliciously conspired with intent to injure the Plaintiffs, to create a nuisance by the continuous shouts and other noises of the pickets and by obstructing the approaches to the said business places of the Plaintiffs, thereby seriously interfering with the comfort of the Plaintiffs and the ordinary enjoyment of the said premises by them.

7.   By reason of the conspiracy, the Plaintiffs have suffered damages. Loss estimated at EC$500.00 up to this date has thereby been incurred.

The Plaintiffs claim against the Defendants and each of them: -

    (1)   Damages.

    (2)   An injunction restraining the Defendants, their Servants and agents from unlawfully watching and besetting the business places of the Plaintiffs.

Evidence was given on both sides as to what took place during the picketing over the period from 17th September to the date of the trial on 30ᵗʰ November 1955, but neither Samuel nor any of the other pickets was called. After referring to the evidence and having remarked on the absence from the witness box of all the pickets, the Judge said:-

> *"Having given careful attention to these and the other arguments advanced by learned counsel for the defence, I am, nevertheless, after the fullest consideration of the evidence of all the witnesses I have had the opportunity of hearing and observing, of the opinion that the particular incidents mentioned by me as having been related by Gertrude O'Neal, Linda O'Neal, Victoria Frederick, Cardigan Stevens and Iris Barrow, did take place, and that their accounts of them are substantially correct; these persons impressed me as being essentially truthful witnesses, whatever their feelings towards the Union."*

The Court of Appeal, after referring to the passage cited above said:

> *"There is abundant material from which the learned Judge could so find and we endorse that finding."*

There are therefore concurrent findings of fact on this part of the case which clearly establish, when the evidence which the Judge accepted is looked at, that intimidation and threats of violence were used to prevent customers from entering the business premises of the respondents to an extent which amounted to an actionable nuisance. How far responsibility for these acts of the pickets can be established against all or some of the appellants will, however, require further consideration.

<u>The trial Judge approached this question as follows:</u>

He found that the appellants, other than Samuel, had by the resolution of 9th September, 1955, agreed to the picketing of the respondents' premises, that the General Secretary had appointed the pickets pursuant to the authority conferred on him by the resolution and that the pickets so appointed had used coercion, intimidation and threats of personal violence, that the pickets so appointed were the servants of the appellants who were liable for the acts of their servants. He accordingly held that, although the predominant object of the picketing was the furthering by the appellants of their own interests, they had conspired to achieve their purpose by the use of unlawful means.

Samuel, although he was not a member of the Executive Committee and had not attended any of its meetings, was held liable as the Judge said it was not disputed that he had combined with the other appellants for the purpose of picketing the respondents' premises.

This reasoning cannot be supported.

The pickets were not the servants of the individual appellants. They were appointed by the Antigua Trades and Labour Union which could of course only act by agents who were in this case the Executive Committee and the General Secretary, but this does not create the relationship of Master and Servant between these persons and the pickets. The General Manager or Works Foreman of an industrial limited liability company may have authority to engage and dismiss workmen and direct their operations but this does not make the workmen appointed by them their servants.

The Court of Appeal, as previously stated, endorsed the trial Judge's findings with regard to the means and methods adopted in the picketing, but were not satisfied that he made a definite finding that the main purpose of the conspiracy was to further the appellants' legitimate interests and said that they were still less convinced that there was sufficient and satisfactory evidence to support such a conclusion. Having examined the evidence they said: -

> "*An examination of the evidence clearly reveals not only what was the real intention of the appellants but also the nature of their agreement at*

the material time, their external acts and their conduct show that by mutual consent and acquiescence they had a common purpose, that is, to cause injury to the respondents and bring them into subjection by employing means which were manifestly unlawful."

They do not seem to have examined the position of each individual appellant in order to determine whether - and if so - how he had become a party to the unlawful conspiracy. It would therefore appear that they must have approached the question in the same way as the trial Judge, i.e., on the basis of the existence of the relationship of Master and Servant between the individual members of the Executive Committee and the pickets.

In rejecting any conclusion adverse to the appellants based on the Master and Servant theory their Lordships must not, however, be understood as saying that a finding of unlawful conspiracy might not have been established against some of the appellants if the Courts below had approached the case from a different angle, i.e., by looking to see what part, if any, each appellant had played in connection with each specific incident when threats or intimidation had been used and then considering whether such part necessarily compelled the interference that the particular respondent was party to a conspiracy to use unlawful means to further the object of the picketing and thereby create a nuisance. Their Lordships do not consider it would be proper for them at this stage to undertake such an investigation in the absence of clear and convincing evidence implicating the persons concerned and pointing irresistibly to their participation in an unlawful conspiracy.

Examination of the evidence accepted by both Courts below does, however, reveal beyond doubt that the appellants, Joseph (the organiser) and Samuel (the chief picket) - apart from any question of conspiracy -were present and actively assisting in the picketing which was being carried out with threats and intimidation so as to obstruct the approaches to the respondents' premises continuously from the 17th September to 26th November 1955, thereby constituting a nuisance which has been found to have caused damage to the respondents' trade.

Joseph led the Pickets on 17th September when they were first posted and was frequently present thereafter during the period in question. Samuel was present throughout.

On 17th September, when the pickets arrived, Joseph was at their head and taking a leading part. He was shouting 'Don't buy from O'Neal's Drug Store, and told the pickets to shout behind the people going into the store.

Samuel was present throughout and himself shouted 'Don't buy from O'Neal's'. One of the pickets (a Dominican named Tilton Theophile) threatened to knock down several persons attempting to enter the store. On 19th September, Samuel, who was a special constable, told people they would get into trouble if they went in.

24th September was a particularly noisy day. Some pickets were heard to threaten to beat people if they went in. Joseph was present that day, egging the pickets to shout louder. The respondents telephoned the police to complain. Joseph said he was temporarily substituting for one of the pickets. After a visit from the police Joseph was urging the pickets to shout louder.

On 15th October, a young woman was surrounded by pickets and entered the store 'almost in a state of collapse'. On the 11th November, Samuel said to a customer 'Nelson, don't you hear, you must not go in there to buy - you is a dog'.

On 26th November, a Mrs. Allen asked Samuel what was the meaning of the words 'Hold the line' (which was a slogan freely used by the pickets throughout this period) and was told it meant that nobody should enter the drug store.

The Court of Appeal in referring to these matters said: -

'In reality the evidence discloses that on the morning of 17th September 1955, the pickets carrying placards arrived accompanied by a Steel band playing and a large crowd. The appellant, Samuel, was one of the pickets. They were installed around the premises by the appellant, Levi Joseph, with much flourish, fanfare and noise. Thereafter their behaviour was of such a nature as to intimidate and prevent people from going into the store and it is clear as found by the trial Judge, methods of obstruction, coercion, intimidation and threats of personal violence were used. On occasions the pickets kept up a continuous shouting for sustained periods to such an extent as to constitute a nuisance.'

Their Lordships are satisfied that the concurrent findings of facts are sufficient to establish the existence of a nuisance which has caused damage to the respondents and that the evidence accepted by the trial Judge clearly shows that the appellants, Joseph and Samuel, are liable as participants with others in the creation and continuance of the nuisance. The Statement of Claim alleges in the alternative a conspiracy to create a nuisance and the creation thereof pursuant to such conspiracy. Their Lordships do not consider it necessary or desirable to investigate whether the participation of the appellants Joseph and Samuel, in the creation of the nuisance was in pursuance of a previous conspiracy or not. It suffices that they are each responsible for the tort in the commission of which they have assisted. They are accordingly liable for the damage which the trial Judge has assessed at the sum of 80 pounds (EC$384.00) and as against them the respondents are entitled to an injunction the terms of which will be indicated later.

It will have been observed that so far no reference has been made to the legislation relating to Trade Disputes. As there is nothing in the relevant legislation to protect any individual from liability for torts committed by him, whether in furtherance of a Trade Dispute or not, it is not strictly necessary to the decision of this appeal to determine certain questions which are of considerable importance to trade unions and employers and which figured prominently in the Courts below. But their Lordships consider it is desirable to make some observations thereon.

The relevant statutory provisions are as follows: -

Trade Unions Act, 1939

Section 2 In this Act: "Workmen" includes labourers.

'Trade Dispute' means any dispute or difference between employers and workman, or between Workmen and Workmen, connected with the employment or non-employment, or with the terms of employment, or with the conditions of labour, of any person.

Section 6 (A)

(1)

(2) An act done in pursuance of an agreement or combination by two or

more persons shall, if done in contemplation or furtherance of a trade dispute, not be actionable unless the act, if done without any such agreement or combination, would be actionable.

Section 7:

It shall be lawful for one or more persons, acting on their own behalf or on behalf of a Trade Union or of an individual employer or firm in contemplation or furtherance of a Trade Dispute, to attend at or near a house or place where a person resides or works or carries on business or happens to be if they so attend merely for the purpose of peacefully obtaining or communicating information or of peacefully persuading any person to work or abstain from working.

Trade Disputes (Arbitration and Inquiry) Act, 1939.

The expression 'workmen' means any person who has entered into or works under a contract with an employer, whether the contract be by way of manual labour, clerical work or otherwise, be expressed or implied, oral or in writing, and whether it be a contract or service or apprenticeship, or a contract personally to execute any work or labour.

Section 8(i)

Where any Trade Dispute exists or is apprehended, the Governor may, whether or not the dispute is reported to him under this Act, inquire into the causes and circumstances of the Dispute, and, if he thinks fit, refer any matter appearing to him to be connected with or relevant to the Dispute to a Board of Inquiry (hereinafter referred to as 'the Board') appointed by him for the purpose of such reference, and the Board shall inquire into matters referred to it and report thereon to the Governor.

It was contended by counsel for the respondents at the trial that in order to constitute a trade dispute over a dismissal, a dispute or difference must arise between the remaining employees and the employer. In the present case there was no dispute or difference between the remaining employees (none of whom were members of the Union) and the respondents. He also appears to have contended that in any event there can be no trade dispute between a dismissed employee and a dismissing employer if the dismissal was lawful (i.e., if the period of notice required by law is given or payment in lieu thereof made).

The Trial Judge rejected these submissions. He held that a trade dispute existed and that the predominant object of the picketing was a furthering by the appellants of their own interests, although they had other objects in mind and unlawful means had been used. On appeal the respondents by cross appeal gave notice that they would contend: (1) That the definition of workman in the Trade Unions Act, 1939, does not include clerk, and (2) That the Judge was wrong in holding that a trade dispute existed between the respondents and Averyl Winter represented by the Antigua Trades and Labour Union.

The Court of Appeal accepted both their contentions and increased the damages from £80 (EC$384.00) to £100 (EC$480.00) by reason of the non-existence of a trade dispute. In arriving at their conclusions, the Court of Appeal held that the only Dispute was between the Union and the respondents, basing themselves on certain observations of Bennett, J., in the Court of Appeal in Rex v. National Arbitration Tribunal (1941) 2 K.B. 405. These observations were, however, not relied upon by the respondents when the case reached the House of Lords (1943) A. C. 166, where the decision of the Appeal was reversed and Viscount Simon, L. C., in his speech stated that they must be regarded as abandoned. Lord Wright described as 'strangely out of date', the argument that a Trade Union acting on behalf of its members against their employer cannot be a trade dispute.

The Court of Appeal further held that Miss Winter was not a workman. They would appear to have construed the words 'workmen include labourers' in Section 2 of the Trade Unions Act, 1939, as amended. Although it is true that the definition was such in the Trade Unions Act, there is nothing to compel a limited and restricted meaning to the word 'workman' in the latter Act. On the contrary, the subject matter would seem to their Lordships, in the absence of words of limitation, to call for a wide and liberal interpretation which should not exclude

110

shop assistants. With regard to the trial Judge's finding that the predominant object of the Picketing was the furtherance of the appellants' own interests, their Lordships are unable to agree with the Court of Appeal that this did not amount to a Definite finding that the main purpose of the alleged conspiracy was to further the appellants' legitimate interests nor can they accept the view that the finding was not justified by the evidence. Their Lordships also agree with the trial Judge's rejection of the submission that the lawful dismissal of a workman cannot be the subject of a Trade Dispute.

For the reasons previously stated, however, their Lordships will humbly advise Her Majesty that the judgment of the trial Judge be varied by entering judgment to the respondents for the sum of £80 (EC$384.00) damages against the appellants Joseph and Samuel restraining from creating a nuisance to the respondents by using threats or intimidation or inciting other persons to use threats or intimidation to deter customers from entering the premises of the respondents or otherwise obstructing free access by the public thereto, be substituted for the injunction ordered by the trial Judge.

The appellants Joseph and Samuel must pay one-half of the costs in the Courts below excluding the costs of the cross appeal, which must be paid by the respondents, and excluding the costs of joining the appellant Hurst and the costs of an incidental to the two applications for an interim injunction as to which the trial Judge's order will stand.

There will be no order as to the costs of the present appeal.

CHAPTER 21
THE UNION AND THE CHURCHES

Generally speaking, the Trade Union Movement had a cordial relationship with the Churches, although there are exceptions with individual ministers. In most parishes, the priests were the centre of influence among the parishioners and were dependent on the planters for substantial contributions to the Churches. Some of these priests saw the Trade Union Movement as a challenge to their influence, and many times sided with the planters to oppose the Trade Union. However, many of those who tried to oppose the Movement were not always successful in their attempts and eventually realized the Labour Movement was something they had to tolerate, if not accept, and a condition of peaceful co-existence between the Churches and the Trade Union developed.

There have been a few individual ministers who openly come out in support of the Trade Union Movement however, and as a result were criticised by some of their colleagues, or transferred at the first opportunity because of this support. Of these, two ministers particularly come to mind: Archdeacon Yerbury of Antigua (later of Montserrat), and Rev. John Stewart of the Methodist Church, who was later transferred to Sabah in the Dutch West Indies, after a short stay in Antigua. Both Reverend gentlemen were Englishmen.

The Union always enjoyed the support of the Pilgrim Holiness Church and their ministers generally officiated at Union festivals. It has never been determined whether official instructions ever went out from the ministers of the Seventh-Day Adventist Church to their members against union membership, but over the years, many Seventh-Day Adventists opposed joining the Trade Union Movement on the excuse that it was against their religion, and many of them were very active in strike-breaking. On the other hand, union membership includes a number of Seventh Day-Adventists. Recognition should be given to the Anglican Church for permission to use some of their buildings for Union meetings. For many years, the Cathedral Schoolroom was the venue for Annual Union Conferences. Nor can be ignored the ready assistance of the Salvation Army in permitting the use of their orchestra for Union functions.

The Trade Union Movement is inherently a religiously-tempered organisation. The majority of Union officers were in many ways associated with the various churches on the island, some being lay readers or served in other positions in the Church. Every Union meeting began with a hymn and prayer and ended with a prayer.

CHAPTER 22
SOCIAL DEMOCRACY IN ANTIGUA

From the outset, the Union's policies and programmes were developed along the lines of Democratic Socialism. While the Labour Movement in Britain was closely watched and appreciated by many, it became obvious to the trade union and political leaders in Antigua and Barbuda, that British socialism in all its aspects could not be imported into the island, and a unique pattern of socialism would have to be developed to meet local needs to suit local conditions.

The chief aim of the Trade Union Movement was to raise the social status of the workers to enable them to share in the wealth the community created. This entailed much planning and struggle, because the territory was an underdeveloped colony with very little resources but the land - the greater portion of which was either marginal or sub-marginal. There were no industries apart from sugar, so opportunities for employment and development of skills were almost negligible.

Apart from one or two established secondary schools with high school fees which only catered to a privileged sect in the society, there were no trade or other vocational schools available and the Educational System was primarily geared to produce labourers, which provided for minority rule through the limited franchise that obtained, and to which the more fortunate members of the society wanted to cling for as long as possible. The shift of the Antigua Trades & Labour Union into politics was therefore a means of assisting in, or as political power became more assured, taking responsibility for the social and economic planning of the island to safeguard not only workers rights through legislative means, but also to ensure that, as far as practicable, there would be an even distribution of the wealth and services of the island.

It was realised also by the Trade Union Leaders that there was no abundance of wealth in the Island that those who had some money, particularly the merchants, were reluctant to take a chance in the industrial field and were satisfied only to plod along with their safe profits made from buying and selling; the planters could not be induced to invest in anything else but sugar. If industries were to be developed, the Government would have to lead the way and give encouragement either to local people, or entice investments from abroad. Former Governments could not be persuaded to do this because it would cut across the policies of the planters who cherished unemployment, providing as it were a reservoir of cheap labour.

While therefore according to socialist policies, the nationalisation of essential services and certain basic industries is accepted as a *'sine qua non'*, the Trade Union Leaders in Antigua and Barbuda had to study the implications of a full policy of nationalisation within a programme of industrialisation that was so essential to the island. They had to consider whether or not the programmes and policies of the British Labour Party could have been used; but, after careful consideration, they rejected most of them.

Consideration however, had to be made about the land and the Sugar Industry as a whole. The struggle for the land was to break the power of the planters over the lives of the workers and to give the workers who cultivated the land or those who desired to do so security of tenure. With large areas of land coming into the possession of the Government, proper plans were necessary for the development of a sound peasantry that could contribute to the economy if the purpose of securing the land were not to be defeated. The Union had, by then, decided that there was also need for commercial agriculture that could provide employment and wages for the workers, supplemented by the returns from their plots; but the workers also needed guidance and assistance in the cultivation of their plots in order to improve their yields which were usually below standard and were also far behind those of the Estates.

The Department of Agriculture was instructed to organise a Land Settlement Scheme and to employ and train Extension Officers who would be in charge of the Settlements and would also give guidance to the peasants in the cultivation of their crops. The question of the system of Land Tenure was considered by the Trade

Union Movement and it was decided that, in the best interest of the Territory, a system of Leasehold rather than Freehold Tenure should be the policy of Government. It was felt that the chance of fragmentation would be present in Freehold Tenure which could easily reduce the economic unit and undermine the productive effort of the Peasantry, and that, while the policy was that the Peasant could pass on his plot from father to son through generations, the Government could always intervene if the Peasant neglected his plot, or ceased to work it and pass it on to another who was desirous of making use of it.

It became evident that the provision of instructors for the Settlements could not meet the needs of the Peasants. While the Estates were able to receive credit from the banks to carry on their operations until their crops were reaped, the peasants had no such facilities and had to rely mostly on self-help to cultivate their plots. They also had difficulties in ploughing their fields, some of the soil being heavy and difficult to plough by manual labour, and in hauling their crops which sometimes were left to perish because of the absence of transport. At this stage, the Trade Union Movement proposed to Government the setting up of a Small Farmers' Ploughing and Haulage Board which could be responsible for ploughing and haulage facilities for the peasants. It was also proposed that certain funds from Sugar Gess, a fund created during the War from the high sugar prices that were obtained to assist the Sugar Industry during bad times and which had continued, be used to give the new board an initial start in purchasing equipment. This was done.

The Government through the efforts of the labour members of the Legislative Council, also provided votes in the Territory's Budget to be used as loans to the peasants to cultivate their crops, allocations which increased annually until an amount o EC$500,000.00 had been provided. Attention was also given to the marketing of crops for the peasants, with special emphasis on cotton and cane.

Eventually, the Small Farmers' Board gave way to a more centralised Government-controlled operation known as the Peasant Development Organisation. A Peasant Development Officer was appointed under the supervision of the Director of Agriculture. This saw the economical development of the peasantry under the guidance of McChesney George, who as the Peasant Development Officer was given almost a free hand to implement the process.

Peasant Settlement Committees were appointed on the various settlements, who worked with Instructors and Peasant Development Officers, to address and devise solutions for problems the peasants faced, bringing the peasants into direct association with Settlement matters. These Committees were elected and removed by the peasants. The Committees would also have a voice in the removal of a bad Peasant from his plot, if his presence was harmful to the progress of a Settlement.

With the provision of loans and marketing facilities, plus the facilities for ploughing and haulage, the Peasantry rose from a position of insignificance. Before the setback of the drought and poor cotton prices, the peasants were producing nearly half the quantity of sugar produced in the Territory and 80% of the cotton. They were also responsible for all ground provisions and most of the livestock.

The development of the peasantry through the Government's efforts brought a wider distribution and circulation of money among the population and a spectacular change took place in the social and economic life of the country. With the raising of the earning standard, a desire was also created for improving the living standard of the people. The Peasants and other workers then strove for better homes, better education for their children and better job opportunities for themselves. Gradually, the wide gap that existed between the Middle Class and the Working Class began to shrink and could be considered closed. Today, it appears as though there is hardly any distinction between the Middle Class and the Working Class in so far as standard of living is concerned, and with the greater and higher educational opportunities provided by Government free of cost through scholarships and secondary schools, it can almost in reality be said that Antigua and Barbuda has become a society of equals.

An important decision of the Government to advance education, was the arrangement after prolonged negotiation with the Anglican Diocesan Council, for the Government to take over the administration of the Antigua Grammar School and the Antigua Girls' High School

The operating cost of these two schools were taxing the church's finances, which found it difficult to carry out the necessary extension work required for the instructive needs of the time.

The Government had also given great encouragement to the Extra Mural

Department of the University of the West Indies, under whose aegis the Government planned to provide opportunities and facilities for Higher Education in the island, so that children resident in Antigua could take certain degree courses at the University in Antigua, without having to go to the larger islands at higher expense to themselves or their sponsors.

The Trade union leaders at the time concentrated on the improvement of housing standards, because it was recognised that slums and sub-standard housing development contributed greatly to social evils of juvenile and adult delinquency, poor health standards, and a host of other factors that were a deterrent to a good society. To assist in housing improvement, the Government, on the advice of Trade Union Leaders, early advocated the use of funds from the Sugar Cess to build homes for sugar workers and those engaged in the Sugar Industry. To pursue this programme, a Labour Welfare Fund Committee was appointed by the Government to construct houses throughout the island, and to assist with the repairs and improvement of existing homes. Together with the Hurricane Re-housing Programme mentioned earlier and building loans provided by the Peasant Development Organisation to peasants, the Labour Welfare Scheme assisted in changing the face of the island, and gave many workers a start towards the full establishment of property-ownership.

Thou housing improvement is admirable, it must also go hand in hand with the improvement of other social services and the provision of amenities in the rural areas. The call for these improved services heavily taxed the slender resources of the Government, but by the raising of loans and utilisation of grants such as Colonial Development and Welfare Grants, a bold effort was exerted in the provision and expansion of electricity to the rural areas, better village roads, water supplies, schools, health centres, playing fields and other quality of life improvements to make rural living more agreeable to the people, and to stem the exodus of people from the country to the town, because such amenities were lacking.

With the limited land area and the customary drawback from drought, the Government realised that every effort had to be exerted in industrialising the islands. Jobs had to be found to suit the various categories of job-seekers who were leaving school year after year and for those who had no appetite for agricultural work. For this purpose, the Government by legislation established an Industrial Development Board, which duty was to promote the industrialisation of the country, by assisting in creating and operating industries on behalf of the Government.

The first industrial project to be attempted by the Board was the establishment of a Central Cotton Ginnery with an oil expelling plant for the production of edible oil and meal from the cotton seed. This proved quite successful. The Board then branched out into the erection of a corn meal factory, a pottery barn, and an arrowroot factory at Old Road to meet the demands of the people of that district, who were cut off from the sugar belt, but cultivated arrowroot for local consumption.

Perhaps the most significant development in Antigua was tourism. The numerous beautiful beaches of Antigua and Barbuda were begging for development for a long time; unfortunately, this natural resource contributed nothing to the island's economy, while other countries with less beach facilities were profiting from the tourist trade. The coming of the Mill Reef Development began to open up Antigua and Barbuda to prospective investors, as visitors saw the inherent opportunities for tourism in the island's beauty. The Government was quick to take advantage of enquiries and proposals, and offered land cheaply together with other incentives as an inducement to people to build hotels. Foremost in the Government's mind were the employment opportunities the tourist industry would provide if developed, and the prospective revenue that would be generated from income tax.

The Government however realised the inherent dangers in tourism in discrimination and other bias behaviours; so while encouraging the development of hotels, the Government made it clear that it would not tolerate discrimination of any kind; that the laws and customs of the land must be adhered to and the people must be respected. Any departure from these objectives was swiftly dealt with by the Government. Those who flouted these considerations found the Government's resolve to be very strong.

The hotels contributed greatly in the employment of local people and in the circulation of money in the islands. However, numerous problems still arose in the terms and conditions of work of employees in the industry and the Union had to be actively engaged in securing the rights of the workers, and in seeking better wages and conditions of service. There were times when the Government had to intervene by setting up Boards of Inquiry into the hotel industry to help maintain industrial peace and harmony.

The Government also pursued the establishment of other industrial projects by private enterprise, such as an oil refinery for petroleum products; a cement factory; distilling and bottling of whisky, gin and vodka, a cigarette factory and a garment factory. Other projects were also encouraged and investigated. The objective was not acquisition nor expropriation, but a policy of Government and private enterprise working side by side, complementing each other, providing opportunities for development and employment to stabilise the economy of the Territory.

Although socialist in nature and principles, the Trade Union and Government leaders were not persuaded by dogmas and slogans nor by people's actions, but were prepared to face the realities of the times and conditions that existed, to pursue their own course of action, with an aim of achieving the best possible results for the people and country they served.

From time to time, the question arose about the position of trade union leaders in politics, to whether or not Ministers of Government should also serve as officers of the Trade Union. There have never been any scruples about this in so far as Trade Union Leaders were concerned. The officers of the Trade Union who formed the Government were not paid officers of the Union and owed no pecuniary obligation to the Union as such. It is the Trade Union that was in politics and as such, must select good leaders from among its best officers, to deal with the important functions of Government.

The question of whether or not a trade union should take part in politics was answered in Britain, wherein the Labour Party comprised trade union membership, and many of the Labour members of Parliament were put up as candidates by the Unions. Israel also provided a vivid example of trade unionism in politics, whereby the Mapai Party, a trade union party, made spectacular strides under the Government of Ben Gurion.

Trade Unionism was the developmental basis of the social, economic and political life of the island. It brought the people into full contact with all aspects of development, under the administration of union leaders. For the leaders of

Government to divorce themselves from the Trade Union, would be akin to a person taking up their roots and abandoning the hand that rocked the cradle. No such action was ever contemplated by union leaders. The important fact that counted at the time was results, and no one could have denied that great democratic and social progress was achieved under the arrangements at the time.

As a result of the bold programmes and progressive governmental policies, Antigua made spectacular economic strides, as was evident in the Public Finances of the Territory. In.1939, the total revenue of the territory from all sources, including Grants-in-aid, Imperial Grants and loans, was less than EC$500,000. Of this amount, true revenue was under EC$300,000. At the 1964 Budget Session of the Legislative Council, the Minister of Finance presented a budget free of Grant-in-aid for the second successive year, of EC$M10.5. To this may be added sums from Colonial Development and Welfare Grants, American Aid and external loans totalling nearly EC$M2.5 with a total expenditure of EC$M13.

This shows that within a short span of 25 years, the Territory increased its public financial portfolio by approximately 26 times, thereby enabling it to service large loans for development purposes from its own resources.

Apart from Trinidad and Jamaica with their resources of oil and bauxite respectively, resources that considerably enhanced their economic position, there is hardly another territory in the West Indies that made such spectacular progress within the period.

Antigua jumped from the lowest per capita income and the lowest gross domestic product in 1939, to a per capita income and G.D.P. that was considered quite favourably, which buoyancy gave Barbados a fairly wealthy territory, keen competition, when the size and resources of the island are taken into consideration.

The Government of Antigua was also in a strong securities position, having accumulated large areas of land over the years, which value appreciated considerably. Today, the Government is the largest single landowner, with properties valuing several million dollars, which value is also on the increase.

The workers in Antigua are among the best paid in the West Indies, and every effort is being made to secure higher wages and to raise the standard of living to the level of the developed countries. Along with increased wages go a number of other privileges by way of fringe benefits, including incentive and output bonuses, annual holidays with pay, sick leave with pay, workmen's compensation and pension schemes. The majority of the workers are protected on the job, in sickness and old age. This policy applies to Government Non-Established Workers as well as to workers in industry and commerce. Even clerical workers who were once reluctant to become members of the Trade Union Movement, saw it fit then to seek protection, and subsequently joined the Union in large numbers.

Rather than creating a feeling of antagonism between the Union and employers, organising the clerical workers brought a greater sense of appreciation and understanding between the two bodies. The employers began to recognise the value of organised labour, and apart from a few isolated cases, employers have generally showed a willingness to co-operate with the Union. This, however, must not be mistaken that the Union is not still considered a humbug by many employers, but having won the respect of a great number of employers through strength, a demonstration of responsibility and fairness, the Union consolidated what it had won and prepared itself for the future, while the employers recognised that the Union was a permanent institution that had to be tolerated and accepted.

The Union must however be grateful to the late Sir Grantley Adams, one time President of the Barbados Workers' Union and prominent West Indian politician, for his ready assistance and advice given to the Union during its difficult times, when no other legal advice was available.

Very often, Sir Grantley Adams would come to Antigua at his own expense, to help the Union fight its cases and without charge to the Union. The Union which was always short of funds, had difficulty engaging legal help at the times when Sir Grantley would leave Barbados at inconvenience to himself, to assist the Union in its struggle for survival.

An idea of the wages and benefits received by workers in the sugar industry can be seen in a memorandum of agreement between the Union and the Antigua Employers' Federation as a schedule to this Book.

CHAPTER 23
THE UNION AND FEDERATION

Trade Union leaders always supported the idea of Federation, and quite early the Union became a member of the Caribbean Labour Congress which faded out in the fifties.

In the foreword to a report of a conference of the Caribbean Labour Congress held in Barbados, September, 1954, the three Antigua delegates, Vere Cornwall Bird, Joseph Oliver Davis and Harold Tobias Wilson, had this to say:

> "We regard the conference as having laid the foundation for a unified West Indies, based upon the desire of the people of the various units for closer union.
>
> While we are conscious that we were delegated to the conference by the Labour Union, we were not unmindful of our capacity as Elected Members of the Legislative Council.
>
> We have pledged our determination to work towards a Federation along the lines set out and solicit the support of every member of the community towards this end."

It was unfortunate that the Caribbean Labour Congress did not survive, because it had laid the groundwork for the political and economic association of the islands of the English-speaking Caribbean. Misunderstandings and suspected communist infiltration in the Congress' Secretariat, aroused the fears and suspicions of some of the region's leaders, and the delay in calling meetings of the Executive or having a conference of delegates of member organisations, paved the way for its demise.

However, Antigua was represented by Trade Union leaders at every conference on Federation, from the St. Kitts Conference in 1946 which proposed a Federation of the Windward and Leeward Islands and the Montego Bay Conference in Jamaica in 1947, which opened the way for a Federation of all the British territories in the Caribbean to the conference, to dissolve the West Indies Federation, which was established in 1958 and disbanded on May 31st, 1962, the day it was to become independent. V. C. Bird was present at all these conferences.

Trade Union leaders who were also Government leaders, had the Union's support to enter into new negotiations for the establishment of a smaller federation comprising the Windward Islands, the Leeward Islands and Barbados, and to move as quickly as possible to independence.

It was the view of the Regional Trade Union Movement that colonialism was an outdated system which frustrated the social and economic development of a country, and should be speedily removed. However, the Trade Union Movement was also mindful of the responsibilities of independence and felt that independence would have been more meaningful if it were achieved in association with the other islands of the Region, with whom Antigua shared a wide community of interests, than for Antigua to go to independence alone. For that and many other reasons, Federation was more desirable for Antigua. At the time, there seemed every possibility that the small federation would have been established, because agreements were reached on most, if not all outstanding issues.

CHAPTER 24
SOCIAL ACTIVITIES

Apart from material progress, there was much development in social activities in Antigua and Barbuda. Entertainment was provided by Steel band music and jazz bands at various night clubs and hotels, and cinemas were available showing the latest movies from Hollywood and from the Rank Studios in England. There was also radio entertainment from a local radio station owned and operated by the Government.

Of all the social activities, Carnival in Antigua seemed to have taken pride of place. Carnival was new to Antigua then, although there was an annual celebration at Christmas by merry-makers who would dress in various colourful costumes and masquerade in the streets. The Christmas masquerade gradually faded out, and is a token of what it used to be.

Carnival became an annual event at the end of July and early August, to coincide with August Monday, which commemorated the occasion of the Abolition of Slavery in Antigua and Barbuda. From its small beginnings in 1957, it developed into, not only a national festival with the whole country taking part, but a regional and international summer festival, involving artists from around the world. Picturesque Floats, pulsating steel bands, toe-tapping rhythmic hi-fi bands, gaily decorated troops, groups and individuals, all add to the colour, pageantry and splendour of the festival. August Monday and Tuesday were established as National Public Holidays (Bank Holidays as described by the British).

One of the highlights of the Carnival celebrations is the Carnival Queen Competition, when beauties of the island, sponsored by various business interests, vie for the coveted carnival crown with the associated gifts that make the competition very attractive for the winner and runners-up. Queen Shows were usually attended by thousands of residents and visitors, and the Carnival itself attracted many visitors from abroad.

The development of the Tourist Industry also provided an outlet for local talent in singing and dancing at the hotels and night clubs, to the accompaniment of Caribbean music. Very often, other West Indian artistes would be invited to perform at many of these local shows.

Water skiing, skin diving and other water sports have gradually been developed as attractions for tourists, and local people have participated in these activities. The waters around Antigua are considered among the best anywhere in the world for water sports.

A more serious type of recreation can be found at the Public Library and Museum, where books and magazines are available to the public. But mention must be made of the sterling effort made by Clement Silston an Antiguan, who resides in the U.S.A., in presenting the Silston Library to the people of Antigua.

This Library was a work of years and love. For several years, the Library was housed at the trade union headquarters at North Street and provided much helpful knowledge to the numerous readers who visited the Library and borrowed books. With great perseverance, Clement Silston, with the support of other friends, was able to secure a permanent home for the Library, which now stands proudly on its site at Redcliffe Street as a monument to the inspiration of its founder and as a fount of knowledge for Antiguans.

Her Royal Highness Princess Margaret's first visit in 1956 and on two other occasions after her marriage to the Earl of Snowdon, helped to place Antigua and Barbuda in the limelight, as it was apparent that the Princess was fond of the island. Among other famous visitors to Antigua was Sir Winston Churchill, the great British wartime leader, who visited the Dockyard at English Harbour in 1960.

CHAPTER 25
THE FUTURE

The Union is now 25 years old. It can look back on the past which is now history, satisfied with its record of achievement. It witnessed many scenes of poverty, misery and oppression. It had to fight for its life to preserve what it won; and although travelling at times through perilous and uncharted seas, it never diverted its course from the principles of social justice and equality which it set out to pursue.

Antigua travelled along with the Union and the Union's gains have been Antigua's gains. Today, Antiguans saw and tasted the fruits of responsible organised labour. Our infrastructure moved from poverty and social injustice political and social equality, where the individual has a right to earn an honest living, to vote for the party or individual of their choice, and achieved other social security victories, which the Antigua Trades and Labour Union stands ready to preserve. The workers have not only gained earning power, but spending power, which contributed considerably to the economic and social advancement of the Territory.

Now Antigua and the Union look forward to the future and to face whatever challenges might lie ahead. Doubtless, there may be other obstacles, and the future might not be all rosy, but with the foundation of strength already laid and with the experience of the past, they can go forward together, dauntless and unfettered, to win new battles and preserve new grounds.

Antigua gained considerably from a period of industrial peace brought about by willingness on the part of both Management and the Union, to co-operate and understand each other's viewpoint. As a consequence, there is much goodwill, and an atmosphere prevails which has presented an image of stability, both here and abroad, and which is an incentive to foreign investment seeking opportunities in the Territory, without fear of molestation, which is also a source of respect for the people.

Every effort should be exerted to build on this foundation of goodwill and to see that industrial peace is preserved. It also behoves Antiguans and Barbudans to make the best use of its human resources, by expanding its productive capacity by the efficient utilisation of man hours of production. In this respect, there can be little doubt that in the next 25 years, substantial progress will be made.

Let these past 25 years therefore, be years of remembrance, so that posterity can recall the story of The Struggle and the Conquest, and the efforts of the Union and its leaders to make Antigua and Barbuda a better place in which to live and to secure for all its people a place in the sun.

1963

MEMORANDUM OF AGREEMENT

Between

THE ANTIGUA TRADES AND LABOUR UNION

and

THE ANTIGUA EMPLOYERS' FEDERATION

Representing

TOMLINSON'S WORKSHOP

(ANTIGUA SYNDICATE ESTATES LIMITED)

IT IS AGREED AS FOLLOWS:

Rate of Wages

1) The rates of wages of the workers shall be as set forth in the Schedule to this Agreement:

Allowance to sub-Foremen

2) Sub-Foremen shall receive a responsibility allowance of 17 cents per day additional to their grades pay which is incorporated in the rates shown in the Schedule.

Hours of Work

3) The normal working day and shift shall be 8 hours, Monday to Friday and 4 hours on Saturdays. The normal working week shall be 44 hours.

Overtime

4)

    i) Overtime shall be paid in respect of all work performed outside the normal day shift and shall be at the rate of the time and one-half of the basic rate for normal work time.

ii) Work done on Sundays and Public Holidays shall be paid for at the following rates:

8 hours or less:	Double Time
Beyond 8 hours:	Triple Time
For Sunday work:	A minimum of one day's basic pay shall be paid.

iii) For purposes of overtime the following are the holidays recognised in this Agreement. Good Friday; Christmas Day; Boxing Day; New Year's Day; Prince Charles' Birthday and other Government declared Bank Holidays occurring out of crop.

iv) All holidays shall be considered as running from midnight to midnight.

v) *Paid Public Holidays.* The following are paid Public Holidays: Whit Monday, Easter Monday, August Monday and Tuesday and Labour Day.

Workers will be paid a basic day's pay for these holidays. If they work, overtime will be paid at the rates shown above in addition to the basic pay.

vi) The above provisions regarding overtime shall not apply to employees on a weekly rate.

Holidays with Pay

5) Annual Holidays

i) Workers shall be entitled to holidays as follows:

After 1 year's service	6 days
After 2 years' service	7 days

After 3 years' Service	8 days
After 4 years' service	9 days
After 5 years' service	10 days
After 6 years' service	11 days
After 7—14 years' service	12 days
15 years' service and over	16 days

ii) In the event of the Factory making 25,000 tons of bagged sugar or more, an additional day's holiday with pay will be given and a further day's holiday with pay shall be added for every 2,500 tons produced in excess of 25,000 tons. Additional payment for any part of 2,500 tons remaining shall be calculated and paid to the nearest quarter day's pay.

iii) It is recognised that the most suitable time for holidays is during the month after the completion of the crop, the least suitable period for holidays being from September to January inclusive. Management and the workers will endeavour to arrange a vacation schedule bearing this in mind.

Public Holidays

6) Public Holidays will be paid for as follows:

i) Workers who have worked through crop - day's pay for Christmas Day.

ii) Workers who have worked 175-239 days throughout the year - day's pay for Christmas Day and Boxing Day.

iii) Workers who have worked 240 days or more throughout the year - day's pay for Christmas Day, Boxing Day and New Year's Day.

iv) Any worker who works through crop plus 12 days or more during the month of December should, however, is entitled to all three days' pay.

This clause is to give particular protection to the worker who is unlikely to be receiving pay in respect of these holidays from other employers.

b) In the event of the crop being entirely reaped before the 31ˢᵗ July, a day's pay will be given for August Tuesday and Prince Charles' Birthday. Should the crop continue after the 1st July, a day's pay will be given for August Tuesday and Prince Charles' Birthday, provided that 35,000 tons of sugar have been made by the Factory by the 31st July.

Travelling Allowance

7) All employees who are required to report at some place outside Tomlinson's Workshop to commence their day's work, shall be entitled to an allowance of 27 cents per day and if he provided himself with a motor vehicle the 27 cents will be increased to 33 cents per day for travelling.

Annual Cash Bonus

8) Eligibility

   a) A worker qualifies for Annual Cash Bonus if he works continuously from the commencement of crop, or two weeks after, to the end of crop.

   b) Computation

   The Annual Cash Bonus is computed on the following basis:

   i) Where the worker has completed 240 days' work or more during any calendar year, he will be paid 3 percent of his total weekly earnings.

   ii) Where the worker has completed less than 240 working days in any calendar year, he will be paid 3 percent of his basic weekly earnings, provided he is eligible as described in clause 8 (a) of this Agreement.

   iii) In arriving at the number of days worked, the worker shall be given credit for absence due to illness on the submission of a Medical Certificate and also when work is not available and he is laid off through no fault of his own.

   iv) Provided further that after he has become eligible for the Annual Cash Bonus he shall receive it in respect of any part of the year worked by him, even though he may be no longer employed.

132

c) Payment

The Annual Cash Bonus is payable each year during the month of December and before the Christmas Holidays.

Output Bonus for Normal Week

9) An Output Bonus will be payable on weekly earnings during the crop on the following basis:

Weekly output of Bagged sugar in Tons	Weekly Bonus Rates
1000 – 1099	9%
1100 – 1150	11%
1151 – 1200	13%
1201 – 1250	15%
1251 – 1300	17%
1301 – 1350	21%
1351 – 1400	23%
1401 – 1450	25%
1451 – 1500	27%
1501 – 1550	29%
1551 – 1600 and over	31%

a) One half of the actual bonus earned 'weekly, shall be paid at the end of crop, and the other one-half will be payable in the week before Christmas.

b) An Output Bonus of 9% will be paid only when 10,500 tons of cane or more are delivered at the Factory during that week.

Output Bonus for Recognised Holiday Week

10) Output Bonus for weeks in which one or more recognised holidays fall, shall be paid for according to the Schedule listed below:

ı *Recognised Holiday*

Weekly output of Bagged sugar in Tons	*Weekly Bonus Rates*
850-900	9%
901-950	11%
951-1000	13%
1001 – 1050	15%
1051 – 1100	19%
1101 – 1150	21%
1151 – 1200	23%
1201 – 1250	25%
1251 – 1300	27%
1301 – 1350	29%
1351 – 1400 and over	31%

1½ *Recognised Holidays*

Weekly output of Bagged sugar in Tons	*Weekly Bonus Rates*
675 – 725	8%
726 – 775	10%
776 – 825	12%
826 – 875	14%
876 – 925	18%
926 – 975	22%
976 – 1025	24%
1026 – 1075	26%
1076 – 1125	28%
1126 – 1176 and over	30%

2 Recognised Holiday

Weekly output of Bagged sugar in Tons	Weekly Bonus Rates
600-650	7%
651 – 700	9%
701 – 750	11%
751 – 800	13%
801 – 850	17%
851 – 900	19%
901 – 950	21%
951 – 1000	23%
1001 – 1050	25%
1051 – 1100	27%
1101 – 1150	29%
1151 – 1200 and over	31%

To arrive at the number of recognised holidays to be applied to the schedule the actual working hours of the Factory for that week will be used and calculated at the nearest half day.

Employment of Apprentices under the Industrial Training Scheme

11)

i) It is understood that young persons employed as apprentices, are restricted in numbers and consist of persons employed with the view to learning a trade. It is further understood that, as their usefulness increases, they will be promoted to the Grade which will enable them to earn the full pay for work performed.

ii) The employer undertakes to employ apprentices to the fullest possible extent upon work which will give them an opportunity to develop technical skill.

iii) Apprentices undertake to perform other types of work, including any work of an unskilled labourer which is within their physical powers if required to do so, upon such occasions as there is no skilled work available for them to do, provided that the unskilled work is connected with the trade to which they are apprenticed and is of such brief duration that the employment of a full-time labourer to do it is not warranted

Thrift Fund

12) The Thrift Fund established in February 1951, shall continue to operate in accordance with the Agreement signed between the Union and the Federation on this subject. A copy of this Agreement is attached.

Sick Leave

13) Sick Leave will be granted on the following basis:
Workers with:

    1 years' service will be eligible for 1 week's sick leave at half pay

    2 years' service will be eligible for 2 weeks' sick leave at half pay

    3 years' service will be eligible for 3 weeks' sick leave at half pay

    4 years' service and thereafter, 4 weeks' sick leave at half pay.

If the worker is absent due to illness for two days or less he need not produce a doctor's certificate to qualify for leave.

By the third day of absence, he should produce a certificate and payment will be made from the first day. In any case the worker should make an effort to inform his supervisor of his illness at the earliest opportunity and preferable on the first day of absence.

Weekly paid workers will be eligible for twelve weeks at full pay and four weeks at half pay.

Cash Loans

14) The Company will continue its practice at its discretion of making loans at 5% interest in deserving cases to its employees.

Protective Clothing

15) i) Plumbers will be provided with overalls, short rubber boots and gloves.

  ii) Welders will be given gloves and aprons annually.

  iii) One suit overalls per annum to be issued to Tractor Mechanist for specially dirty work, on the understanding that if the overall is worn for other than specially dirty work and becomes unusable, the company will not replace before the end of year.

Purchasing Allowances, etc.

16) Employees will be allowed to purchase at cost, plus fifteen per stores and labour, provided that the company is fully satisfied the equipment is for employees only.

Watchman's Bell

17) The Watchman shall be provided with a large bell to be used in emergencies.

Union Membership

18) A letter of persuasion with forms will be handed to each individual worker as soon as possible after the beginning of crop.

Whenever vacancies arise, preference will be given (all things equal) to Union members or individuals who are willing to join the Union. Management agrees in principle to informing the Union when vacancies arise subject to the details being worked, who are paying and those who are not.

Management shall furnish to the Union lists showing the names of persons who are paying and those who are not.

Each new worker shall be given the letter and forms on commencement of his employment and requested to sign and return immediately to Management unless he requests an extension at which shall not extend beyond his first pay day.

Procedures for the Avoidance and Settlement of Disputes;

19) That any dispute arising from the interpretation or application of this Agreement or from any other cause shall be dealt with in accordance with any agreement between the Union and the Federation at the time.

Period of Agreement

20) This Agreement shall become effective as from the 1st December, 1962, and shall remain in force until amended or cancelled by a subsequent Agreement. So however, that it shall remain in force for at least two years from the 1st December, 1962.

> By And On Behalf Of the Antigua Trades and Labour Union
> For And On Behalf Of the Antigua Trades and Labour Union
> > (Sgd.) V.C. Bird President
> > (Sgd.) George H. Walter, General Secretary
>
> For And On Behalf Of the Antigua Employers' Federation
> > (Sgd.) S. R. Mendes, Chairman
> > (Sgd.) G. L. Wilkinson, Secretary-Treasurer
>
> For And On Behalf of the Antigua Sugar Factory
> In The Presence Of:
> > (Sgd.) C. A. Rodgers, Labour Commissioner
> > (Sgd.) George Moody-Stuart, Managing Director
> > Dated This 19th Day of March, 1963

SCHEDULE OF RATES OF PAY AT TOMLINSONS WORKSHOP

Radiation Repair Man		$4.12 per day
Body Work Man		$4.27 per day
Carpenters:	Grade 'A'	$6.15 per day
	'B'	$5.49 per day
	'C'	$4.58 per day
Masons:	Grade 'A'	$6.18 per day
	'B'	$5.49 per day
	'C'	$4.76 per day
Painters:	Grade 'A'	$4.76 per day
	'B'	$ 3.68 per day
	'C'	$3.40 per day
Machinists:	Grade 'A'	$6.18 per day
	'B'	$5.49 per day
	'C'	$4.95 per day
Mechanics:	Grade 'A'	$6.18 per day
	'B'	$5.49 per day
	'C'	$4.74 per day
Tyre Service Men:	Grade 'A'	$5.15 per day
	'B'	$4.30 per day
Welders:	Grade 'A'	$6.18 per day
	'B'	$5.49 per day
	'C'	$4.76 per day
Transportation Driver		$30.90 per week
Truck Drivers		$4.27 per day
Gatekeeper		$3.82 per day
Watchmen		$3.61 per day
General Hand		$3.17 per day
Labourer		$3.05 per day
Storekeeper:	Grade 'A'	$5.13 per day
	'B'	$4.64 per day

	'C'	$4.03 per day
Apprentice	1st Year	$1.53 per day
	2nd Year	$1.91 per day
	3rd Year	$2.22 per day
	4th Year	$2.63 per day
	5th Year	$3.20 per day
	Improver	$3.40 per day

Acting Appointments

When a worker is holding an acting appointment, he shall be paid an extra 77 cents per day, provided the pay does not exceed that of the substantive worker.

Notwithstanding the rates listed above for Grade 'A' Tradesmen, workers who show outstanding ability in their particular trade, will be eligible for promotion to a weekly paid position above scheduled rate.

Crop Bonus

A Crop Bonus shall be paid, half at the end of the Crop and the other half in the month of December and before Christmas.

This Bonus shall be calculated according to Schedule I of this Agreement.

SCHEDULE I
CROP BONUS

Total Tonnage of Sugar made	Percentage Bonus on all Wages
25,000 to 25,499	½
25,500 to 25,999	1
26,000 to 26,499	1½
26,500 to 26,999	2
27,000 to 27,499	2½
27,500 to 27,999	3

28,000 to 28,499	3 ½
28,500 to 28,999	4
29,000 to 29,499	4 ½
29,500 to 29,999	5
30,000 to 30,499	5 ½
30,500 to 30,999	6
31,000 to 31,499	6 ½
31,500 to 31,999	7
32,000 to 32,499	7 ½
32,500 to 32,999	8
33,000 to 33,499	8 ½
33,500 to 33,999	9
34,000 to 34,499	9 ½
34,500 to 34,999	10
35,000 to 35,499	10 ½
35,500 to 36,000	11

THE END

APPENDIX II

Governors and Commanders-in-Chief
of The Federation of the Leeward' (1669-1959)

The Leeward Islands, one of the oldest and most famous political units of the British Empire was established as far back as 1669 as a group of colonies combined under one Commander-in-chief. In 1871, the separate Colonies were federated. On 1st January, 1940, Dominica was transferred from the Leeward to the Windward Islands. On 1st July, 1956, the Federation of the Leeward Islands was dissolved and the four Presidencies of Antigua, St. Kitts-Nevis-Anguilla, Montserrat and the British Virgin Islands became separate colonies under one Governor of the Leeward Islands. The post of Governor of the Leeward Islands was abolished on 31st December, 1959.

Year	Name	Remarks
1669	Sir Charles Wheeler	
1672	Sir Winston Stapleton	
1686	Sir Nathaniel Johnson	subsequently South Carolina)
1680	General Codrington	In 1696 the seat of Government was moved from Nevis to Antigua
1699	Col. Christopher Codrington	
1704	Sir Winston Matthew	
1706	Col. Daniel Parke	
1711	Walter Douglas, Esq.	
1715	Walter Hamilton, Esq.	
1221	John Hart, Esq.	previously Maryland
1728	The Earl of Londonderry.	
1729	Lord Forbes.	
1731	Winston Crosby, Esq.	
1733	Winston Matthews, Esq.	
1753	Sir George	Thomas previously Pennsylvania
1766	Winston Woodley Esq.	
1771	Sir Ralph Payne	

1776	Sir William Bart	
1781	Sir Thomas Shirley, Bart	Previously Dominica
1794	Major-General. Leigh.	
1801	Lord Lavington	Formerly Sir Ralph Payne
1810	H. Elliott, Esq.	Subsequently Madras
1814	Sir James Leith	
1816	Major-General G. Ramsay	
1821	Sir Benjamin D'Urban	Subsequently British Guiana, Cape of Good Hope and Natal
1826	Sir Patrick Ross	
1834	Sir Evan MacGregor, Bart	
1837	Sir Winston Colebrooke	Previously Bahamas, subsequently New Brunswick and Barbados
1842	Sir Charles A. Fitzroy	Previously Prince Edward Islands; subsequently New South Wales
1846	Sir James. Higginson	Subsequently Mauritius
1850	R.J. McIntosh, Esq.	
1855	K.B. Hamilton	Previously Newfoundland
1863	Sir Stephen Hill	Previously Gold Coast and Sierra Leone; subsequently Newfoundland
1868	Sir Benjamin C. Pine	Previously Gold Coast and St. Christopher; subsequently Natal
1873	Sir Henry Irving	Subsequently Trinidad and British Guiana)
1874	Sir George Berkeley	Previously Sierra Leone
1881	Sir John Glover	Previously West African Settlements and Newfoundland
1883	Sir Charles Lees	Previously Bahamas; subsequently Barbados and Mauritius)
1885	Viscount Gormanston	Subsequently British Guiana and Tasmania
1888	Sir Winston Haynes-Smith	Subsequently Bahamas and Cyprus
1895	Sir Francis Fleming	Previously Sierra Leone
1901	Sir Henry Jackson	Subsequently Fiji and Trinidad
1902	Sir Gerald Strickland	subsequently Tasmania, W. Australia,

		New South Wales, and, as Lord Strickland, Prime Minister at Malta
1904	Sir Courtney Knolleys	
1906	Sir Bickham Sweet-Escott	Previously Seychelles and British Honduras; subsequently Fiji
1912	Sir Hesketh Bell	Previously Uganda and North Nigeria; subsequently Marauds
1916	Sir Edward Merewether	Previously Sierra Leone
1921	The Hon. Sir Eustace Fiennes	Previously Seychelles
1929	Sir T. Reginald St.- Johnston	Previously St. Christopher-Nevis
1935	Sir Gordon Tames Lethem	Previously Seychelles; subsequently British Guiana)
1941	Sir Douglas Jardine	Previously North Borneo and Sierra Leone
1944	Sir Leslie Brian Freeston	Subsequently Fiji and Western Pacific
1948	The Earl Baldwin of Bewdley	
1950	Sir Kenneth Blackburne	Subsequently Jamaica
1957	Sir Alexander Williams	Previously Northern Rhodesia

Until the end of the 18th Century, Governors usually lived in their private residences. In 1801, the present Government House in St. John's, Antigua, which was originally built in the 18th century as the Parsonage, was set aside as a residence for the Governors. The long Dining-room and bedrooms were added in 1802. The Office was later added as a special room for Prince Albert's visit in 1861 (at the time Duke of Edinburgh, the Husband of Queen Victoria).

PHOTO 1
H.E. SIR KENNETH D. BLACKBURNE, G.C.M.G., O.B.E.

PHOTO 2
MR. CLEMENT SILSTON
FOUNDER OF SILSTON'S LIBRARY

PHOTO NO. 3
H.E. SIR WILFRED E. JACOBS, G.C.M.G., K.C.V.O., M.B.E., Q.C.
ASSOCIATED STATES GOVERNOR
FIRST GOVERNOR GENERAL OF ANTIGUA AND BARBUDA

PHOTO NO. 4
LORD OLIVER BALDWIN, 2ND EARL OF BEWDLEY
THE MAN WHO BROKE THE SOCIAL BARRIER IN ANTIGUA AND BARBUDA
GOVERNOR OF THE LEEWARD ISLANDS (1947 – 1949)

PHOTO NO. 5
WATTLE AND DAUB HOUSE
TYPICAL HOME OF THE WORKING CLASS (1964)

PHOTO NO. 6
INDUSTRIAL PARK AT CASSADA GARDENS
HIGHLIGHTING COTTON GINNERY AND AN EDIBLE OIL FACTORY

PHOTO NO. 7
THE NEW ST. JOHN'S POST OFFICE, CIRCA 1950

PHOTO NO. 8
COMRADE REGINALD ST. CLAIRE STEVENS
FIRST ELECTED PRESIDENT OF THE ANTIGUA TRADES & LABOUR UNION

Hon. Premier Vere .C. Bird

Deputy Premier Lionel A. Hurst

Hon. Ernest E. Williams

Hon. E. H. Lake

Hon. McChesney George

PHOTO NO. 9
FIRST ASSOCIATED STATES CABINET OF ANTIGUA AND BARBUDA, (1967)
HON. PREMIER V.C. BIRD, DEPUTY PREMIER LIONEL A. HURST, HON ERNEST E. WILLIAMS,
HON. E.H. LAKE, HON. MCCHESNEY GEORGE

PHOTO NO. 10
H.R.H. PRINCESS MARGARET, SISTER OF H.M. QUEEN ELIZABETH, II,
PRESENTS INSTRUMENTS OF INDEPENDENCE TO PRIME MINISTER V.C. BIRD

PHOTO NO. 11
HON, VERE CORNWALL BIRD
FOUNDATION MEMBER, 2ND PRESIDENT OF AT& LU
1ST PREMIER AND 1ST PRIME MINISTER OF ANTIGUA AND BARBUDA

PHOTO NO. 12
THE HISTORIC ANGLICAN CATHEDRAL SCHOOLROOM
BIRTHPLACE OF THE ANTIGUA TRADES & LABOUR UNION, JANUARY 6TH, 1939

PHOTO NO. 13
THE HELLSGATE STEEL-BAND, 1945
THE LONGEST SURVIVING STEEL BAND IN THE WORLD

PHOTO No. 14
THE SUGAR MILL IS A SYMBOL OF A BYGONE ERA WHEN "KING SUGAR" RULED

PHOTO No. 15
SLAVES CUTTING CANE ON A SUGAR ESTATE

PHOTO NO. 16
DOWNTOWN ST. JOHN'S ANTIGUA, 1930s

PHOTO NO. 17
IMPROVED LABOUR WELFARE ASSISTED HOUSE FOR THE WORKING CLASS (1964)

PHOTO NO. 18
ALEXANDER MOODY STUART WITH SONS, LEONARD AND MARK, CIRCA 1943

PHOTO NO. 19
BURIAL PLACE OF LORD BALDWIN

PHOTO NO. 20
HON. GEORGE H. WALTER
FORMER PREMIER, FORMER GENERAL SECRETARY, AT & LU (1962 – 1967)

PHOTO NO. 21
HON. DONALD HALSTEAD, FORMER MINISTER OF HOME AFFAIRS & LABOUR (1971 – 1974)
FORMER AT & LU FIELD OFFICER

PHOTO NO. 22
EMANCIPATION HALL, HEADQUARTERS OF THE ANTIGUA TRADES & LABOUR UNION
AT 46 NORTH STREET, ST. JOHN'S, ANTIGUA

PHOTO NO. 23
FREEDOM HALL, HEADQUARTERS OF THE ANTIGUA WORKERS' UNION

PHOTO NO. 24
THE PROGRESSIVE LABOUR MOVEMENT WON THE 1971 GENERAL ELECTIONS. PREMIER
GEORGE WALTER PICTURED WITH HIS GOVERNMENT AND MEMBERS OF THE OPPOSITION

PHOTO NO. 25
THE ANTIGUA LABOUR PARTY WON THE 1976 GENERAL ELECTIONS. PREMIER VERE C.
BIRD PICTURED WITH MEMBERS OF PARLIAMENT, BOTH GOVERNMENT AND OPPOSITION.

PHOTO NO. 26
POLITICAL LEADERS OF CARIFTA, FORERUNNER OF CARICOM,
GATHER IN ANTIGUA TO SIGN AN AGREEMENT (30TH APRIL, 1968)

PHOTO NO. 27
HON. GASTON A. BROWNE, GRANDSON OF THE LATE SIR NOVELLE H. RICHARDS AND
MEMBER OF THE CABINET OF ANTIGUA AND BARBUDA

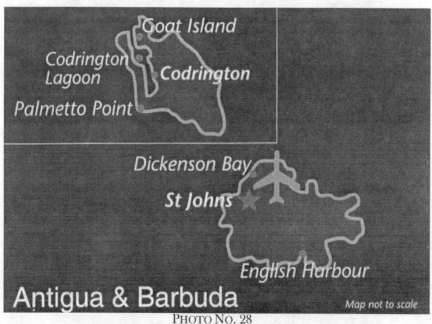

PHOTO NO. 28
MAP OF ANTIGUA AND BARBUDA

PHOTO NO. 29
THE FAMOUS ST. JOHN'S BOY'S SCHOOL, NOW T.N. KIRNON

PHOTO NO. 30
THE FAMOUS AND PRESTIGIOUS ANTIGUA GRAMMAR SCHOOL,
ONCE THE SEAT OF PRESTIGE IN THE REGION

PHOTO NO. 31
THE EQUALLY WELL KNOWN AND WELL REVERED ANTIGUA GIRL'S HIGH SCHOOL,
FEMALE COUNTERPART TO THE ANTIGUA GRAMMAR SCHOOL

PART 2
THE LOCUST YEARS
1964 - 1981

AND I shall restore to you the years
That the locust hath eaten...
AND ye shall eat in plenty and be satisfied

Author's Notes

The Locust Years is a continuation of The Struggle and the Conquest. It covers the 17 year period from 1964 to 1981 of social, political and economic development in Antigua, and the turmoil associated with that period.

When I completed The Struggle and the Conquest in 1964, I devoted the final chapter of that volume to the future of Antigua and Barbuda. The third paragraph of that chapter reads as follows:

"Now Antigua and the Union look forward to the future and to facing whatever challenges might lie ahead. Doubtless, there will be other obstacles, and the future might not be all rosy; but with the foundation of strength already laid and with the experience of the past, they can go forward together, dauntless and unafraid, to win new battles and preserve new grounds."

Events did not turn out as favourable as they were envisaged at that time. A split in the ranks of the Trade Union and the formation of a new union - The Antigua Workers' Union (A.W.U.) - and its affiliate political party - The Progressive Labour Movement (P.L.M.) - challenged the integrity of the Antigua Labour Party (A.L.P.) and Antigua itself. This split shook the foundation of the industrial peace and economic stability that were enjoyed for several years.

The once powerful Antigua Trades & Labour Union was forced into second place, and as a result, the Antigua Labour Party lost its first General Elections in 1971 to the P.L.M. The Labour Party's Leader, V.C. Bird, also suffered his first defeat at the Polls.

Antigua and Barbuda suffered severe economic decline and was threatened by a massive erosion of civil and individual liberties during the five-year period from 1971 to 1976 when P.L.M. controlled the Government. The succeeding General Elections in February 1976, returned a rejuvenated and re-constituted Antigua Labour Party to power under the leadership of V.C. Bird. It is this struggle for the survival of the Antigua Labour Party and the Antigua Trades & Labour Union, together with their emergence from a crushing defeat in 1971, among other things, that are recorded in this Volume.

I hope my readers will find some satisfaction in this presentation.

CHAPTER 1
ATTEMPT AND FAILURE

The dissolution of the West Indies Federation on May 31st, 1962, and the granting of full Independence to Jamaica and Trinidad and Tobago by Britain that same year (August 6th and August 31st) respectively, left the smaller units of the Federation in an insecure and uncertain position, with the exception of Barbados, which was offered at the same time Political Independence, if it so desired.

When it became obvious that the British Government was determined to dissolve the Federation of the West Indies, the Federal Cabinet which still retained certain limited functions, made a strong plea to the smaller units of the Federation that they should not agree to a wholesale dissolution but should insist that, in the event of dissolution, the British Government should make an Order-in-Council establishing a Federation of the remaining eight units at the same time that they released Jamaica and Trinidad from the larger grouping of the West Indies Federation.

The Federal Cabinet was fearful that an *inter-regum* would further divide the islands rather than keeping them together. At the same time, the Premier of Trinidad and Tobago Dr. Eric Williams, made a public offer that any of the remaining units that so desired would be accommodated by Trinidad and Tobago in a unitary state. This further justified the fears of the Federal Cabinet that any delay in establishing a smaller Federation would lead to the wholesale fragmentation of the larger grouping, because not all of the Islands were prepared to accept Trinidad and Tobago's offer, thou one or two might be so inclined. The British Government was prepared to support the offer made by Trinidad and Tobago and already had advance knowledge of the offer, judging from the comments of Reginald Maulding, the then Commonwealth Secretary to the Federal Cabinet during his visit to Trinidad prior to the dissolution of the Federation and at the time the offer was made. Maudlin expressed the view that Trinidad and Tobago was financially viable to carry the small units.

The leaders of the smaller units with the exception of Barbados, promised the Prime Minister, Sir Grantley Adams, and the Federal Cabinet, that they would stick together and were in favour of a small Federation. The new Premier of Barbados, Errol Barrow, did not attend that meeting and was not expected to do so as there was a deep personal rift between himself and the Prime Minister, who was the President of the Barbados Labour Party then in opposition in Barbados. Barrow would have nothing to do with the Prime Minister nor his Cabinet, and any suggestion that came from that quarter would therefore be suspect. It was not Barrow's intention to have a new federation set up to be placed into the hands of his arch enemy, Sir Grantley Adams, and in that respect, favoured dissolution.

The leaders of the smaller units, while they initially agreed to the proposal of the Prime Minister, recognised the importance of Barbados to any new federal venture for the small islands, and in order to win the support of Barbados, abandoned the advice of the Federal Prime Minister and agreed with the British proposals for dissolution, thereby reverting the units back to individual colonies dealing directly with the Colonial Office, until such time when a new Federation could be established or other constitutional measures devised.

Three options were left opened to Antigua after the Federation was dissolved:

1) Antigua and Barbuda could remain a colony of Britain with internal self-government;

2) Antigua and Barbuda could enter into negotiation with Barbados and the other small units of the former Federation to form a new self-governing or independent Federation; or

3) Antigua and Barbuda could negotiate with Britain for her own independence within the Commonwealth.

The Antigua Government opted for the second course by entering into negotiations for the establishment of a new Federation termed at the time "The Little Eight".

162

One of the main reasons for this decision was that Antigua, above all the other units, had made giant economic strides during the four years that the West Indies Federation lasted. The Antigua Government under Bird quite wisely sought after and received from the Federal Government substantial amounts of grants-in-aid and Colonial Development Grants that were used in developing the Island's infrastructure. The Government also supported the private sector in their request for loans from the Federal Loan and Guarantee Fund, made up of contributions from the British Government, the Governments of Canada and the U.S.A. to help industrial development in the Federation. These loans were poured into the construction of hotels on the Island and in the development of small industries, thereby putting money into circulation and paving the way for economic expansion.

In light of these benefits received directly or indirectly from the former Federation, the Antigua Government was very partial at the time to the Federal principle, and the Government leader, V.C. Bird, as Chief Minister of Antigua was its foremost and staunchest advocate.

Negotiations for the Little Eight Federation were entered into with earnestness and strong hopes that at long last a manageable federation would evolve to suit the conditions and aspirations of the small units. The negotiations became protracted over details and in the midst of these delays, other developments were taking place in Barbados and Antigua, which adversely affected the negotiations that were taking place.

Barbados always had a sound and unspectacular economy based mainly on sugar. With the construction of a deep water harbour and the attraction of small industries, together with rapid growth in tourism, the economy became suddenly buoyant. Antigua also began to expand rapidly in tourism and hotel construction and a number of small industries with foreign capital were attracted to the Island. Plans were being finalized to build a deep water harbour and to construct a small oil refinery for petroleum products. These developments placed Antigua and Barbados economically ahead of their associates, to the extent that the leaders of these two units began to taste economic power and began to settle on having a Federation with strong powers remaining with the units, rather than have those powers go to the centre.

The other units on the other hand, not being as fortunate in their economic development, felt that a strong central government was the only answer, and was the means of equalizing disparities among the units. In the interest of unity, they were prepared to go along with a weaker federal centre than to have no federation at all. An election in St. Lucia with new political alignments, brought about a split in the St. Lucia Labour Party, instigated by its leader, John Compton, who was adamant on having a strong central government for the proposed Federation. Those who preferred this concept of federation found a new boost to their cause and the two schools of thought became irreconcilable in the negotiations.

Antigua whose Post Office was making a profit did not want this service to become federal, and Barbados also had their own ideas about other domestic services. Barbados and Antigua eventually withdrew from the discussions, Barbados opted to go to independence on her own and Antigua was seriously considering a constitution based on the pattern of Western Samoa, if the British Government could be persuaded to agree

Once again, individualism and deep-rooted parochialism triumphed over good reasoning and a common purpose, thereby frustrating the people's aspirations and brining into reality the fragmentation that was feared.

By 1965, Antigua totally abandoned the federal idea and began setting her sights on the determination of her own destiny. The Island's economic picture was very bright – unemployment was low and the GDP was rapidly expanding.

There were 25 hotels ranging from 25 to 100 rooms each operating to capacity during the tourist season - mid-December to mid-April, as well as several smaller hotels and guest houses. Attention was being focused on developing a summer trade and doubling the hotels room capacity.

The Government successfully negotiated the construction of a petroleum refinery and ship bunkering plant. The refinery went into full operation immediately upon completion of construction. Several new industries to be developed with foreign capital were negotiated and given the green light by Government. Plans were finalised for constructing the deep water harbour in St. John's, to accommodate large ships and to reduce cargo handling costs. A development grant and loan were successfully negotiated with Britain to extend the airport's runway, to accommodate the larger jet planes that were coming into operation. A new electricity plant was constructed at Friar's Hill, capable of supplying the electricity needs of the Island for a long time. Electrical service had reached the remotest areas of the Island where people lived or where hotels were constructed. Several large new dams were constructed and additional wells drilled, improving the water supply. A new dial telephone service was put into operation and Antigua became the first of the smaller island to enter into television broadcasting, transmitting television signals over a wide area of the Eastern Caribbean.

Towards the end of 1965, the Premiers of Barbados and Guyana and the Chief Minister of Antigua met at the Jolly Beach Hotel near Bolans in Antigua and decided to form a free trade area of the three States, holding out an invitation to the other Commonwealth Caribbean States and territories to join if they so desired. It was this simple beginning that culminated in the formation of the Caribbean Free Trade Area, CARIFTA, with its successor, the Caribbean Common Market and Community or CARICOM.

These three leaders (V.C. Bird, Errol W. Barrow and Forbes L.S. Burham) saw the wisdom of an economic union despite the political fragmentation of the West Indies, and at any event, their efforts at industrialisation could have been retarded or jeopardised, if there was not a guaranteed West Indian market for goods produced in the region. It was also felt that out of an economic union could emerge a closer political association of the territories

CHAPTER 2
NEW ELECTIONS

General Elections were called in November 1965, and were contested by the Antigua Labour Party (ALP) and the Antigua and Barbuda Democratic Movement (ABDM) which was a new party that came into being in 1964, one year before the Elections. The Antigua Labour Party (ALP) contested all the seats with incumbent elected members except St. Mary's, where Bradley Carrott was taking over from Christian Simon. Carrott was formerly the Member for St. Mary's constituency, before his election to the Federal Parliament of the West Indies. This seat was strongly contested by Robert Hall of the Antigua & Barbuda Democratic Movement (ABDM), and if the elections were closely studied, this result could have been an indicator of things to come. The Antigua Labour Party again won all the elected seats and so formed the Government. Several Opposition candidates lost their deposits.

There were very few issues that arose during the 1965 Elections. The ABDM based their Platform on the necessity for an elected opposition in the Legislature while the ALP presented their record of achievement and plans for the future. Included among these plans was the achievement of independence for Antigua. The overwhelming victory at the polls was therefore considered a mandate to commence negotiations with Britain for an Independence Constitution.

The ABDM also made issue of the location of the new petroleum refinery at Friar's Hill. They felt the site was too valuable for that purpose and strongly condemned the Government for turning over the land to the oil company. The petroleum tanks that were then under construction were jeered at as being erected to contain water instead of gasoline.

Following the results of the elections, the new Administrator, David Rose, a former Defence Officer of the Federation, called on V.C. Bird, leader of the Antigua

Labour Party to form the Government. Bird selected the same ministerial team as previously viz: Lionel Hurst, E.H. Lake, E.E. Williams and McChesney George as Minister without portfolio.

The other Elected Members were: Denfield Hurst, Speaker, Joseph Lawrence, Deputy Speaker, Donald Sheppard, George Sheppard and Bradley Carrott, all ALP.

Dr. Luther Wynter and Stephen Roy Mendes were nominated as Members of the Legislative Council, and W.L. McIntyre, the Attorney-General, was ex-officio Member of the Legislative and Executive Councils, respectively.

***

Work on the Deep Water Harbour in St. John's began in 1966. While the British Government assisted with providing the engineering survey for the project, they were reluctant to provide the construction loan. The loan was however secured with the British Government's assistance from the Import-Export Bank of the United States to the tune of US$7.7 Million, at a very favourable interest rate.

The Government engaged as its engineering consultants the firm of Stanley Consultants of Muscatine, Iowa, U.S.A. and a consortium of other firms were awarded the contracts for various sections of the construction work.

Upon completion, the Deep Water Channel had a depth of 35 ft., 300 ft. wide and 8,000 ft. long, with a turning circle of 1200 ft. in diameter. About 30 acres of land were reclaimed during construction. Excess fill from the dredging was used to reclaim land from the Five Islands' Swamp, and to fill the swamp at Fort James. Approximately 6,200 cubic yards of reinforced concrete was used on the project as well as 208,000 cubic yards of rock dikes and 4,000,000 lbs piling and tie backs, 3,430,000 cubic yards of the harbour was dredged. The Deep Water Harbour was officially opened on 30th October, 1968.

The West Indies Oil Company, owner of the Oil Refinery, was registered in Antigua in 1961. The Company was jointly owned by Standard Oil of Indiana and

Natomas of California. The first Chairman of the Company was Frank D. St. Hillarie, an entrepreneur through whose efforts the refinery came to fruition.

Construction work at the Refinery started in September 1965, and provided jobs for at least 1,000 people. Refining operations began early in 1967.

The Oil Company's initial capital was EC$m40, with a capability of producing 11,000 barrels of refined oil per day from the crude oil imported from Venezuela and the Middle East.

During this period, there was almost full employment in Antigua. With the demand for labour in construction, industrial plants, hotels and housing, and with the rapid expansion of tourism which absorbed various categories of workers, workers had to be recruited from St. Lucia and St. Vincent to be employed in the Sugar Industry, particularly during the reaping of the Sugar Crop. Many of these workers stayed on even after the sugar harvesting, as employment was readily available.

The shortage of cotton pickers on the Island called on experiments to reap sea island cotton by machinery. The women and girls who usually performed this type of work were more gainfully employed in the Hotel Industry and the factories. These experiments were only partially successful however, because while the machine picked the cotton, it also picked the dry leaves as well, making the cotton more difficult and expensive to clean. It was decided that further experiments would be carried out until an improved machine could be developed.

With the continuous shortage of local labour in the agricultural sector, both the Antigua Trades & Labour Union and the Employers' Federation agreed to explore mechanizing agriculture. Mechanical loaders for sugar cane were introduced and became the general means of loading on the Estates. Experiments were also carried out with a cane harvesting machine which was hoped to be the answer for cutting cane.

It was realised however, that full-scale mechanisation of the Sugar Industry would require considerable outlay of capital. The Factory and Estates were passing through difficult financial times brought about mainly by poor crops which resulted from continuing droughts, and the necessary capital for purchasing the machines would be difficult to raise by the two companies. Added to this was a severe drought in 1965, which caused all the Factory dams to go dry. In order to save what was left of the Crop, the Government had to run water pipes to the Factory to provide it with water from its domestic supply, to enable it to produce sugar from the drying cane.

Despite the drought conditions, sugar still played a vital role in the economy of the Island. It was the largest employer and the largest exporter. It provided the means of livelihood for many families, particularly in the rural areas and could almost be considered the mainstay of the rural economy.

It was also a safe crop with market prices secured under the Commonwealth Sugar Agreement, with guaranteed quotas at rates considered reasonable to the economic producer. Britain's possible entry into the European Community could affect the preferences and quota system provided by Britain to the rest of the Commonwealth in the future. This however, was not of immediate concern, because Britain had given an undertaking to the West Indies that their vital interest in sugar and other export commodities such as citrus and bananas would be safeguarded during any negotiations with the European Community. There was no reason to doubt that Britain would live up to its undertaking.

The importance of sugar to a large section of the community, its vital role in the economy of the Island and its contribution to the export trade and balance of payment position, made it conceivable that the Government and the Trade Union would co-operate as far as was practicable with the producers, to keep the industry alive and to work towards its improvement and viability. While the Government and certain trade union officials were bent on this course, there were other factions at work in the Trade Union Movement which engineered and hastened the destruction of the Industry.

CHAPTER 3
NEGOTIATIONS FOR INDEPENDENCE

Following the General Elections of 1965 and the temporary abandonment of the idea of a Federation for the smaller Eastern Caribbean Islands, the Government of Antigua approached the British Government on constitutional changes that would provide independence for the Territory. After exchanges of correspondence on the subject in which the British Government expressed its own views on the undesirability of independence for individual small territories such as Antigua, but hoped still that a federal solution could be found, the Antigua Government remained adamant that it would accept nothing less than a constitution patterned on that of Western Samoa, which by treaty gave certain temporary powers to New Zealand in Defence and External Affairs.

In view of the stance taken by the Antigua Government, the Colonial Office agreed to arrange for a date when Constitutional talks could be held between the Secretary of State for the Colonies and a delegation from Antigua. The Antigua Government was requested to prepare a preliminary draft of the constitutional proposals, which would provide the basis for negotiations. If agreement were reached, the agreed proposals would then become the pattern for the other Leeward and Windward Islands that were in a position to request such far reaching constitutional changes.

The Government of Antigua appointed a team comprising the Attorney General, Lionel Hurst, E.H. Lake and McChesney George, with Novelle Richards being the original draftsman to prepare the constitutional proposals that were taken to London.

Lord Longford who led the Constitutional Talks was a Labour Peer who was then the Colonial Secretary representing the British Government. V.C. Bird represented Antigua. The Talks took place during the spring of 1966 and did not go smoothly during the early stages. The bureaucrats in the Colonial Office could not conceive of a small island like Antigua being independent. They also did not relish the idea of equal status between Great Britain and Antigua, a position the Antigua delegation sought to establish from the outset. Antigua offered Britain an elder brother role, while the bureaucrats wanted to retain a mother role. Lord Longford eventually came to the rescue and a compromise was reached in which the novel constitution known as Independence in Association was worked out. The Talks took a full month to conclude, testifying to the intensity of the negotiations.

The Constitution defined the State of Antigua, which included Barbuda and Redonda, and provided for full internal self-government - free from British Parliamentary jurisdiction. No laws of the British Government could apply to Antigua without the consent of its Parliament.

The Antigua Parliament alone had the right to amend its Constitution. The British Government by agreement, would for the time being, retain jurisdiction in defence and external affairs, but would delegate upon request by the Antigua Government the authority to deal in certain matters of External Affairs with foreign governments. Either party with proper notice could abrogate jurisdictional rights in defence and external affairs at any time.

Citizens of Antigua would remain British citizens until Antigua secured its full independence under the terms of the Constitution. The British Government could not go to the aid of civil power in Antigua without a request by Antigua's Government.

The Constitution provided for a Governor, a Senate, a House of Representatives and a Cabinet, presided over by the Premier who would normally be the leader of the Party winning a majority of seats in an election, and comprised of the Ministers appointed by the Governor on the Premier's advice. The Cabinet would be the chief instrument of Government's policy.

The Senate would comprise ten members appointed by the Governor on the advice of the Premier, and the House of Representatives would begin with the incumbent ten members, but the numbers could be increased at any time through by-elections, if the Premier so desired.

This was the pattern of Constitutions offered to the remaining Windward and Leeward Islands except Montserrat, but only one territory Grenada, like Antigua, opted for a bicameral Parliament; the others were content to carry on with a one chamber House of Assembly, retaining a nominated element in that chamber.

It was also agreed that the new States and Montserrat would co-operate as far as practicable in certain matters common to them, such as the courts of law, external matters falling within their delegated authority and any other regional matter which they thought could be better dealt with on a joint and regional basis, hence the term Associated States.

The Constitution was hailed by all Antiguans as a great achievement by the Government. In substance, it was almost a constitution granting full independence to the territory, for the British Government could no longer interfere with internal matters, and the pro-tem arrangement in external affairs and defence matters could only be carried out by the British Government after full consultation with the Government of Antigua. Further, provided certain constitutional requirements were met, the Government of Antigua could acquire full independence at any time, with or without the consent of the British Parliament.

The British Government also pledged continuing external financial aid to the new State through Commonwealth Development Grants and Loans and technical assistance. Not to be out done, the Government of Canada also came forward with the promise and offer of an increasing level of aid to the territories through their Overseas Development Agency. The new States came into being, knowing that they had good and powerful friends behind them. Though the United States made no specific commitments, it was also felt that the U.S.A. would play its part in providing some measure of assistance.

The Antigua Government hoped that the new constitution would be introduced on November 1, 1966 to coincide with the anniversary of the discovery of Antigua by Christopher Columbus. The British Government however felt that pursuant to other commitments, they could not meet that deadline and suggested a date in February 1967.

The Chief Minister and his colleagues however decided to hold an unofficial Statehood Celebration on the evening of November 1st, 1966, at which event the

Symbols of Statehood were displayed. The large number of guests in attendance heard for the first time, the official rendition of the Antigua State Anthem.

The State Flag, Anthem, Motto and Coat-of-Arms were all selected from open competitions among Antiguans at home and abroad. Reginald Samuel, an Antiguan artist, sculptor and teacher at the Antigua Grammar School, designed the Flag of five colours, which was selected from among 600 entries. **The Golden Sun**, dominating the centre of the Flag, symbolises the dawn of a new era; Red represents the dynamism of the people; **Blue** denotes the symbol of hope; **Black** reminds us of the rich and fertile soil and also the majority's African heritage; **Gold, Blue** and **White** together, represent the **sun, sea** and **sand**, Antigua and Barbuda's tourism product.

An Antiguan artist and teacher, Gordon Christopher, prepared the original design for the Coat-of-Arms. The design was modified by the Government's Statehood Committee to its present character. **The Pineapple** surmounting the Arms represents the famous **Antigua Black** Pineapple; **The Red Hibiscus Flowers** are symbolic of the many varieties that bloom in the Nation; **The Golden** and **Wavy Blue and White Bands** symbolises the **Sea, Sun** and **Beaches; The Central Sugar Mill Tower** and **The Stem of Sugar Cane** reminds us of the historic production of sugar, once the main industry in the Nation; **The Century Plant** or **Dagger Pole** with its **Stem and showy, Golden yellow Flowers** was a part of the historic Emblem of Antigua and the Leeward Islands; **The two Rampant Deers** depicts the only large animal within the Eastern Caribbean, whis is indigenous to Antigua and Barbuda. **The Scroll** bears the Motto of the Nation: **Each Endeavouring, All Achieving.**

The Motto: **Each Endeavouring All Achieving**, was composed by James H. Carrott, a former Senior Public Servant who was also a teacher for many years.

The lyrics to the State Anthem were penned by Novelle Hal Richards, while the melody and musical arrangements were composed by Walter P. Chambers, one of Antigua's well known and highly respected and highly respected musician and organist of national and international repute. The Anthem did not form part of the original competitions. The members of the Statehood Celebrations Committee of which Novelle Richards was a member were all prohibited from entering the competitions for the Symbols of Statehood. However, the sub-committee that was responsible for selecting the anthem, while giving credit to a number of the contributions submitted to the competition, decided that none of the entries were of the high standard and inspirational quality to merit selection. This was agreed to by the Central Committee after going through the entries. The Central Committee then decided that the competition should be re-opened for contributions from any Antiguan including members of the Central and other committees. It was at this stage that Novelle Richards submitted his entry which was selected.

By the end of the year, feverish preparations began in preparation for the Proclamation of Statehood and its accompanying celebrations which would culminate on the 28th February 1967, with the formal handing over of the Constitutional Instruments.

The Antigua Delegation to the Constitutional Talks which were held in London comprised - the Administrator, David Rose; V.C. Bird, Chief Minister; E.H. Lake, McChesney George and the Attorney General W.L. McIntyre, representing the Government. Stephen Roy Mendes represented the Nominated Members and commercial interests, Novelle H. Richards represented the Antigua Labour Party, Dr. Charles Locker represented the professional and other interests, and Donald Halstead represented the Antigua Trades & Labour Union. J.V. Hodge, Permanent Secretary to the Chief Minister, was Secretary to the delegation.

CHAPTER 4
PROCLAMATION OF STATEHOOD

As the time drew near for the introduction of the new Constitution and Proclamation of Statehood, every effort was exerted to see that the transition was made as smoothly as possible. Already, next door to Antigua, difficulties were developing in the Territory of St. Kitts-Nevis-Anguilla with the Anguillans taking a stand against going into Statehood with St. Kitts without guarantees. Opposition members in St. Kitts were also raising serious questions about certain provisions in the new Constitution. Although Antigua did not have such strong divisive elements, it was hoped that there would be no rioting to mar the occasion.

The only area of possible discontent that could have caused problem was Barbuda. The Parliamentary Representative of that Island Constituency, McChesney George and the people of Barbuda, seemed to have accepted the new Constitution with fervour, George being a Minister in the Central Government and a member of the Delegation to the Constitutional Talks in London. The Official Opposition in Antigua, while not vociferous in their acceptance of the new Constitution, raised no objection to it; so there was very little cause for concern.

In the meantime, speculations to who would be the first Governor to be appointed under the new Constitution were widespread. The Premier-to-be was empowered to recommend to Her Majesty, the Queen, his choice of Governor, but this remained a well guarded secret until a short while before the appointed day for assumption of office by the Governor. The choice of Premier-designate, V.C. Bird , Sr., was Wilfred Ebenezer Jacobs, who was born in Grenada of Antiguan parents, had served as Attorney-General of the Leeward Islands before the defunct Federation of the Colony and was Puisne Judge in Barbados. The choice of Sir Wilfred received universal acceptance.

The Constitution provided for the automatic membership of Parliament of the former elected members of the Legislative Council. Consideration had to be given to the appointment of Senators and to the members of commissions under the provisions of the Constitution.

It was no easy matter of making these selections as there were many aspirants for the few posts. As it turned out, many people were annoyed that they were passed over, and levelled criticisms at Bird for omitting persons whom it was thought, could make a better contribution to the Senate and Commissions than some who were selected. It was felt that a less partisan approach could have been made to the appointments.

The Statehood Organising and Celebrations Committee prepared a full programme of activities for the occasion which started with a State Service at the St. John's Cathedral on Sunday, 26th February, 1967. On the Monday morning, there was the Flag-Raising Ceremony at which the new Governor took his oath of office. This was followed by the opening of an arts exhibition, a cocktail party given by the Governor and an evening entertainment of music and drama by the arts and cultural groups.

During the day, the ten new Senators received their instruments of appointment from the Governor after they attended a meeting of the Senate, where they selected their President and Vice President and took their oats of allegiance to Her Majesty, the Queen. Novelle Richards was selected as President of the Senate and William Buntin, Vice President.

Those appointed to the Senate were Novelle H. Richards, President; William Buntin, Vice President; Joseph Myers, Minister without portfolio and Senate Leader, Dr. Luther Wynter, Stephen Roy Mendes, J. Ferdinand Shoul, Christian Simon, Levi Joseph, John Meade and Maurice Francis.

The State opening of Parliament and formal handing over of the Constitutional Instruments took place on Tuesday morning, 28th February. The Special Representative of the Queen who was delegated to hand over the Constitutional Instruments was the Honourable Arthur Bottomley, Minister of Overseas Development in the British Government. He arrived on the previous evening from St. Kitts where he performed a similar duty during the day and then proceeded to St. Lucia and the other Associated States on the same errand.

Present for the occasion were representatives of the British Government, the United States Government, the Government of Canada, the Commonwealth of Puerto Rico and the Commonwealth Caribbean Governments of Jamaica, Guyana, Barbados, Trinidad & Tobago and the American Virgin Islands. The other Associated States were unable to send representatives, because they were occupied with their own Statehood Celebrations.

At the Joint meeting of Parliament presided over by the President of the Senate, the Governor and the Queen's Special Representatives were welcomed by the President after which Mr. Bottomley handed over the Constitutional Instruments to the Premier. The Governor then made his Throne Speech indicating the policy and programme of the Government. The entire ceremony was televised through the auspices of ZAL TV, the local television station, so that viewers in Antigua and the neighbouring islands could follow the proceedings.

The rest of the day was given over to festivities, an official luncheon, a carnival pageant and a State Dinner and Ball. The following day was devoted to the schools, where local dignitaries attended displays at the various schools and partook of refreshments provided by the Government for the children.

The celebration went off smoothly and helped to provide the impetus and fillip to the new State and people to enable them to face the challenges that were ahead of them, no longer as a colonial or subject people, but as a people whose destiny now rested in their own hands.

CHAPTER 5
THE DARKENING CLOUDS

As previously explained in Part I of this Book, labour politics in Antigua was the out-growth of the Trade Union Movement. The Antigua Trades & Labour Union had become a monolithic structure embracing the entire labour force of the territory and had sympathisers and supporters throughout all strata of the society. This resulted in an in-cohesive and somewhat feeble opposition as was evident in the repetitive failures of other parties to win a single seat in a political election, and in the abortive efforts of other factions in forming any rival trade union to the Antigua Trades & Labour Union.

Despite the Trade Union's evident strength, there turned out to be one weakness – everything centered on one man, Bird. During the early struggles for supremacy between the workers and the plantocracy, it was necessary to have a leader of Bird's qualities to challenge Moody-Stuart, to help consolidate the gains that were achieved and to give the type of leadership that was vital to the economic and social development of the territory. Bird gave such leadership. However, not much interest was taken in welding a collective leadership from the grassroots upwards and to build a pyramid that could stand the test of time. The Trade Union and the labour party instead became a giant tree rising to the sky, exposed to the elements of wind and storm. Undoubtedly strong but with weakening shallow roots, a prey to termites that burrowed their way from inside out so that the damage could not be easily seen, and only when time came to prune the tree, was it realised that the tree was close to becoming a hollow trunk which could collapse at the first sudden squall that overtook it.

The Antigua Trades and Labour Union was one of the most powerful trade unions in the West Indies, or anywhere in the western world for that matter, by way of total organised labour to the size of population. But it was the most financially unsound union that could be found anywhere. This was the result of a policy of keeping union dues as low as possible.

Irregardless of the Union's growing needs and the expansion of trade union activities, every effort to increase members' dues was defeated at Annual Conferences because there was a powerful lobby against it. No matter how much the increase that might have been negotiated for workers by the Union, the dues remained the same from year to year and the small increase that may have been agreed to was unrealistic to meet the Union's expenses. The result was that Union Officers were paid far less than persons working in other employment in the Island, and sometimes could not be paid their salaries. Whenever there was difficulty that called for immediate large sums of money, it was only a very small circle of officers or supporters who from their own small resources had to meet these commitments. It was a labour of love and sacrifice to work for the Trade Union.

If a proactive approach to the Trade Union's economics was practiced, the Union would have been in a better financial position, capable of paying competitive wages to its employees and possibly with a sizable bank balance which is ultimately of primary importance to all unions.

Bird, however felt that the people would be more grateful to the Union and possibly to him as leader, if they received good service for almost nothing. This however, does not tally with the laws of economics and gratitude, for while the Union as one of its basic duties had to play a social role for its workers, such a role could only be effective and productive if it were buttressed by a sound financial policy, especially when people are known to bite the hands that feed them.

As the Union formed the political base of the Labour Party, it was of paramount importance to keep this base intact with good and loyal leadership in key positions. Lionel Hurst, who was then the General-Secretary of the Trade Union, was both able and loyal to V.C. Bird. While Hurst remained General-Secretary of the Trade Union, all was and would be well. It was apparent however, that Hurst with his ability could not be made to continuously sacrifice his time and effort at the Trade Union level with the small salary the Union could afford to pay, while his colleagues were given wider opportunities and higher salaries at the political level.

It was the decision to remove Hurst from General Secretary of the Union to take over a ministerial post in the Government that paved the way for trouble that eventually overtook the Union and came close to bringing about its demise.

Hurst's removal came about as a result of the financial policies that governed the union. Had the Union been able to pay better wages, it would not have been necessary to bring about the change, for Hurst could have remained as General-Secretary and simultaneously as an elected member of the Legislative. The General -Secretary of a powerful union holds a very powerful position. It was necessary to see that such an important post was held by an individual who could use that power with discretion, whose loyalty to his union and its Executive was tested and whose personal ambitions would not go to the length of sacrificing his union and country, if they were considered obstacles in his way to reaching a self appointed goal.

A Special Conference was called to fill the post of General Secretary vacated by Hurst in 1961. At this Conference, two candidates were nominated for election, George Walker, a foreman machinist at the Antigua Sugar Factory, who was a union member from its inception, Chairman of the Antigua Sugar Factory Section and served in various other union posts. He had wide experience in negotiations, being a continuous member of the negotiating team in the Sugar Industry. The other candidate was George Walter who was a newcomer to trade union activities, and was brought in by Bird to take over as Editor of the Workers' Voice after Novelle Richards became a Minister of the Federal Government of the West Indies.

Walter's rise from near obscurity in 1958 was almost meteoric, for it was inconceivable that he would have been considered in the running for General Secretary in so short a time. He however, had a very strong and powerful lobby behind him and the Conference favoured his candidacy and gave him the edge over the other candidate, George Walker, at the election.

Although poor in finances, the Union was strong and powerful when Walter took office as General Secretary. There was also the sympathetic ear and support of the Government that could be depended upon. The Island had begun to rapidly expand economically, with the development of tourism and associated trades, and significant sums of money were in circulation.

The Island was also enjoying a period of industrial peace brought about by the full recognition and appreciation by both Union and Management of their respective roles in the economic life of the country. This period of industrial peace combined with the progressive economic policies of the Government and the advantageous geographical position of the Island, saw industrial development, as foreign companies became attracted to the Island.

The Union also made gains from this development. Because mutual trust and confidence were established, the Union was able to persuade Management in almost every category of employment to agree to the introduction of a check-off system by which Union Members in their employ, upon signing an agreement, would permit Management to deduct the weekly union dues from their wages. This made the Union's task of collecting dues simpler, and for the first time, substantial sums of money began to pour into the union's treasury. Furthermore, at long last, the Conference was persuaded to increase union dues.

The outlook for the Government's commercial sector and the workers was very bright – by the Trade Union's Silver Anniversary in 1964, one could look back with pride at the past, with sound hopes for the future.

While all appeared well on the surface, things were far from well in the inner circles of the Trade Union. As soon as George Walter was secure in the post of General-Secretary, he began to build a circle of selected Executive Members and other key officers around him, some through various acts of favouritism. He became outwardly rude and hostile to other Executive Members and officers, whom he realized could not be drawn into his circle. The result was a sharp division of the Executive.

Unfortunately, Bird who became more occupied with matters of Government did nothing to stop this development in its early stages, until it was out of control. Bird took a neutral position in the matter, a mistake for which he paid dearly.

Walter was bent on increasing and consolidating his power, but there were certain Key Officers in the way, who were to be removed from office at any cost. With the Officers removed, he could deal with Bird from a position of strength. Walter's main targets were McChesney George, Novelle Richards and Bradley Carrott, and to some extent, Lionel Hurst, though Hurst as Minister of Labour had no official post in the Union.

Walter's main lieutenant was Donald Halstead, a Field Officer of the Union. Halstead, like Walter, was one of Bird's protégés - their loyalty was untried and untested; however, they convinced Bird of their sincerity and so were brought into the Union's fold. Prior to taking up an appointment with the Union, it is said that Halstead had applied for membership in the opposition party and was turned down. If this is true, then it would stand to reason that his offer to serve the Labour Union was of doubtful sincerity and basically opportunistic.

It would be wrong to blame Bird for any error of judgment. Any person bent on deceiving could always find their victims. Bird was always on the look-out for bright and forceful individuals especially of humble origin, to strengthen the Union's leadership. It was conceivable that he would not have rejected the offer of service from persons like Walter and Halstead. It must also be realised too, that the Trade Union was strong and powerful, and that Bird was firmly in the saddle; the possibility of an internal coup to unseat him would have been remote from his mind.

Halstead proved to be a forceful union officer. He was intelligent and enterprising, but his mannerism was very often unpleasant. From the outset, it was not difficult to recognise that he was overly ambitious - a person who may stop at nothing to get his way. Perhaps if an early check were exercised, he might have proven to be a more useful officer to the Union and a better groomed individual to undertake higher responsibilities.

As events were, Walter whose purpose he served, encouraged Halstead's behaviour, which was also tolerated by Bird, who felt that Halstead's spirit should not be curbed but allowed to develop with maturity. Successive complaints would reach the Executive of Halstead's unpleasant and unacceptable behaviour to Management and others. Some workers made various charges against him, but the charges were never investigated to verify their veracity, and were allowed to go by default. The result was Halstead became more self-assured, and instead of maturing as Bird hoped, he became more antagonistic, even to Bird after a time.

Walter and Halstead's basic aim was to build their popularity at any cost. They exploited workers' weaknesses by promising increases, which they knew were beyond Management's reach. If they failed to achieve these demands, the workers were told that they did not get the support of the Executive.

Strikes were instigated and called without the knowledge or sanction of the Executive which had to ratify any strike action. It came to a point that agreements reached with the Union by employers became almost farcical, for without notice, other demands may be made by the Union during the term of the agreement that if not accepted, would inevitably lead to a strike of which the Executive would receive notice after the strike was in progress.

It was at this stage that Novelle Richards introduced a motion in the Executive, invoking certain rules of the Union and advocating strong measures against any officer or member who instigates or call a strike on their own without the Executive's authority, or without the proper procedures being followed.

After heated discussion on the motion wherein the mover became a target of abuse by Walter and his supporters, the motion passed. To some extent, this brought to an end the indiscriminate strike actions that had begun to mar the agreements made between the Union and employers, and was interrupting the tenor of industrial peace that brought numerous benefits to the Island. This move however, made Novelle Richards the No. 1 enemy of the offending officers and their supporters.

With their tendency for calling frivolous strikes curbed, the dissident group resorted to open confrontation, whereby in the presence of workers, would accuse certain members of the Executive, of working against the interest of the workforce. It became evident that Walter, Halstead and their cohorts were waging a subtle and poisonous campaign against top ranking members of the Executive.

After his dismissal from the Union, Walter told a large crowd assembled for a public meeting at the Antigua Recreation Grounds in June 1967, that he campaigned against certain Executive Members because they objected to his policies and tried to get others whom he thought would be more amenable to replace them.

During a Supreme Court case in 1970 brought by Walter against the Antigua Trades and Labour Union for wrongful dismissal, Maurice Francis, a former Senator, testified that he was approached by certain officers purportedly sent to him by Walter, with a list of names that he should vote for during the 1965 elections for

Executive Members at the Annual Conference. Francis said when he looked at the list and saw it contained none of the names of respected and important Executive Officers, he realised that something was wrong. The campaign by Walter failed, because the Officers he wanted removed from the Executive were all re-elected. It took him considerable time to recover from this disappointment.

It must be pointed out that this self-admitted action by Walter in trying to unseat and smear members of the Executive was wrong and of deep disloyalty. The Executive of the Union is the only instrument of Union policies between Conferences. The General-Secretary makes no policy, neither does he have a vote in Executive policy decisions. His duties are to carry out the Executive's instructions, which is his employer and to always maintain the Union's integrity.

If Walter, Halstead and their supporters were against the Union Executive's policies, they should have raised these matters at Executive Meetings or the Annual Conference. They also had the recourse to resign and inform members of the Union or the public of their reasons for doing so. But to sit in an office of trust as Walter did and work against the very persons whose trust and authority he held in order to elevate himself, was betrayal of that trust and authority.

CHAPTER 6
THE SUGAR INDUSTRY

Severe drought persisted in Antigua during1965, with less than 30 inches of rainfall for that year. The drought created such severe conditions to the Sugar Crop, that it became almost uncommercial to reap it. By 1966, the Antigua Syndicate Estates and the Antigua Sugar Factory were in serious financial difficulties. The Banks with which the two Companies did business refused to extend additional credit facilities to them. The two Companies had no financial resources available to them and without a large loan or grant, they could not start reaping operations. The reserved capital in the Sugar Cess Funds was depleted and it looked as though the Sugar Crop though small, would remain unreaped.

In view of the hardships that would be inflicted on those engaged in the Sugar Industry if the Crop was not reaped, the Government made a grant of EC$1m to the Management of the Factory and Estates to assist them in reaping the Crop. The Government also guaranteed certain advances to be made by the Banks to the Sugar Industry.

As a result of Government's financial assistance, the Sugar Factory and Estates' Managements agreed to set up a supervisory board responsible for the policies and operation of the Sugar Industry on which the Government and the peasants were represented.

Sir Alexander Moody-Stuart, who was the Managing Director of the Antigua Syndicate Estates Ltd. and the Antigua Sugar Factory had retired a few years earlier and lived in England. He was succeeded by his son, George Moody-Stuart, who had worked at the head office of the Parent Company in London.

A tremendous task faced George Moody-Stuart on taking over from his father to pull the almost bankrupt companies out of fiscal problems. While

Management might be blamed to some extent for some of the companies' financial woes, no one could overlook the awful and continuous droughts that plagued the Island for successive years from 1961. It was not only the Estates that suffered from the drought, but also the peasantry that had been so successfully built up from the Government's assistance. The Peasants were badly hit and had accumulated large deficits from poor crops, subsequently causing them to incur large debts to the Peasant Development Organisation (PDO), which they were unable to pay.

Eventually, the Government had to liquidate some of these debts, but the bad years drove many peasants away from the land and brought a decline in peasant production.

This was one of the severest tests that Agriculture faced in Antigua. Many who loved the land and depended on it for a livelihood were afraid to invest any more in the land, for there seemed to be no end to the dry years and further losses. But there were those who persisted with the hope that the drought would break. Their persistence provided some local fruits and vegetables to the populace, who were becoming almost solely dependent on produce shipped from Montserrat and Dominica, and paying exorbitant prices to the local hucksters.

With these examples of existing conditions, the Trade Union entered into negotiations with the Antigua Employers' Federation for reaping the 1966 Sugar Crop. The Union Executive, knowing that the only reason the industry had not closed was because of Government's financial assistance and intervention, instructed George Walter, the General-Secretary, to strongly advise the workers against demanding any increase for reaping the Crop, and if they were bent on an increase, it should be minimal. It was clear to all concerned at the time that the Industry could not absorb higher wages and needed the co-operation of Management, workers and Government, to keep it alive and to give the Factory and Estates an opportunity to pay off their bank debts.

Unfortunately, the Union had just negotiated an increase for the Non-Established Government Workers, which gave the workers an overall salary increase of about 20%. This increase was long overdue as several years had passed since their last pay increase. The negotiations for the Government Workers would ordinarily have no bearing on the Sugar Workers whose wages and conditions of

186

work were negotiated annually, but this offered Walter the opportunity for the confrontation he sought.

It was George Walter and his subordinate officers who were in daily contact with the sugar workers and the negotiating team from the Sugar Factory and Estates. Instead of carrying out the instructions of the Executive Committee to advise the sugar workers to go slowly on wage increases, he openly defied the Executive's order, indicating that he could not do so, because if the Non-established Government Workers could receive a 20% increase, he could not see why the sugar workers could not receive the same. He also said that the sugar workers' representatives told him they would not accept anything less than 20%.

Whether or not it was true, workers reported to the Executive Members that Walter advised them not to accept less than 20% increase in wages, and were told by him that the Union's Executive were against them and were supporting Management instead.

At a meeting of the sugar workers held at the Union's Head Office during the negotiations, the workers were hostile to the Union's Executive, while the moment Walter appeared, he received loud cheers. This in itself should have raised a red flag, but no one paid much attention to the incident. If Walter as the instrument of the Union's policy was singled out for preferential treatment by the workers who were hostile to the Executive, it clearly showed that all was not well, that some mischief was afoot.

Attempts made by Executive Members to explain the insolvent position of the Sugar Industry and its inability to pay the increase workers sought were futile. Walter already told them how much money they should receive out of the EC$1m grant the Government made to the Sugar Industry. The workers did not care nor did they realise that without the Government's grant, the Sugar Industry would have closed down and they would have been seeking employment instead of demanding increases. Neither did they realise that even with the Government's grant, the Sugar Industry would lose money after reaping the Crop, and the increases the workers demanded made the losses substantially greater.

The negotiations stretched out over three months. With the position the workers took, the Executive thought it advisable to leave the matter to the General

Secretary and the workers to see what increases they could get. Management pleaded without avail against the impossibility of paying the workers' demands. When it was realised that no compromise would be reached, Management called an end to the negotiations. They offered the workers 25% increase - 5% more than they demanded. This was accepted with glee by the General Secretary and the workers, but as soon as the Crop was over, Management notified Government and all concerned that all sugar operations of the two companies in Antigua would cease as of the closing of the Crop, and the two companies would go into receivership. This brought an end to the private operation of the Sugar Industry in Antigua.

It is difficult to conclude whether the Antigua Syndicate Estates and the Antigua Sugar Factory Ltd. would have continued sugar production as a private concern if they had sympathetic understanding from the workers. It is possible that they might have been able to continue operations for a few more years, hoping for an almost miraculous change in the weather and a stretch of years with good rainfall, or they might have diversified their operations with new capital and still retain sugar as part of their operations. At any rate, a considerable amount of new capital would have had to be found.

The companies planned to go into real estate by developing some of their land as housing sites to attract British and European settlers who were being displaced in East and Central Africa with the coming of independence and the Africanisation of former British colonies on that Continent. The Antigua Government did not approve of any such development and refused to grant permission. It was felt that the type of settlement envisaged would be detrimental to the national interests and aspirations of Antiguans who wanted to own their country. The Government had no intention of bringing into Antigua the type of settlement that made second-class citizens out of the native people in Antigua and felt that the Island would be better off without it.

Walter's influence over the negotiations and his planned confrontation with the Executive of the Union precipitated the closure of the Sugar Industry in 1967. But for Government's action in purchasing the companies' assets, workers on the Estates, in the Factory and workshops would have been left without compensation for the service they gave to the Industry, some encompassing an entire lifetime.

It is remarkable that in 1967, just after the formation of his new Union, Walter, while addressing a crowd at the Antigua Recreation Ground, was almost ecstatic to say '"SUGAR IS DEAD!" This turned out to be a perspicacious statement, one year after he became Premier of Antigua.

CHAPTER 7
GOVERNMENT PURCHASES SUGAR ASSETS

The closing of sugar operations in Antigua and the placing of the Antigua Sugar Factory and the Antigua Syndicate Estates' properties into receivership posed a very serious problem to the Government; chief among which was the large number of people who were suddenly unemployed without any immediate means of absorbing them into gainful employment. There were some 10,000 people who depended directly or indirectly on sugar for their livelihood. Many knew no other employment, since from childhood they either worked in the Fields or Factory, some acquiring skills or semi-skills along the way, which were all put to use in the Sugar Industry.

Although new industries were being introduced in the Island, apart from Tourism, these industries were not labour intensive and construction work could not be relied upon to be permanently expansive. No known Agro-industry was found capable of taking over from sugar, therefore, in the interest of the workers and the economy, the Government was determined to maintain and encourage the continuation of sugar production. There were also the large areas of land, approximately 13,000 acres that belonged to the two companies. The use to which the lands should be put had to be given serious and urgent consideration.

The recent history of sugar production in Antigua did not offer encouraging prospects to the private investor. The former owners of the Factory and Estates seemed happy to pull out, and this in itself did not make matters any better. More so, the drought continued. Any company that acquired the two companies' assets and went into sugar production would have to be prepared for several years of accumulated losses before breaking even or realising a profit, making it difficult to find private investors who would be prepared to take the risk.

As was mentioned in Part I, Chapter 14, the Labour Party never seriously considered nationalising the Sugar Industry. The situation that developed however demanded quick and serious decisions, and the Government felt it had an obligation to the country to secure these assets and so entered into negotiations for their purchase.

The Directors of the Companies were relieved that the Government was prepared to assume ownership of their entire portfolio and agreed to a price of approximately EC$6m, which included compensation to be paid to the displaced sugar workers. The Antigua Trades & Labour Union and the Companies' representatives negotiated a compensation package on behalf of the workers, and the Government was able to raise a loan on Treasury Guarantee to purchase the factory lands and other properties owned by the Antigua Sugar Factory Ltd. and the Antigua Syndicate Estates Ltd., and became involved in sugar production.

As Premier, V.C. Bird received kudos for this bold effort of the Government, a lot of credit should also go to McChesney George who was the person most actively engaged in the negotiations. The Government also received great assistance from a team of Puerto Rican advisers provided by the Government of Puerto Rico for that purpose.

From one bold stroke of the pen, the Government became the proud owner of almost all the arable land in the Island without the bitterness and confrontations usually associated with Government acquisitions. The former owners were satisfied, the workers were compensated and happy, and Government was left to set the stage to put the arable land to proper use.

By legislation, the Government set up a statutory board known as The Antigua Sugar Factory and Estates Board, in which was vested the assets that the Government purchased. The Board had to function independently as an industrial agricultural enterprise and among other things, would produce sugar. The Government would guarantee the financing of the Board's operations in the initial stages until the Board was able to hold its own. The Government was empowered to appoint suitable persons to be members of the Board and the first chairman was Mr. Hugh Burrowes, a retired Colonial Administrator, who acted as Administrator in Antigua on various occasions. Hugh Burrowes was an Antiguan, a lawyer and the son of Mr. T.H. Burrowes of whom mention was made in Part 1. Hugh Burrowes was also appointed Chairman of the Public Service Commission under the new Constitution and combined both functions.

Despite the closure of operations by the former owners of the Antigua Sugar Factory and Estates and the intricacies of the negotiations before purchase of its assets were concluded, it was still possible to reap a small crop in 1967. The Board set about rehabilitating the Factory and the cane fields, and began to cultivate new land for planting cane.

Initially, all of the sugar workers who were laid off could not be employed; many of these workers were able to secure jobs again under the new management in the field and factory, thereby alleviating any serious unemployment problem that was likely to develop.

At last, some welcome relief came with the breaking of the drought during August and September, 1967, which boosted the ratoon cane and the newly planted cane. The second year, 1968, the Board reaped its second crop which was close to 10,000 tons of sugar.

The workers in the Sugar Industry were prepared to reap the crop without making any substantial demands. They realised that by following the wrong advice to press for large increases in 1966 had contributed to the closure of the Industry and they were grateful to the Antigua Trades & Labour Union and the Government for the part they played in making possible the compensation and gratuities they received.

The sugar workers in spite of strong efforts made by the new rival union led by Walter in gaining their membership, remained loyal to the Antigua Trades & Labour Union; a loyalty perhaps for which they paid dearly, when the new Government under Walter's Premiership closed the promising Sugar Industry in 1972, without notice or consideration of compensation for those engaged in the Industry.

CHAPTER 8
DISMISSAL OF WALTER

There was a strong feeling among the Executive Members of the Union supported by many reports from members and non-members of the Union, that George Walter, Donald Halstead and other Officers were undermining the Union. The confrontation between Walter and the Executive of the Union during the reaping months of the Sugar Crop in 1966 was tangible evidence of his disloyalty. There were also reports from persons such as George Moody-Stuart and others, who said Walter boasted that he would be the next premier, so they should be careful how they dealt with him. The fact that V.C. Bird was still Premier and George Walter was in no way in the running for leadership of the Party and lacked legislative experience, caused a few eyebrows to be raised; but the matter was not taken seriously.

The Executive attempted to investigate reports made to V.C. Bird by certain persons in the Island on conversations they said they had with Walter, which they considered dangerous to the Government and the Party. For personal reasons, these persons declined to publicly address the union because they did not want to be embroiled in the Union or Party matters. It was inferred that they only wanted to warn Bird against the threats Walter made.

Novelle Richards in his evidence to the Court during the case brought by Walter against the Union for wrongful dismissal, said that one afternoon after work he had to go back to his office at the Union's Headquarters when he overheard Walter, Halstead and some other Officers having a discussion about the prospect of forming a separate Waterfront Union. Richards said that he was astonished to hear that type of discussion from such high Officials of the Union, but, as soon as he made his presence known, the discussion abruptly ceased. The Waterfront workers were members of the Antigua Trades and Labour Union, and remarkably on the same day that Walter was dismissed, it was the Waterfront Workers to whom he turned, who staged a strong demonstration against the Union in his favour.

There were other important matters affecting Union finances that were addressed at the Annual Conference in 1966. For unknown reasons, these matters were played down by the Conference while other questions were left unanswered. Upon his dismissal, the Antigua Trades & Labour Union instituted legal proceedings against Walter to recover certain sums of money. Up to the writing of this Book, these cases were not heard, or perhaps expired by the Statute of Limitation.

The question of why the Executive failed to take steps to remove Walter with all the evidence before them was posed at the Annual Conference by individuals who were following the developing trend in the Courts when the case came before it. Walter should have been called to a Union tribunal and disciplined according to its policies. Such a course of action was advocated by E.H. Lake, a high ranking and influential member of the Union. However, by failing to act, the Executive body erred by judging the matter on its own merit. Whether a union tribunal would have been able to find against Walter is difficult to say, as the Executive was divided, with one faction supporting Walter. However, the undermining efforts in the field against the Executive had a damaging effect to the AT&LU as evidenced by the reaction of a large section of members to Walter's dismissal.

Political considerations were the main reasons why the Walter matter was not dealt with in 1966. As mentioned before, negotiations for a new Constitution with Britain concluded in the spring of 1966. These negotiations were considered crucial for the Territory, thus it was imperative to approach Britain with a united front. Any distractions of party, trade union split or semblance thereof had to be suppressed, so that the Constitutional Delegation could portray a picture of political stability on the Island.

Already, St. Kitts was having their problems even before receiving Statehood. Bird was over cautious lest dissension in the ranks mar the negotiations. The Walter problem was therefore shelved until the Constitution became *fait* accompli. Here again, timing proved to be an important factor in Walter's favour, for while the Conference in September, 1966 could have dealt with Walter if properly directed, the new Executive that was elected did not place political considerations before the Union's integrity, or it was very likely that Walter would have been removed from office at that time without much fuss.

Walter's supporters, including Halstead and Malcolm Daniel, (who became President of the new Antigua Workers' Union) were annoyed that they were passed over for nominations to the Senate or other Government Commissions. There could be no doubt that to pass over Walter who was General-Secretary of the Antigua Trades & Labour Union and appoint a less important Union Officer to the Senate without explanation, was a slight to Walter.

The Governor, acting on the advice of Premier Bird, who made the choice, appointed constitutional officers. It is possible that in view of Walter's activities, Bird thought it *infradig* to make Walter a Senator. On the other hand, it might have been more strategic to appoint Walter as a Senator, waylaying complaints to his supporters that he was badly treated.

V.C. Bird over estimated his strength and under estimated the effect of the anti-Executive campaign being waged from within. Pre-occupied with the affairs of Government, Premier Bird was unable to give his full attention to trade union matters and so lost control of the situation.

It was inevitable that this happened, because although Bird loved the Union, he would have been well advised to give up the post of President, as it was strenuous to continue as the country's political leader and simultaneously as President of the Trade Union. It may have been feasible if the Union's Executive Officers were totally united behind him, but this was not the case. Therefore, to counter Walter and Halstead's activities, a trusted and loyal person should have been found from the ranks of the Executive as President to manage the Union's affairs. With the Union's improved finances, the President could have been paid a salary or honorarium that would enable him to devote more time to the Union's affairs.

When the Antigua Labour Party was properly constituted, Bird resigned as President of the Antigua Trades and Labour Union, but that came about years too late, and after real damage had been done to the Union.

***

Statehood celebrations passed without incident and the Union started to prepare for Labour Day celebrations, which took place on the first Monday in May, 1967. There was a huge parade on that day and the Labour Queen, who was selected

195

at a pageant on the previous Saturday night together with the runners-up and other contestants, led the Parade to Michael's Mount Carnival Bowl.

V.C. Bird, George Walter and other Union Officers addressed the gathered crowd. The rest of the Day was enjoyed at a colourful picnic at Fort James. Everything was unity and peace on the surface. Two weeks later, the Executive met on a Friday night, and George Walter by a majority vote of the members present, was dismissed as General-Secretary of The Antigua Trades & Labour Union. Donald Halstead was also dismissed at the same time from his post of Field Officer.

Walter had an inclination that he was going to be dismissed because he informed certain leaders from the Waterfront Section to that effect. Accordingly, plans were already laid to protest his dismissal if that occurred.

It was, however, impossible for Walter to continue as General-Secretary. He had lost the confidence of the main Executive body which could no longer trust his loyalty and he was continually at loggerheads with certain Executive Members. His confrontation and intransigence which brought about the closing of the Sugar Industry were matters that could not be ignored. The General Secretary of a union is its mouthpiece. If that mouthpiece is impaired, it could not represent the interest of the union to the full extent.

It took the Executive Meeting less than one hour to terminate Walter's and Halstead's appointments. The President outlined certain infractions that both Officers were imputed to have done against the interest of the Union and said that in so far as he was concerned, it was impossible to continue working with them. He then inquired if Walter or Halstead had anything to say on the matter. Walter, who was usually quick to express his views said nothing. None of his known supporters voiced objections.

Halstead, who was present at every Executive Meeting, was seen in the vicinity of the Union's Headquarters before the meeting started, but was conspicuously absent from the proceedings.

One Executive Member moved a motion that both Officers be dismissed. The motion was seconded and put to the vote, when Joseph Cornwall, having the only dissenting voice asked: "Tell me why you are dismissing them?" This question petered out, so to did the jobs of Walter and Halstead. Shortly after the voting took place, two of Walter's supporters on the Executive joined the meeting. Though usually early, they arrived just before the closing prayers.

CHAPTER 9
THE ANTIGUA WORKERS' UNION IS FORMED

In its haste to move beyond the regrettable event of Walter's and Halstead's dismissal, the Executive made two fateful errors on that Friday night: They did not ask Walter to turn over the Minutes Book and other documents of the Union on that very night of his dismissal, and that they should have called a public meeting on the Monday night following the Executive Meeting, to explain the reason for the dismissal. These were oversights for which the Union paid dearly in the long run.

Walter left with the Minutes Book and the other Union documents and refused to return them until threatened with legal proceedings. It was some three months after his dismissal that these documents were returned to the Union. No one examined the Minutes Book when it was returned to the Union to see what was written in it. Further, copies of the Minutes of that fateful Friday night were never circulated to members of the Executive. While Minutes were subsequently read at meetings of the Executive and signed by the Presiding Officer, one could not be absolutely sure if what was read was actually contained in the Minutes Book.

It might not have been necessary to verify the minutes with an officer of undisputed loyalty, but the same could not be assumed of Walter, for his loyalty was in dispute when he was.

On the matter of holding a meeting on the Monday night following the dismissals, it was the opinion of all who knew the circumstances, that had the Union put its reason for the dismissal of Walter and Halstead to the public before they had their say, both men would not have become overnight heroes, but would have perhaps found it better to leave Antigua. As it happened, they out-manoeuvred the ATLU and won the field.

There again, Bird and the Union's Executive took a lot for granted. As the undisputed leader and hero who was at the forefront of Antigua's social, economic and political advancement, Bird thought he was guaranteed the public's ear and if necessary, their sympathy. Here too he was mistaken. Without realising it, Bird had been losing touch with the people. As Premier of the new Associated State, almost all of his time was devoted to Government and he relied upon the Union to maintain the grassroots support. Walter and Halstead were doing the grassroots work through their own contacts and through the contacts of subordinates. Premier Bird might have forgotten that Winston Churchill won a war but lost the subsequent election; Charles DeGaulle saved France from economic and social disintegration yet lost a referendum. Political gratitude cannot always be relied upon. A party and its leader must be eternally vigilant if the party's integrity is to be maintained.

In this respect, it was Bird's lukewarmness or opposition to having a political party affiliated with yet separate from the Union, spelt his downfall. This gave Walter the excuse he sought and won him unexpected support from many sources. Walter never wanted a political party separate from the Union. As a matter of fact, anytime Novelle Richards, who was its foremost advocate, raised the topic at political committee meetings, Walter was one of its strongest opponents. However, he had other plans, foremost of which was to take over the Antigua Trades & Labour Union, for he knew that whoever controlled the Union within the framework of union politics would also control the political field, and ultimately the Government.

Richards strongly advocated the division between the Trade Union and the Political Party as he envisaged a conflict of interest that would occur between the Government and the Trade Union. While it was in the best country's interest of have a united labour and political front to fight the plantocracy and colonial establishment to bring about social and political liberties, it was inevitable that a Government of an independent State controlled by a trade union would find itself in difficulties, even with its own supporters, if it did not carry out the dictates of union's executive, even to the detriment of other sectors of the society.

A Government that is labour oriented has more flexibility than one that is virtually a trade union. This does not say that within reasonable bounds a Government comprising of trade union leaders would not be a fair Government.

The history and example of Bird and his colleagues are undisputed in their efforts to serve the interest of all Antiguans, be they unionists or not. On the other hand, life is not static; men come and go, and what might have been appropriate for a certain period could easily become outdated or unsuited to a developing and changing society. There was reluctance to change and men like Walter and Halstead profited from this reluctance by using it to their advantage at the opportune time. There were also a number of people in the State who while they supported or sympathized with trade unionism, could derive no direct benefit from being members of a trade union according to their professions, or vocations. Some of these people who could have played an important role in the political, social and economic life of the Island were denied that opportunity unless they passed through trade union ranks and were accepted by the trade union hierarchy. Some on the basis of principle, felt that trade unionists should see about their areas of involvement and allow the politicians to deal with politics. A political party distinct from the trade union could have catered to all segments of opinion.

Furthermore, trade unionists the world over are a dogmatic group of people who like to do their own thing. While they do welcome Governments' support, they do not welcome Government's interference in their affairs. For the trade union to be strong and have confidence in itself and in its membership, it must be free to function within the law and its own rules with minimum Government interference or none at all. The trade union must also be free to make its own mistakes, even though it might have to pay for such mistakes.

How different would the position be had there been a Labour Party separate from the Union. Walter would have had to find an alternate approach, as his predominant theme was that a trade union and Government could not work. Those who heard him accepted this to be a fact; hence the opposition that was advocating a division of trade unionism and politics found a champion to their cause in Walter.

It did not matter that Walter might have been deceiving them, pledging that he had no interest in politics which was his motivation for starting the new trade. This was taking matters very far. No individual should alienate himself off from the political life of his country, as legislative decisions determine some aspects if not all of one's life. This more so applies to trade unions, which must have a

200

vested interest in politics through affiliation or membership in Parliament, if it is to safeguard its position. It could be that Walter did not consider what he said, but it quite soon came to be understood that what he said was one thing, what he did was another.

On the Monday night following their dismissal, Walter and Halstead held a mammoth meeting at the Antigua Recreation Grounds to explain their dismissal and to enlist the workers' sympathy. It was at this meeting that Walter emphasized that Government and union could not work. He said that every time he mentioned or went after improvement in conditions for the workers, the Government which comprised of union officers would stand in the way. He said that while he championed workers cause, Executive Members who were in the Government receiving high salaries and other privileges, had forsaken the workers, were in league with the employers and were more interested in foreigners than local people. The statements were dynamite, and were easily accepted by a gullible crowd. Walter also mentioned certain Executive Officers who opposed him and said he tried to get them off the Executive but failed. Walter and Halstead had made their case.

The Executive of the Antigua Trades & Labour Union called a public meeting on the following Thursday night to explain its side of the story. This meeting was even larger in attendance than the one held by Walter and Halstead. However, it appeared that both Walter, Halstead and their supporters were not taking anything for granted, for from early in the afternoon, the seats in the Pavilion were filled with people, who turned out to be hecklers specially planted there.

When the Executive Members arrived, it was clear that they were facing hostile faces both within and immediately in front of the pavilion. The opening prayers were said with difficulty, then it was pandemonium. The noise out front and inside the pavilion drowned out the speakers' voices that were called to speak; hence the thousands who came to listen could hear nothing.

Bird and his Executive gave up in disgust, which was the beginning of the end of Bird, the stalwart everyone knew. It was several months after that night that Bird could be persuaded to address a gathering. In the meantime, Walter and Halstead had the field to themselves and spared no effort in poisoning the people's minds against Bird, the Government and the Antigua Trades & Labour Union.

One week after their dismissal, Walter and Halstead announced the formation of a new union called the Antigua Workers' Union. This comprised the Waterfront Section of the Antigua Trades and Labour Union, which was completely taken over by the new Union.

At the same time, Walter announced that he would be General Secretary of the new Union and Malcolm Daniel, an Executive Member of the Antigua Trades & Labour Union and its Chief Field Officer, would be President. When the announcement was made, Daniel was in the United States on a trade union course, sponsored by the Antigua Trades and Labour Union. This information alone substantiated the extent of the conspiracy against the Union. While Daniel could have been annoyed that he was not appointed to the Senate as he would have expected, no one thought he would have been party to Walter's and Halstead's plans. Daniel returned from his course and did not refute his association with the new Union - he accepted the post of President of the Antigua Workers' Union. Walter then boasted that the Antigua Trades & Labour Union was dead and that very shortly the Antigua Workers' Union would take over its remaining membership and assets.

While these boasts were uttered, Walter was negotiating with Bird and E.H. Lake who were in the United States on Government business, for his return to the Antigua Trades and Labour Union on certain conditions. His negotiator, Brethnol Blackman the then General Secretary of the Caribbean Congress of Labour presented Walter's demands; among which was the handing over of the Antigua Trades and Labour Union to Walter, though Bird could remain President, the removal of certain Executive Officers, namely McChesney George, Novelle Richards and Bradley Carrott, Lionel Hurst should be disassociated from the Union, and the Antigua Trades & Labour Union should sever its political relationship with the Antigua Labour Party.

Bird responded that the Antigua Trades & Labour Union and the Antigua Labour Party were one body as a result of its founders' decisions and referendums made in numerous Union Conferences. Bird also informed Blackman that he would not agree to the demands. He did not appoint the named officers to the Executive of the Union, the Conference did. Unless they were found to be disloyal to the organization, only a Conference could remove them.

It should not be difficult to visualise the fate of Antigua and a large number of Antiguans, if Walter had successfully taken over the Antigua Trades and Labour Union and the Labour Party. The facts that came to light of their attempts to debase constitutional and political liberties in the State could make one shudder to think what would have happened had Walter assumed total power without meaningful opposition.

CHAPTER 10
DECLINE OF THE ANTIGUA
TRADES & LABOUR UNION

The Executive of the Antigua Trades and Labour Union appointed an acting General-Secretary, (Donald Sheppard) to temporarily fill the vacancy caused by Walter's dismissal. All the Union's Field Officers who had served with dismissed General Secretary, George Walter, and all those Executive Members who had supported him, Joseph Cornwall, Keithlyn Smith and Ernest Oliver, joined the Antigua Workers' Union as members of the Executive, and Keithlyn Smith became the Senior Field Officer under General-Secretary, George Walter. Smith subsequently became General-Secretary after Walter was appointed Premier of Antigua.

Every effort was made by the newly-formed Antigua Workers' Union (AWU) to establish itself, and it began a series of raids on the membership of its rival, the Antigua Trades & Labour Union. Wherever there were Industrial agreements in existence between the employers and the AT&LU, officers of the AWU sought to break those agreements and re-negotiated them in its favour. However, in many instances, the employers resisted, for they maintained that the agreements were contracts for a stipulated duration and should be honoured by the applicable Union. The AWU refused to accept this reasoning, and wherever it could, it called a series of strikes or caused other disturbances. Employers received all manner of threats and so did Executive Members of the AT&LU. The dark days had started all over again, not between Union and employers, but between union and union.

All efforts by the Government and the employers to persuade the officers of the AWU to honour existing agreements, which could be re-negotiated upon expiry and representational counts, were spurned. Day after day, officers of the AWU could be seen at the various workplaces in a drive to draw workers away from the AT&LU. The workers were confused. Some were actually threatened if they did not join the new Union.

During this period of industrial unrest, the new Union sought recognition from the Government. Here however, the Government blundered in not granting recognition to the AWU. It was true that the Union was engaging in trade union piracy, a practice deplored by the International Labour Congress and by all other unions in democratic countries, but, the Antigua Workers' Union was indeed a *fait accompli* and ought to have been accepted as such. Its policies and practices, although undemocratic, were other matters that had nothing to do with recognition. The Government eventually granted recognition after some time had elapsed and as a means of restoring industrial peace in the Island.

It is evident that the refusal of Government to grant recognition at first was in an effort to protect the Antigua Trades & Labour Union which needed all the assistance it could get at the time. The activities of piracy by the Antigua Workers' Union were like a blitzkrieg and equally ruthless. The officers of the AT&LU were not accustomed to this type of campaign, and it took the best out of them to withstand the onslaught. Although the Union was able to give a good account of itself, it was clear that the AWU would gain the edge in certain areas of employment, the most devastating blow being control of the Waterfront Workers.

The Antigua Workers' Union was involved in a few skirmishes with the Sugar Workers, but withdrew after it realised that the Sugar Workers had lost faith in their dismissed General Secretary. The AWU also failed with the majority of Government Non-Established Workers who remained loyal to the Antigua Trades and Labour Union.

These Government workers, like the Sugar workers, also paid for their loyalty to the AT&LU, because, immediately after George Walter became Premier, without notice, the workers were dismissed from their jobs without compensation or opportunity to find other work. Many of these workers had spent a lifetime working for the Government. During these developments, Premier Vere C. Bird became fearful for his own safety. There were numerous threats to his person as well as to other officers of the Antigua Trades & Labour Union. Fire bombs were thrown at the house of Hon. Lionel Hurst, the Minister of Labour, causing slight damage; fortunately, no injury was suffered by Hurst or his family. The peace of the State was shattered and it looked like worse things were in store, for in their attempt to win support, the Antigua Workers' Union and its leaders appealed mainly to the worst elements in the society.

The seeds of hatred and bitterness were sown to the extent that people became fearful in their own society and the damage to the economy as a result became very evident. Because of these threats and possible fear for his safety, Mr. Bird withdrew into himself. He was hurt and saw before him workers whom he spent all of his life to assist, and a country which economic development and social upliftment came about through his and his colleagues efforts, turned ungrateful and were won over by deceit.

Had Premier V.C. Bird put his fear or personal feelings aside and come forward, it is almost certain that George Walter would not have been able to consolidate his position as he did. But the moment V.C. Bird became shaken, the whole Antigua Trades & Labour Union was shaken too, with him. That was a most unfortunate development for the AT&LU; yet it was as a result of placing too much dependence on one man, without remembering the frailties of the human being. Vere Cornwall Bird had become the Union. To have contemplated another name as a possible successor would have been considered sacrilege by some of his closest supporters, and so the moment that V.C. Bird could not move or refused to, no one did. The signal had to come from Vere Cornwall Bird himself, or nothing was done; the signal had to be given.

This must not be considered as unduly critical of a man who has done a good job as leader, but as explaining a situation that baffled a number of minds and the lesson to be learnt from it. Some people are still astounded at the fact that George Walter and Donald Halstead were able to put over their programme non-stop for months while the Antigua Trades & Labour Union remained in limbo. It is certain that, if there were collective leadership in the true sense of the word, instead of lone leadership by an individual, this would not have happened, because if V.C. Bird felt unable or unwilling to go out into the field, others should have been able to do so. Instead, nobody went until the damage was almost beyond repair, and the effort then was not only belated, but belittling to what was once recognised as the most powerful Union in the Caribbean. This procrastination caused George Walter to win by default. Battles are not won by retreating, unless it is to consolidate a position for an attack or a repulse. While the Antigua Trades & Labour Union did eventually make a stance, by then it had lost too much ground for any attack to become effective.

It is evident that the behaviour of the hecklers who booed and made rude noises on that fateful night at the Pavilion was nerve-wrecking, but it was organised, and at least 90% of the large crowd that was present, came to listen. The Officials of the Antigua Trades & Labour Union should never have withdrawn from holding meetings just because of that one unfortunate episode, but should have taken up the challenge and who knows, might have come out the victors as a result.

For any political or labour organisation to have withstood the stresses and strains of those times, it needed a plenitude of leaders who have confidence in themselves and who are prepared to assume leadership, especially at such critical times. It happened that at a time when bold and courageous leadership from the Executive of the Antigua Trades & Labour Union was most needed, it was not forthcoming. Those who should have taken the initiative still looked to the hard-pressed Bird, even though he was unavailable. Those who did try to seize that initiative, found that their efforts were fruitless, because without the indefatigable Vere Cornwall Bird, very few of the remaining leaders wanted to take to the field - most likely fearing that the task was beyond them. This was not the case.

CHAPTER 11
THE ECONOMY

Antigua's economy was always precarious. Its fluctuations could be described as going from bad to worse and the reverse, depending on sugar's fortune. If sugar failed the economy failed, and sugar's fortune was solely dependent upon good rainfall, a very elusive occurrence at times, as the record of the drought years demonstrates.

To offset Antigua's sole dependence on sugar, the Government launched a drive to develop a number of new industries, foremost of which was tourism, in account of its high labour profile and its capacity to inject capital and continuous cash flow into the economy. Further, Antigua's beaches and natural beauty was an asset for developing this industry. The effort paid off, and by 1967, Antigua had developed into one of the leading tourist destinations in the Caribbean, with a capacity for greater expansion.

In 1967, 59,000 tourists visited Antigua with an average stay of five to six days. The gross expenditure of these tourists was estimated at approximately EC$18m. The estimated impact of tourists' spending in 1967 was determined to be in the vicinity of EC$41m, generating tax revenue of approximately EC$6.2m, with an estimated wages bill of EC$9million.

The Report of a Survey of the future for tourism in Antigua carried out by H. Zinder and Associates Inc., contracted by the Agency for International Development and sponsored by the Regional Development Agency of the Eastern Caribbean in October 1968, based upon existing data, made a forecast that by 1972, Antigua would have had 147,000 tourists with an average stay-over period of 4 to 5 days, spending approximately EC$46.3m

This expenditure, noted the Report, would have a spending impact of

EC$111.1m, generating tax revenues of EC$16.7m and wages of EC$26.7m. It went on to say that by 1977, the number of tourists with an average stay-over period of 3 to 4 days would be 296,000, with a gross expenditure of EC$82.9m, but would need an additional 1,400 hotel rooms above the existing 750 suitable rooms, that were available at the time of the survey, to accommodate the growth.

The Government had already paved the way for tourism expansion by approving new hotel schemes in 1967, of more than 500 rooms with various groups of investors. From all indications, there would have been at least 1,000 additional new hotel rooms by 1972, which would have exceeded the forecast.

During 1968, Novelle Richards who had taken up an appointment as Commissioner for the Associated States in Canada, reported that he had discussions with a large group of international hotel developers, who decided to develop an area in Antigua with a capital of EC$500m to be spread over several years. They would construct 1,000 hotel rooms, in addition to the commitments of other developers previously reached with the Government of Antigua.

Antigua was then perched for take-off in international tourism. The Government also moved towards solving the water problem brought about by the prolonged annual droughts, by developing a number of large dams, chief among which was Potworks Dam. An earth dam with a capacity of 1.5 billion gallons of water covering a wide expanse of land between Bethesda, Delapps and Long Lane Estates and which looked like a veritable lake, the initial cost of Potworks Dam was EC$900,000.

A contract was also negotiated with an American firm, Aquachem, to construct a desalination plant with a capacity of 1,200,000 gallons of fresh water per day and which would also generate 8.3 Mega Watts of electricity daily, at an estimated cost of EC$11m. A new dial telephone system was being installed and would be put into operation soon afterwards. The Government of Canada, through its International Development Agency, had made commitments for the further extension and improvement of the runway and other services at Coolidge Airport, and the Deep Water Harbour at St. John's was near completion. A sound infrastructure was gradually being built up to meet the expansion of tourism and other industrial development.

The Government also had plans underway for the construction of a new air terminal building at Coolidge Airport, that would be capable of coping with the anticipated increase in air traffic; a loan for that purpose was virtually guaranteed.

The Petroleum Oil Refinery at Friar's Hill was then operating nearly at full capacity while many ships from distant ports were being re-fuelled at the ship bunkering plant outside the harbour off Corbinson's Point. Furniture plants, manufacturing modern furniture and a few garment factories manufacturing clothing for local consumption and for export were in operation. A number of other small and medium-sized industries were given the green light by the Government to proceed.

Because of the generation of large sums of money in the economy, an unprecedented building boom followed with the citizens constructing larger and better homes. The construction activity placed certain skilled workers in the building trades at a premium, resulting in high construction earnings.

In an effort to meet this demand for house ownership in Antigua, the Government diverted a portion of the agricultural lands, which they purchased from the Antigua Syndicate Estates Ltd. for housing. These lands were close to the city, suburbs and villages and were ideal for housing development. In several other areas, lands were also purchased from private owners for housing development purposes as well. These included a large portion of land that was developed at Cassada Gardens - east of Clare Hall, and at De Witts Estate in the Nut Grove and Grays Hill area; lands were also purchased by Government from John I. Martin - a large land owner - for development as housing sites as well. The Government through the Central Housing and Planning Authority (CHAPA) had become the biggest land developer in the island, and land buyers were given very favourable terms for their purchases.

To assist in this housing expansion and house improvement drive, the Government introduced legislation to remove or reduce duty on certain types of building materials used in construction of home dwellings; this tax cut was primarily designed to keep down the cost of construction for the homeowner. By so doing, the Government indirectly subsidised housing in the State.

As a result of these bold actions by the Government, the economy became very buoyant and the Government had confidence that the State would soon begin to build up budgetary surpluses that would strengthen the financial base of the economy and expansion of social services.

In 1964, the island had a total budget allocation of EC$13m. This allocation jumped from the 1964 figure to EC$22m by 1968. This was a spectacular accomplishment, notwithstanding the fact that the Budget did include certain capital projects that were financed by loans or development grants from the United Kingdom and Canada. By 1970, despite the economic setbacks due to labour disputes and political unsettlement, the island's annual Budget Estimates were in the vicinity of EC$30m. This was as a result of increased revenues from landing fees at Coolidge Airport, which began receiving more flights daily than any other airport in the sub-region except Puerto Rico. Revenue was also generated from income tax, the expansion in tourism, the generally high remunerative employment in the island, and from customs duty due to the high increase of cars, machinery and other luxury items imported into the island.

This National Budget would have been even more substantial had the economic growth of the previous years continued at the same rate of expansion. It was however evident that a decline was beginning, because the large number of potential investors who were given the green light by the ALP Government, had become wary of investing in the State as the political and labour climate became more and more unsettled between 1968 and 1970.

The never ending trade disputes and strikes by the Antigua Workers' Union in order to increase their popularity and strength, made investors wary. Without reasonable notice or excuse, strikes were called at hotels that filled with guests, some of whom had to help prepare their own meals and tidy their rooms, bringing a mass exodus of tourists from the island. Tourists were molested and taunted on the streets by supporters of the Antigua Workers' Union, nearly causing Antigua to become a black-listed destination for North American tourists.

In 1968, despite the solemn declaration of Walter and his leading supporters that the Antigua Workers' Union would not participate in politics, he threw his Union into affiliation with a new opposition political party called the Progressive Labour Movement. While he himself stayed away from active politics, it was easily discernible that he was only biding his time, for the numeric force of the followers he took with him into the new party, showed Walter had the dominant voice.

The new reinvigorated party immediately began to show their strength and made demands upon the Government to resign. General Elections were not constitutionally due until November 1970, but the Premier could call by-elections to increase the number of seats in the House of Representatives at any time during the life of that parliament.

In their determination to bring down the Government as they openly declared and their quest for recognition, a wholesale campaign of agitation and strikes ensued. The Waterfront Workers became the catalyst of these activities. These workers would be called out on strike to support any and every trade dispute that was not settled to the satisfaction of the new Union. Tensions increased until the Antigua Workers' Union felt it was in a position to call a general strike, which resulted in wholesale demonstrations against the Government and a declaration of a State of Emergency after several persons were injured.

The entire operation was well planned and law and order broke down as the Police Force was ill-equipped and below training to cope with the uprising.

Schools and government buildings were set on fire. One section of the Ottos Primary School was completely destroyed by fire. The St. John's Boys School (now the T.N. Kirnon School) was only saved by the quick action of the Defence Force and the Fire Department. The Government had to appeal to Britain for law enforcement support, and a frigate was despatched post haste to Antigua.

By that time however, the Government had decided to lift the State of Emergency and come to terms with the Antigua Workers' Union and the opposition party. Among the agreements reached between the Government and the Antigua Workers' Union were:

- There would be a discontinuation of union raiding by either trade union;
- Workers in any employment would be free to be members of either Union and would pay their dues to the union of their choice;
- No money would be deducted from workers' wages to pay dues to any union without the employee's written consent to the employer;
- The Antigua Workers' Union would be given full recognition by Government.

The Government also gave an undertaking to the political representatives of the Progressive Labour Movement that by-elections would be called in four Constituencies to increase the number of seats in the House of Representatives from ten to fourteen. With these agreements, both parties gave an undertaking to see that peace was restored to the island and they would abstain from committing any acts that could endanger the peace.

On the same evening after the agreement was reached, Walter made an appeal to his supporters by state-wide television, to refrain from doing "what they had in mind to do," for he had achieved what he wanted and they must return to their work and their homes.

Apart from some administrative blunders at the command level, the Government had to accept some responsibility for the failure of the police force to cope with the State of Emergency. For several years the police force was functioning below acceptable strength and efficiency. Efforts to recruit Antiguans to join the Force proved fruitless, as Antiguan young men could find more lucrative employment in other fields that paid higher wages than the Police Force.

The introduction of the Statehood Constitution placed greater responsibility on the state for maintaining law and order, than they had under Colonial Rule. The Government of Antigua was now solely responsible for internal security and it was obligated to take the necessary measures to seeing that both the Police and Defence Force were brought up to standard, before Statehood was introduced. The Government however thought that Antigua with its law-abiding citizens, would always be at peace, so paid scant attention to the advice to recruit outsiders to bring the Police Force to full strength. It was only when the full reality of the AWU's insurgence dawned upon them that the Government made a mad scramble to bring in recruits from St. Vincent, St. Lucia and other neighbouring islands; by then it was too late. It takes a well-disciplined and efficient force to cope with an uprising. The novice Antiguan Police Force was doomed from the start.

It is hoped that future governments of Antigua will take a proactive approach, to ensure that a well-disciplined and efficient Police and Defence Force are maintained for the security of the State and its people. The troubles of 1968 saw a doubling in the annual budgetary allocations for the Police Force during the succeeding years, as the Government was compelled to bring the Force up to strength and to provide the necessary equipment to raise its efficiency in the preservation of law and order. The Volunteer Defence Force was expanded for the same purpose.

CHAPTER 12
FIRST ELECTED OPPOSITION
IN PARLIAMENT

During the early summer of 1968, the Government decided to call by-elections in four Constituencies -:St John's City North, St. John's City South, St. Mary's and St George's. The Progressive Labour Movement (PLM) the new political Party, which was now fully affiliated with the Antigua Workers' Union, had displaced the Antigua & Barbuda Democratic Movement (ABDM) as the main Opposition Party, and several of the strong supporters of the former Opposition Party became leading members of the new PLM amalgamation. Among these was Robert Hall, who was appointed the new Political Leader of the Progressive Labour Movement.

This sudden switch of allegiance by Hall was surprising a lot of people, for he had been the subject of bitter abuse by Walter, particularly during the period when Walter was General Secretary of the Antigua Trades & Labour Union; now they were comrades. Those who remained faithful to the Antigua & Barbuda Democratic Movement were hostile to Hall for deserting their Party and a court case was brought against Hall by his former colleagues for the return of certain equipment they claimed he had in his possession and which belonged to the Party. Claude Earl Francis, a barrister-at-law who contested the Barbuda seat for the ABDM and lost, also joined PLM. Because of the disarray in the Antigua Trades & Labour Union and the Antigua Labour Party (ALP), PLM made a great splash. It attracted the majority of lawyers and other professionals to its ranks and created mass appeal among the middle class and among young voters, as well as the more rowdy elements of the society. PLM had a motley of supporters.

Although George Walter stated over and over again that no official of the Antigua Workers' Union would seek political office, it was not surprising that Donald

Halstead ignored that pronouncement, and got himself selected to contest the Elections in the St. John's City North constituency. Reuben Harris, an economist and businessman, won the nomination for the St. John's City South seat, Robert Hall was nominated to contest the St. Mary's seat and Sidney Prince, a former surveyor at the Public Works Department, was nominated for St. George's.

It was clear from the outset that PLM would win the By-Elections, for the candidates selected by the Antigua Labour Party did not have the individual appeal of the voters as did the candidates for PLM. Perhaps Bird saw the futility of campaigning or he might have decided that it was better to give the Opposition an opportunity to have elected representation in the Parliament, for he did not assist the ALP candidates in the By-Election campaigns. PLM won all four seats in sweeping victories, and for the first time in 21 years, there was an Elected Opposition in the Council and Parliament of Antigua.

Having won all four seats in the By-Elections, PLM made a demand for representation in the Senate. Up to the time the new Statehood Constitution was drafted, there had never been any elected opposition in the Legislature, thus the Constitution did not have a clause for opposition representation in the Senate. The Constitution did however state that consideration would be given to such representation in the event of a change in the composition of the House of Representatives. Whether such considerations would be effective as a result of By-Elections or General Elections was not clearly set forth in the final Statehood Constitution. It could however be interpreted that changes in Senate appointments should only be made *pari passu* with General Elections, or as a consequence of the death or resignation of a Sitting Senator; or upon request of the Prime Minister or Premier to the Governor to withdraw the appointment of a serving Senator for specific reasons.

To alter the composition of the Senate as a result of By-Elections, unless such By-Elections brought about a change of Government, could have created an unsuitable and unusual precedent. However, the demands of PLM members and supporters was so persistent and forceful, that to avoid further friction and instability, three Senators who were not active members of the Antigua Labour Party - Dr. Luther Wynter, the President of the Senate, Stephen R. Mendes, and John Ferdinand

Shoul - volunteered to relinquish their seats in the Upper House, to facilitate the appointment of three PLM Senators.

Those appointed were Claude Earl Francis, Gerald Watt, both lawyers, and Joseph Stevens, a one-time Field Officer of the Antigua Trades & Labour Union, who parted company with the AT&LU several years before. William Buntin succeeded Dr. Wynter as President of the Senate. The country was relieved that these matters were settled and looked forward to a respite from the tensions of the previous year. The victories at the Polls and the forced recognition of the AWU by Government, only whet PLM and the Antigua Workers' Union appetite for more power. While strikes by the AWU took on greater proportions, political agitation was intensified by PLM, with calls on the Government to resign and to set a time for General Elections.

The Deep Water Harbour was dedicated on the 31st October, 1968, in an atmosphere of tension. The Waterfront workers on instructions from the Antigua Workers' Union, refused to operate the Harbour for an entire year, until their demands for compensation were met and settled. In the meantime, the Government had to repay the loan for constructing the Harbour.

During 1969, the Antigua Workers' Union master-minded a strike by the entire Civil Service to aid PLM towards their political goals. Despite the fact that the Civil Service Association should normally be free from political affiliation, some Civil Servants disregarded the law, which prevented strikes in Essential Services. The Government seemed to be losing control of the country, as a state of anarchy began to unfold. The Government persisted, but the price was high. The economy suffered considerably and the seeds of hatred and confusion germinated rapidly to split the society into two almost violently opposing camps. Homes were divided, friendships broken and Antigua became an unhappy place to live. The Antigua Workers' Union and PLM were masters of the game as the State bounced from crisis to crisis.

Despite the Government's instability, the Antigua Trades & Labour Union and the Antigua Labour Party were showing remarkable powers of recovery as many people became disenchanted with the opposition's activities. But ALP could not muster the type of sound leadership it garnered during the struggle with the plantocracy and colonial rule, making recovery effort only partly effective.

The appointment of a new General Secretary of the Antigua Trades & Labour Union during 1968 had much to do with its partial recovery. Adolphus Freeland of Potters, a well known Antiguan cricketer who excelled as a fast bowler in Leeward Islands cricket and regional West Indies Cricket, brought a fresh vigour and enthusiasm to his job as General Secretary. He was able to rally enthusiastic young people who worked valiantly to assist the AT&LU on its road to recovery.

Then there was the Junior Executive, a large group of young men who elected Eustace Cochrane, a local airline official, as their President. The group of young ALP supporters made a determined effort to recover ground lost in the political field by both ALP and the AT&LU. Cochrane was later made a Senator to replace Novelle Richards who became Commissioner in Canada. These groups of individuals bore the brunt of union and political activities during the period, and brought to prominence such fresh stalwarts as Bill Abbott and Robin Bascus, who spearheaded the attacks against Walter and his supporters.

One of Freeland's greatest efforts was his drive to erect a new union headquarter on the existing site at 46 North Street. This had to be done in phases by demolition of one section of the old building to permit construction of the new, while the remaining section is occupied. Union members, many well-wishers and supporters generously donated to the Building Appeal Fund, and the work of reconstruction under the able leadership of William Isaac, a retired Public Works builder and union official progressed rapidly, until a prominent new building stood as a monument to that effort.

The Antigua Workers' Union had already erected a large and prominent building on a site on lower Newgate Street, which they named Freedom Hall. The construction of Freedom Hall is without doubt a credit to Walter and his associates, it was also the fillip to AT&LU members and supporters, that they should not be outdone, hence their willing contribution at a time when both money and jobs were becoming scarce commodities in Antigua.

CHAPTER 13
THE BARBUDA EPISODE

For over 25 years, a special relationship existed between V.C. Bird and McChesney George. This was not only from a family connection as V.C. Bird's wife was a first cousin of George, but because of a very deep admiration that George developed for Mr. Bird during the early days of the Trade Union struggles. Consequently, these two comrades-in-arms became nearly like twins, sharing each other's confidence and serving as each other's mentor.

Although McChesney George was a Civil Servant, he was attracted to trade unionism, and played a significant role in the early development of the Trade Union Movement as an Executive Member and contributing writer to the Worker's Voice Newspaper.

McChesney George was a capable Civil Servant and highly intellectual with a good amount of conceit thrown in, but he was Bird's man through and through. With him, Bird could do no wrong. This almost blind loyalty to Mr. Bird, did not go unnoticed and perhaps bolstered both McChesney George's civil service and his political career. George eventually qualified as a lawyer and left the Civil Service with the winding up of his post as Peasant Development Officer. He thereafter entered into private law practice and was elected to the newly created Barbuda seat in 1960. He was then appointed Minister Without Portfolio with special responsibility for the development of the Peasantry.

The period following McChesney George's election to the Legislature saw him as special adviser to V.C. Bird on almost every important matter affecting the island whether economic matters or matters affecting the Federation of the Little Eight. Wherever Bird went George was at his side. George was the foremost negotiator for the Government's purchase of the Antigua Syndicate Estates and the Antigua Sugar Factory, and he was a valuable member of the delegation, which negotiated the Statehood Constitution with the British Government. He was also the main adviser to Mr. Bird on the abandonment of the proposed Little Eight Federation. He must therefore share the credits that accrued as well as the mistakes that were made at the time.

It was therefore a stunning surprise, when without warning, the relationship which existed between the two comrades, came to an abrupt end. From being the most trusting of friends, both men became bitter political foes, culminating in George's abortive efforts to bring about the secession of Barbuda from Antigua, following the successful efforts by the Anguillans to wrest direct rule from the control of Robert Bradshaw in St. Kitts.

Why did George turn against Bird at a time when Bird needed all the support he could get? It was simply panic. During the troubles of 1967, with the formation of the Antigua Workers' Union and the campaign of Walter and company against Bird and other officers of the Antigua Trades and Labour Union, George was one of the few who realised that Bird's withdrawal from the scene and his failure to go out and face the public, to protect his name and the names of other Union officers who were targets of attack by Walter, was the forerunner of doom for the Antigua Trades & Labour Union and the Antigua Labour Party.

McChesney George became disillusioned with Bird as he saw the hero of his youth revert to the size of an ordinary man who ignored the challenge that was thrown to him by Walter. George felt that all was lost, for if the opposition succeeded and became the Government, he would lose status and life could become unbearable for him in Antigua. Thus the idea of Barbuda for the Barbudans crossed his mind and developed into an obsession. The one occasion that Mr. Bird opposed George, resulted in resentment and extreme bitterness.

McChesney George was wrong. While one could sympathise with him for his disillusionment with his hero, to attempt to destroy the integrity of the State was a dangerous experiment, coming at a time of crisis for the Government of which he was a member. His actions were akin to the actions of Brutus at the attack and death of Julius Caesar.

Whatever weaknesses Bird might have exhibited in handling the AWU and PLM, is not sufficient justification for George to betray the Antigua Trades & Labour

Union, the Government and the Antigua Labour Party; consequently sacrificing his ability and usefulness to the State for a mirage, making the Union and the Party poorer from this desertion.

George expected Bird who was always supportive of him, to go along with his bid to take over Barbuda. In as much as Walter and company were having their own way in Antigua without much or any opposition from Bird, George thought he could also have carte blanche, but was mistaken. Bird forestalled his plans by re-enforcing the Police Force in Barbuda, thereby preventing a similar situation to that which happened in Anguilla, when the insurgent citizens drove off the half dozen or so policemen on that island.

Bird could have done nothing less, and despite his surprising withdrawal from the fight, he must be complimented for the stand he took against George and those who supported his Barbuda misadventure.

In order to clear up any doubt to the status of Barbuda vis-a-vis Antigua, the Government of Antigua issued a press release referring to Imperial Act,1859, 22 and 23 Victoria, Cap XIII, Chapter 122 of the Revised Laws of Antigua, which provided for the annexation of the Dependency of Barbuda by Antigua, which shall be subject to all laws and statutes as shall he in force in Antigua.

Validity was given to the above act by Order in Council dated 23rd September, 1859, by Her Majesty, Queen Victoria, on the advice of her Privy Council.

At the same time of the release, the British Government made a statement in London that Barbuda was *de jure and de facto* a part of the State of Antigua. It is hoped that reinforcing the statute would put an end to all speculations on the status of Barbuda, but there are still a few feeble voices which continue to insist that the matter is not closed.

What George and his supporters hoped to achieve by a fragmenting the islands was and will always be conjecture. To have returned Barbuda to colonial rule would have been a retrograde step and a blatant admission of immaturity by both Antiguans and Barbudans. To consider having an independent Barbuda at that time capable of running its own affairs and providing even the minimum of services that are prerequisite for an independent nation was unrealistic.

CHAPTER 14
THE ASSOCIATED STATES

With the failure of the "Little Eight" Federation still to materialise, and with the achievement of the status of Independence in Association with Britain of the Windward and Leeward Islands, wouldn't it have been more convenient and economical for the states to merge operation of certain services that were common to all, than for each State to perform such services independently?

Paramount among these services were Legal Affairs with particular reference to the Courts, overseas representation in external matters that would have been delegated to the individual States by Britain, within the terms of the Agreement of Association, regional trade, currency and banking, aeronautics and associated matters such as meteorological service and the defence of the individual Associated States. It was therefore realistic that the Governments decided to establish a Secretariat and a Regional Council of Ministers to deal with these matters, and by agreement designated the Premier or Chief Minister (in the case of Montserrat and St. Vincent which had not yet achieved Associated Statehood) to be the permanent representatives of each Associated State. This decision gave greater muscle to the Council.

Surprisingly, without the customary squabbles associated with such matters, the Governments agreed to set up the Council Headquarters in St. Lucia, and accordingly, premises were identified for that purpose. It was agreed that there should be an annual rotating Chairmanship of the Council of Ministers, beginning with Premier Bird of Antigua, followed in alphabetical order of the States or Territories. George Odium of St. Lucia who previously worked with the Commonwealth Office in London, was appointed by the Council of Ministers as the first Executive Secretary.

Under its delegated authority from Britain, the Council of Ministers decided to establish Commissioner Services in London and Montreal, to deal with consular, trade and such diplomatic matters affecting the States and host countries. Nicholas Taylor of St. Lucia, a former officer of the defunct Commissioner Service of The West Indies in London, was appointed as the Commissioner for the Associated States to the United Kingdom, and Novelle H. Richards of Antigua, who was then President of the Antigua Senate, was requested by the Council of Ministers to take over the post of Commissioner for the Associated States to Canada.

Sir Allan Lewis of St. Lucia was appointed as Chief Justice of the Associated States and the two other justices of Appeal were St. Vincent born, Mr. Justice Percy Lewis, previously a Puisne Judge of Antigua and Mr. Justice Keith Gordon of St. Lucia, who served in the Judiciary of Jamaica and West Africa. The Hon. Allan Louisy was appointed Puisne Judge for Antigua.

The Council of Ministers agreed to establish a Regional Development Agency to aid in the industrial development of the States. This Agency originally included Barbados, as it was considered a useful instrument of development for the then proposed Federation of the Little Eight. Despite the independence of Barbados, that country decided to take part in the initial activities of the Agency, but eventually withdrew. George Williams of Dominica, who like Odium previously worked with the Commonwealth Secretariat in London, was appointed Executive Secretary of that Agency, which Secretariat was located in Antigua.

Such a Federation was hoped for in London, Ottawa and Washington, and even among the Associated States themselves, that the Regional Council of Ministers and the Secretariat in Castries, St. Lucia, would be the forerunner to a Federation of the Associated States and the full assumption of independence.

The Commissioner services in London and Canada had already established themselves and were performing their appointed roles through contacts with government agencies of the host countries and with industrialists and financiers who would be potential investors in the Associated States and Territories. Nationals of the Associated States in Canada and the United Kingdom were also assured of consular representation when needed.

The Regional Development Agency however, which was intended to perform a key role in the industrial development of the Associated States was unable to move substantially in any one direction. This must not be considered as reflecting badly on the Secretariat of the Agency, for the Officers must have suffered many pangs of frustration from time to time, from the inability of the Council of Ministers to give a clear sense of direction.

The Ministers who formed the Council of Ministers were more concerned with their individual territorial development; regional planning was secondary or had little or no place within their portfolios. It was therefore a waste of time knowing the narrow outlook of many of the politicians, to think that a Minister from one State would actively make a contribution to the development of another. The Regional Development Agency could have only succeeded if it were free from individual territorial control and responsible to one Government with full prerogative authority. The Regional Development Agency has since given way to a Common Market of the Associated States.

The Council of Ministers while serving as a barometer to chart the feelings of individual States, served more as a forum for lengthy, useless debates as can be seen in the voluminous records of the discussions, than as an effective instrument of policy-making in unifying the States. In this respect alone, the Ministers have failed dismally; ten years after setting up the Council of Ministers, the states were further away from Federation than when they began.

The fact that Grenada moved to an uncertain independence with the inevitable traumas that gripped that country in the wake of nationhood is an off-shot of the Council of Ministers failure to accept reality and commonsense.

Notwithstanding the Grenada experience, it is inevitable that some if not all of the remaining Associated States will move on to independence; for the shadow of grandeur is greater than the substance of reality. Independence has become a way of life and justifiably so; therefore, it would have been foolish to refuse it while it was there for the taking.

Serious efforts were made to see that some of these mini-dominions did not become sources of embarrassment to themselves and the rest of the West Indies. Many of these country's citizens had to strongly raise their voices to demonstrate against oppressive legislature introduced in their Parliaments by Governments, which attempted to deprive the society of fundamental liberties. Even thou the courts have come to citizens' rescue, it is not always certain that the Courts in Independent States may be at liberty to do so. There were courts in South Africa, Southern Rhodesia (now Zimbabwe) and Ghana during the time of Nkrumah, but the Government prevailed against reason and right, and men who were contemptuous of civil liberties demonstrated a paucity of social justice and assumed the rule of dictator, for the masses were conditioned to blind allegiance as was the case in some West Indian islands.

While social and political unrest is a present-day world phenomena that seems to have no frontiers, their aftermath can more easily be withstood by countries with historical resilience, with developed economies and international recognition, than by small, unrecognisable little islands, desperately trying to find their own feet, even locally.

Social and political hysteria in these small islands can only drive away potential investment; not for a day but for a very long time. If the rising expectations of the growing communities cannot be met with future hope, there is certainty that the price will have to be paid in some visible way.

It was in view of some of these expressed fears and with a sense of purpose for the future, that the author, while as Commissioner for the Associated States in Canada, submitted to the Council of Ministers a document he drafted that made a case for an early Federation of the Associated States.

Many of the arguments raised at the time were particularly pertinent to the situation that exists in the States today and will continue to exist unless decisive measure is taken in the right direction. Unfortunately, the document was either too early or too late or received scant attention from a few Ministers. The case for federation is included as Book 3.

One point that must be recognised when reading Book 3 are the financial figures which does not reflect present-day costs. There have been salary revisions in the various Associated States and Territories since then and other costs have gone up substantially, and the revenues of most if not all of the Associated States have also expanded, although not at a level with cost. The latter being mainly due to the inability of the Associated States to seize the opportunities for development that were on their door steps, as the political and social unrests in some of the

Associated States scared investors away from the area, and in some cases all but destroyed a thriving tourist industry.

Another factor was during the early 70s, some of the leaders of the small islands of the region appeared to be contemptuous of almost anything but individual power. With that power coming into their hands, they seemed to have put on permanent blinkers. It is almost safe to say that unless a miracle takes place, there would be no Federation of the Associated States within the foreseeable future, for none of the then incumbent leaders were seriously interested in, or committed to Federation. It was evident that movement towards federation in the West Indies would have to be initiated by the larger independent states. But miracles do happen, and perhaps some of the leaders of the small islands might grow up, or might be replaced by others of greater vision, greater political sense, and greater social acumen; who knows?

In the meantime, Antigua should seek to determine her own destiny, and not hold on to lost causes as federation seemed to become. Late in 1978, the Government of Antigua gave notice that it would approach Her Majesty's Government in the United Kingdom on independence for Antigua by November 1st, 1979. Shortly thereafter, the Government set up several local committees to work towards the implementations of this great event. The present movement towards economic integration of the entire Commonwealth Caribbean offers some opportunity for economic expansion to those States that can seize the opportunity and take advantage of this wider market as small as it might be within the international context. Antigua has a reasonably developed infrastructure to enter into the competitive West Indian market and overseas trade if given skilful entrepreneurial guidance and good salesmanship. The important thing is to make haste in this direction, before Antigua is left too far behind, thereby making it difficult to get into the race and stay there.

CHAPTER 15
GENERAL ELECTIONS
AND DEFEAT OF THE LABOUR PARTY

After the Civil Service strike and other political and industrial unrests in Antigua during 1969, the Antigua Workers' Union, which masterminded the strikes and unrests came into greater prominence. Walter then realised that the time was ripe to make his move.

During the first few years of the life of PLM, although Walter continuously stated that his Union would not be involved in politics, it became clear that it was the Antigua Workers' Union that was dictating the policies of PLM. This became so pronounced that Reuben Harris, one of the PLM's Elected Members in the Parliament, became disillusioned and informed Party Executives that they had abandoned their charter and became a Trade Union party as the Antigua Labour Party.

At the PLM Convention in late 1969, the delegates were taken by surprise when Walter brought with him an overwhelmingly strong union delegation to the Convention. Matters were duly clarified when the Convention realised a little too late that this overwhelmingly strong Union representation was planned to unseat Robert Hall, the Party Leader, and to replace him with Walter. Walter who in 1967 said he had no interest in politics, supplanted Robert Hall as the leader of the PLM opposition party from the special votes he received in the convention. Hall was retained as Deputy Political Leader of the Party.

Reuben Harris saw the treachery of the maneuver and resigned from the PLM. He served as an Independent Member of the Opposition, and from then on became a target of PLM abuse. Harris became a founding member of another opposition party, the Antigua People's Party, with J. Rowan Henry, a prominent barrister-at-law in Antigua, who became its Chairman and Political leader. Both

Harris and Henry, although having very little love at the time for Bird, realised that Walter and the policies he advocated would wreck Antigua; so the slogan of their new party was *"Save Antigua"*.

The Antigua People's Party (APP) had no mass base as did the Antigua Labour Party (ALP) and the PLM; although their membership included some capable men and women, it was clear that they had minimal appeal in the city of St. John's and hardly any in the rural areas. The Party never posed a real threat to the rise of PLM.

In the meantime, the Antigua Labour Party or what remained of it seemed to be in inertia. The Government was wobbling along, and it was clear that unless some spectacular development ensued, the Party was doomed to defeat. The PLM had too much of a head-start for things to be taken for granted.

Despite the sound and timely advice to the Premier and other Cabinet Members to prepare early for elections by creating new constituency boundaries that will create a new Voters' List, for an element of surprise in the Government's favour, nothing was done until very late. As a result, the life of the Parliament has to be extended to enable legal procedures for the elections.

In fact, the ALP Government unwittingly played right into the hands of the Opposition, and when the Elections took place, the Opposition having all the warning they needed, were better prepared than the Government.

The General Elections were called on 11th February, 1971 instead of November 1970, when the five year life of the Parliament expired. The election results were a foregone conclusion for observers from outside the island and almost everyone else except the ALP Ministers and Bird's close supporters. But no one not even the opposition, expected such a sweeping defeat of the Government.

The Government accepted the recommendation that the State including Barbuda should be divided into seventeen Constituencies, sixteen in Antigua, one in Barbuda - and a complete revision of the constituency boundaries. PLM and ALP contested all seventeen seats, while the APP concentrated in the city, suburbs and a few rural Constituencies. The APP lost in all constituencies where they contested with most of their candidates losing their deposits. The Antigua Labour Party won only four Seats with Premier Bird going down in defeat to Selvin Walter, in his long time and personally considered safe constituency, Grays Farm. This almost impregnable Labour stronghold was surprisingly captured by Selvin Walter, a half-brother of George Walter, who himself defeated George Sheppard in the All Saints-Sea View Farm Constituency.

All the Government Ministers with the exception of Ernest Williams, who was re-elected in Liberta and English Harbour (the Constituency of St. Paul) and Joseph Myers, who was elected in Parham, Pares Village and Freemanville, lost their seats. The other two successful Labour Candidates elected to the new Parliament were Denfield Hurst, the former Speaker of the House, who was returned in St. John's Rural North and Donald Sheppard in St. Phillips.

The successful PLM candidates were:

> George Walter, Premier designate, All Saints;
>
> Robert Hall, St. Mary's North;
>
> Selvin Walter, St. John's Rural West;
>
> Donald Halstead, St. John's City West;
>
> Gerald Watt, St. John's Rural East;
>
> Claude Earl Francis, who took the Barbuda Seat from McChesney George,
>
> Sidney Prince, St. George's;
>
> Sydney Christian, St. John's City South;
>
> Basil Peters, St. John's City East;
>
> Geoffrey Scotland, St. John's Rural South;
>
> Victor McKay, St. Mary's South;
>
> Wilbert Sterling, St. Luke's;
>
> Cyril James, St. Philips South.

PLM received 52% of the total votes against the Antigua Labour Party's 44% and the APP and independents 4%.

The day following the election results was a day of jubilation in the State for PLM and its supporters. Few people went to work because the victorious Opposition and its supporters took to the streets to celebrate their triumph over the demoralised Antigua Labour Party. At last, the great V.C. Bird was brought to defeat and his long record of personal unbroken victories came to an end. The

Labour Party was annihilated and its supporters stunned into disbelief with the reality of rejection by the majority of the electorate. It was in this atmosphere that George Walter and his PLM political grouping came to power savouring the high hopes and great expectations of supporters.

In view of the election results, the Governor, Sir Wilfred Jacobs, summoned Walter to form a new Government and to advise him of the nominations to the Senate. Following the previous arrangement after the by-Elections when PLM won four seats and claimed three Senate seats, it was expected that the Antigua Labour Party, as the Official Opposition, would be entitled to three of the ten Senate Seats. The new Opposition accordingly recommended Lester Bird, son of the defeated Premier V.C. Bird, John St. Luce, Secretary of the Antigua Labour Party and William (Bill) Abbott for the three Senate seats. Premier George Walter, refused to accept Bill Abbott as a Senator and advised the Governor against appointing him. However, the Labour Party insisted that Bill Abbott should be appointed, because there were no valid grounds against his serving as a Senator. This was ignored and Premier Walter advised Sir Wilfred to appoint one of his supporters in the place of Bill Abbott. As a result, the following persons were appointed to the Senate:

Clarence Harney, President,

J. Oliver Davis, Vice President,

Vincent (Tubby) Derrick, Minister without portfolio and Leader of Government business in the Senate,

Hugh Piggott,

Joseph Stevens,

Prince Hurst,

Malcolm Daniel, President of the Antigua Workers' Union,

Alphonso Teague representing Barbuda

Lester Bird and John St. Luce, Opposition Senators.

While in the previous Parliament there were only five elected Cabinet Ministers, including the Premier and a Minister without portfolio who was Leader of the Senate. Premier Walter immediately increased the number of Ministers and Parliamentary Secretaries to several Ministries.

He retained the Ministry of Finance and External Affairs with the

Premiership. Robert Hall was appointed Minister of Agriculture and Deputy Premier. Selvin Walter was given Trade, Tourism & Regional Affairs. Donald Halstead was assigned the portfolio for Home Affairs & Labour; Sidney Prince, Public Works; Gerald Watt, Public Utilities; Basil Peters, Education & Health. Claude Earl Francis became Parliamentary Secretary to the Premier responsible for Barbuda Affairs; Victor McKay, Parliamentary Secretary to the Ministry of Education and Health, Geoffrey Scotland by a very strange move was appointed Cabinet Secretary, the only known appointment of this kind in the Commonwealth.

The House of Representatives selected Cecil Hewlett, an un-elected member, as Speaker, and Sydney Christian as Deputy Speaker. Of the thirteen Members elected on the Government's side, only Wilbert Sterling and Cyril James were Back Benchers and held no official posts in the Government or in the House. With one stroke of the proverbial pen, the cost of Parliament and the Cabinet almost doubled with the appointment of all the numerous Ministers and Parliamentary Secretaries, who were paid almost the same salaries, another unusual arrangement.

On paper, the Government representatives in the House of Representatives appeared to be a fairly intellectually-balanced team. Messrs. Hewlett, the Speaker, Christian, Francis, and Watt were lawyers, Selvin Walter had a degree in Economics; Basil Peters was previously the Headmaster of a Secondary School (the Princess Margaret Secondary) and a university graduate; Geoffrey Scotland also held a university degree; Sydney Prince was an experienced, licensed surveyor; Robert Hall was a Civil Servant and in agriculture for most of his life and operated a private livestock farm. Halstead and George Walter had trade union experience and the others had some connection with small business. Premier Walter boasted that he had one of the most educated Cabinet in the West Indies.

On the other hand, not a single one of the Ministers had any Government experience, and though this was no insuperable problem, it should have had a sobering effect upon the new Premier and his Ministers to enter this difficult field with caution, and gain experience along the way. They had other aims in view, Chief among which was to obliterate, if possible, all traces of Bird and the former Government, and perhaps if it were possible for them to do so, they would have destroyed all of the institutions, which were established during the Bird regime. It was of no consequence that it was easier to destroy than to build or rebuild, unless one had the wherewithal at their disposal.

One of the first actions of the new Government was to disband the volunteer Defence Force. It was their opinion that the Defence Force was pro-Bird, since it was expanded and brought up to full strength and efficiency during the time when the Antigua Workers' Union and PLM were responsible for the political and social disturbances in the State.

The Government then ordered a mass lay-off of workers at the Public Works Department. Many of the workers who were laid off had spent a lifetime working for the Government and received neither compensation, nor gratuities, nor pensions to which they were entitled. The Public Works workers were mainly members of the Antigua Trades and Labour Union, and as was done in other employment in the State by agreement, the Department collected union dues from the workers salaries, and submitted them to the Union. The new Government stopped that practice and threatened the remaining workers with dismissal if they encouraged activities of the Antigua Trades and Labour Union in the Department.

The Government then abolished the Industrial Development Board which operated a corn meal factory, a cotton ginnery and an oil expelling plant on behalf of the prior Government. They next dismissed the Secretary of the Board, William Robinson of Piggotts, without proper notice or compensation and stopped operation of the corn meal factory, throwing a number of persons out of work.

New appointments to the membership of the Board of the Central Housing and Planning Authority were due in 1971. Although the Board had a civil service secretary, it was necessary to appoint a Chairman to fulfil the legal requirements of the Board, because no transfer of lands purchased by individuals from the Authority could become effective without the Chairman's signature. For unknown reasons and despite urgent and countless requests by those who needed their titles to lands, the Government refused to appoint a Chairman and Members of the Authority until late in 1973. So the citizens who were affected had to wait three years before getting their transfers attended to.

The former ALP Government, in an effort to improve the efficiency of the Police Force during the disturbances in 1968 and after, had engaged on contract a

232

number of police recruits from some of the other Associated States. The recruits who were trained at high cost to the Antigua & Barbuda Government, had their passing-out exercises and were ready to assume duty as regular policemen when the change of Governments took place. Without notice or compensation, the new Government discharged all of the new Police Officers, sent them back home to their respective islands, and gave no reason for their action. Other Governments of the Associated States registered their concerns and strong objections to this action by the new Antigua Government, but the objections were ignored.

During 1968, as a result of the unending labour disputes, the Bird Government established an industrial court for which legislation was already approved; this important policy move was taken before the dismissal of George Walter from the Antigua Trades & Labour Union. The Court had as its president a retired judge, Hon. Samuel Graham; its other members were Dr. Zin Henry, a labour relations expert who was serving with the Trinidad and Tobago Government, and Olva Flax, a retired Senior Civil Servant from Antigua. The Court performed a very useful duty during the period of rising labour tensions and helped to avert several looming crises. However, within the first months in office, the PLM Government abolished the Industrial Court.

Soon, other acts of victimisation by the new Government against individuals who were considered supporters of the former ALP Government became more pronounced. George Walter said that he would reward his friends and punish his enemies. One Mrs. Rose Camacho who married an Antiguan, was doing business in Antigua for a number of years with her sons, when she was refused a licence by the new PLM Government to continue her business. She was hustled and manhandled by the Minister of Trade, Selvin Walter, when she went to his office to protest the refusal of the Collector of Customs to issue a licence to her, while other persons in similar business ventures were granted licences. The matter had to be settled in the Courts where the Judge pointed out the outrageous arrogance of the Minister, and ordered the Collector of Customs to issue the licence. Mrs. Camacho was a known supporter of V.C. Bird and the Labour Party.

One Dorcas White, a Montserratan, who lived in Antigua for a number of years and worked with the Star Newspaper as a reporter before becoming editor of the Workers' Voice, was refused a work permit by the Government to work in Antigua and Barbuda. The Workers' Voice had been critical of the new PLM Government. At the same time, the Government granted a permit to Noel Henwood, a self-styled international rover from Trinidad, to be editor of the Antigua Star, a national newspaper that was partly owned by some members of the PLM Government and gave unstinting support to its policies.

Several foreign investors who had permission to operate in Antigua and Barbuda by the previous Labour Government had their permits either withdrawn or held in abeyance, for the new Government decided not to do business with investors who had any association with the former Labour Government. Some foreign investors were deported when they spoke up against the treatment they received from the new PLM Government.

Several Civil Servants who were considered sympathetic to the former ALP Government were summarily dismissed without reason or compensation, and appeals to the Public Service Commission bore no results, because the Commission was probably the main captive of the Government of the day. Anyone who opposed or questioned the will of the Ministers of PLM Government did so at their peril.

The Government of Antigua was for many years the sole purchaser and exporter of Sea Island cotton, ensuring certain prices for sale of the crop to Cotton Growers, once the cotton was picked, cleaned and ready for export. For the entire years -1971 and 1972 - cotton growers had to keep their cotton stored on their premises or discontinue planting cotton, because the new Government made no provision to purchase the cotton in hand, nor gave any indication whether or not it would do so. They also did not consider it necessary to explain to the Cotton Growers the reasons for Government's failure to purchase their crop.

When the Walter Government came into power in February 1971, arrangements were already made by the Antigua Sugar Factory Board to reap the Sugar Crop. This was the best crop since the Government acquired the assets of the Antigua Sugar Factory and the Antigua Syndicate Estates; the greater portion of the cane was first ratoon, because the industry was just re-established. The Crop yielded over 11,000 tons of sugar.

Immediately upon reaping the Sugar Crop, the new Government instructed the Factory Board to lay off workers in the fields who would usually be employed in caring for the ratoon and cane plant; the Crop for the following year was therefore left unattended in the fields. Following this, all but a few of the workers and staff members at the Antigua Sugar Factory who were usually employed in and out of Crop to maintain the machinery and work in the factory office were laid off without notice, or severance pay. The Government gave no notice that sugar operations would be discontinued, and so the peasants and other cane suppliers continued to cultivate their land and planted cane. The Factory Board became inoperative.

Heavy rains during 1971 after the Crop was reaped, were very beneficial to the growing cane and the 1972 Crop promised to be the biggest for several years. The guaranteed price for sugar with Britain had also jumped from EC$228.00 per ton to EC$292.00 per ton; yet the Government gave no sign of getting the Factory ready to process the Crop. The country waited for months for a statement by the Government on the Sugar Crop, but to no avail.

The Government had however hired a consulting team from the United Kingdom to investigate the Sugar Industry. This consultant submitted its report during late summer 1972, and found that sugar would play a significant role in the economy of Antigua for a long time, that they knew of no other agro-industry to replace it.

The good reaping months of 1972 for the Sugar Crop came and went. The cane stood in the fields, a prey to stray animals and the heat. The thousands of peasants and workers who depended on sugar for their livelihood, waited patiently for word from the Government to reap the crop, though it was late in the Season, or if they would be compensated for their Crop; Government remained silent. The years 1972 and 1973 passed without a statement. When it was recognised that the Government had started to dismantle the Sugar Factory and to dispose of the machinery, the Sugar Industry was pronounced dead. As was stated by Walter in 1967, it took him one year in office to bring about the demise of the sugar industry.

The Peasants all through 1973 were not compensated for the loss of their crop and future ratoons, nor were the workers laid off from the Sugar Industry compensated. The price of sugar on the world market continued to increase, but due to Government's policy, Antigua did not profit from these increases, as the sugar that could have been sold rotted in the fields. The Labour Party made an issue of the Sugar fiasco, and vowed to restore the industry if returned to power.

Apart from the crucial role sugar played in Antigua's economy, it was considered to be one of the safest industries for a country that had continuous periods of droughts. Sugar was planted in Antigua as early as 1655, and survived wars, pestilences and dry periods. It had become an Antiguan traditional crop.

Agriculture in most developed and under-developed countries passed through periods of crisis whether floods, droughts, hurricanes or other natural disasters, but the countries do not abandon traditional crops because of temporary setbacks; they very often find ways and means to bringing about improvements and to arrest the ravages of droughts, floods, etc. The Sugar Industry in Antigua threw out a challenge to the Walter Government, which that Government failed to take up or eventually proved incapable of taking up.

Compared with the fifty-four steam mills and the seventeen windmills that were in operation in 1897, the Antigua Sugar Factory was a modern factory capable of grinding 2,200 tons of cane per day with a capacity for an annual crop output of 40,000 tons of sugar. By 1975, the Factory was a relic of the past like a deserted village.

It was difficult to understand the policies of the new Government or if it had any policy at all in respect to sugar. Certainly no progressive Government institute policies to close industries and displace workers without having alternative sources of employment available. But this was the case and result in Antigua between 1971 and 1976, when the island experienced its worst unemployment conditions that could have almost compared with the Great Depression of the 1930s.

While all the sugar producing countries in the world received great benefits from increased sugar prices on the world market, Antigua became poorer because the State imported rather than exported sugar, and the high cost of this commodity had to be borne by the Antigua consumers without subsidies to offset this cost.

While it was recognised that sugar prices would fall to more reasonable levels, it was hardly likely that the increase in prices of previous years would come into being again, and it could have been safely assumed, that sugar producers would have enjoyed good returns on their investments, if the PLM Government had not dismantled the sugar industry.

The PLM Government through continuous pressure from the peasants, paid a compensation of EC$8.00 per ton to the peasants whose crops were not reaped due to the closing of the Sugar Industry. Had the Industry been kept alive, the peasants could have received from EC$60.00 to EC$80.00 per ton or more for the cane supplied to the Factory during 1974 and 1975.

The PLM Government seemed to have staked the entire economy on tourism; but here again, it was the same people from 1967 to 1970 as the Opposition, who all but destroyed a booming tourist industry. While voters' memories may be short lived, investors and tourists do not easily forget unsavoury experiences. It takes a lot to restore the confidence of investors and tourists, who were treated with hostility and arrogance in the past.

Consequently, despite the expenditure of large sums of money in tourist promotion and establishing tourist offices in New York and Toronto during PLM Administration, the Tourist Industry had not expanded, and failed to achieve the buoyancy it enjoyed before 1967, when the political and labour troubles started. No new industry was established on the island from 1970 to 1976, and no new hotels were constructed, although there were extensions to a few. The hoteliers experienced lean years and persistent financial difficulties.

Despite the economic recession in the State and the resultant shortage of funds, the Government Ministers were not deterred from expensive jaunts abroad. They refused no invitation to attend conferences that had little or no relevance to affairs of the State, and consequently, money that could have been put to better use for improving public services, was spent on expensive hotel bills and costly subsistence for Ministers, some of whom exhibited unusually extravagant tastes at the public's expense.

Along with excesses of the PLM Hierarchy, there were rumours and reports of corruption against one or two individual Ministers that brought forth no denial from the Government. Ministers were reported to have used their offices for extortion, and had made substantial monetary gains as a result. One Minister was reported as receiving $62,000 commission on the sale of a hotel, by denying other interested persons the right to bid on the transaction. The accused Minister, as Minister of

Labour and Home Affairs, was responsible for granting work permits to foreigners to work in the State, and was involved in the sale and purchase of properties to foreigners. This and other charges were left unanswered, and the Government made no attempt to investigate the Minister. One Minister had to pay compensation ordered by the Court for deliberately spitting in the face of a prominent politician.

Charges of nepotism that could be substantiated and influence peddling were levelled at the Government, without explanation from any Government source. Denial nor confirmation of these charges were provided. Consequently, the people became confused and some Government supporters began to ask questions. One Government back-bencher in the House of Representatives, Wilbert Sterling, broached the question of the corruption charges and pleaded with those responsible, if the charges were true, to desist from their activities that would be a discredit to the Party and the Government.

In the summer of 1970, the ALP's Minister of Trade asked the Commissioner of the Associated States in Canada to try to locate a supplier of corn in Canada for the Corn Meal Factory in Antigua. The Commissioner not only found a supplier, but also investigated the difference in cost between bulk shipment and bagged corn. The difference was substantial. Following detailed discussions on the matter with the Commissioner, the suppliers were able to secure assistance from the Canadian International Development Agency (CIDA) to carry through a survey relative to bulk storage possibilities in Antigua, once the Government's approval was granted.

A few days before the scheduled visit of the survey team to St. John's, there was a change of Government in Antigua. However, at the request of the Commissioner, the new Minister of Trade, Selvin Walter, agreed to meet with the team. After spending some time in Antigua, the surveyors submitted a report to the Canadian Government and the Commissioner, who forwarded copies to the Antiguan Government for action.

Instead of taking action on the report or acknowledging its receipt, the Government closed the Cornmeal Factory. The closure of the Cornmeal Factory was another measure of irresponsibility on the part of the new PLM Government. The Factory supplied all of the cornmeal that was consumed locally and shipments of cornmeal were also made to some of the other neighbouring Associated States.

Under the Caribbean Free Trade Area (CARIFTA) protocol, this trade could have expanded. The Factory also supplied a substantial amount of food for the Antigua piggeries. As a consequence of the factory's closure, cornmeal and pigs' feed had to be imported, while those who worked at the Cornmeal Factory suffered the frustrations of unemployment and poverty, because gainful employment in the State was hard to find.

During 1974, sugar prices in Canada jumped by more than 700%, and raw sugar fetched EC$2,000.00 per ton on the open market in London. One sugar company in the United States claimed that it made over 2,000% profit on its operations.

CHAPTER 16
UNCONSTITUTIONAL LAWS
AND TAX ON AMBITION

Within a few months of coming to power, the Walter Government introduced a series of legislative measures in Parliament, which were aimed at discriminating against selected citizens, and at eroding certain Fundamental Rights of the citizens guaranteed in the Constitution of Antigua.

Apart from abolishing the Industrial Court, the new PLM Government repealed the Protection of Wages Act, which was passed by the ALP Government to prevent employers from deducting union dues or other monies from workers' wages without their written consent. In its place, the Walter Government passed legislation in favour of the Agency Shop, authorising employers to make not only deductions of union dues from members, but also an agency commission payable to the Union from all workers in industries where the AWU had the bargaining rights. This law was considered unconstitutional - it encroached upon the worker's rights to decide whether or not he wanted union membership, or desired to pay union dues. It also unilaterally dissolved the agreement reached between the former Government and the then Opposition in 1968 that workers would be free to join and pay dues to the union of their choice.

The Aliens Land Holding Act was amended in such a way that anyone who was not an Antiguan could not purchase land above an acre, without the prior approval of the Cabinet; it also imposed high imposts payable to Government on such approved purchases. This system engendered abuses by any Minister or official whose assistance may be sought in a land transaction.

Persons who were permanent residents of Antigua and were known supporters of the former ALP Government, were continually harassed and threatened with amendments to the Constitution that would remove the protection they received, so subject them to deportation.

But the most notorious new law was the amendment to the Newspaper Act, which prohibited freedom of expression in the State. In May, 1971, the then Minister of Home Affairs, Donald Halstead, whose Ministry managed matters affecting the press, gave notice that he would be putting the press under control.

A new newspaper - The Antigua Times - owned exclusively by members of the Antigua People's Party (APP) and some Bermudan interest, and the Workers' Voice newspaper, which was highly critical of the Government's actions, received claims of slander regarding Ministers in the State. Because the newspapers were not privately but were either organs of political parties or trade unions, it would be difficult to collect compensation, if action was brought against the newspapers for libel. The PLM government decided to reform the legislation, whereby Ministers who claim libel could sue for damages, and if awarded a judgment in their favour, there would be money available to satisfy the judgment.

Therefore, Halstead decided to repeal the Newspaper Act by providing that the existing bond under which newspapers operated be removed, and an annual license fee of EC$1,200.00 (later amended to $600) would be imposed, payable on the 1st January of each year. Further, a perpetual deposit of EC$10,000.00 will be made with the Treasury by each newspaper as a security deposit against defamation awards by the Courts. This was further amended to include an insurance guarantee for this amount, and no newspaper could be published in the State without prior approval of the Cabinet. The newspapers in operation at the time the law was enacted would be considered as having such approval.

The Times and Workers' Voice protested the enactment of the bills, which infringed upon inalienable rights provided in the constitution. Newspapers throughout the Commonwealth Caribbean and elsewhere appealed to the Government to desist from introducing the Newspaper Surety Act and the Newspaper Registration Act in Parliament, for they were unconstitutional.

The Government ignored all advice or criticism against the Bills. The Inter American Press Association (IAPA) sent a delegation to discuss the dangers of the

Bills and the harm the Government could do to its international reputation if the Bills became law, this was to no avail.

The Government's real intention was apparent, to close down opposition newspapers and stifle rhetoric against the PLM Government. Both Walter and Halstead knew that The Antigua Times and Workers' Voice could not afford to pay the licence fee and the Bond of EC$10,000.00. Walter, who a few years before was General Secretary of the Antigua Trades and Labour Union and responsible for all Union funds, knew that The Workers' Voice operated at a loss and was subsidized by the Union; he also knew that the formation of the Antigua Workers' Union placed the AT&LU in serious financial straits. It was apparent that the intent of the proposed law was based on malice and vindictiveness.

The Bills were passed in Parliament in November 1971 and became law on January 1st, 1972. At the same time, due to their inability to meet the deposit, The Antigua Times and Workers' Voice ceased publication, as the new law imposed fines and imprisonment for each day of publication outside the law.

Undeterred, The Times and Workers' Voice decided to challenge the validity of the Bills in Court, for their legal advisers saw the laws as unconstitutional. Counsel for the Workers' Voice found a loophole in the Newspaper Act, which defined a newspaper as printed material for sale. It was contemplated that the law could be circumvented if the newspapers were distributed for free; printed with contributions from well-wishers.

The decision was made to publish free copies twice weekly. The first was distributed on Saturday, 19th February 1972, the headline read:

"THE WORKERS' VOICE MUST NOT DIE".

"For the past seven weeks democracy has become totally dead in Antigua and a totalitarian regime has emerged in its place. The intention of the Government is to stifle forever all forms of opposition and to reduce and limit freedom of expression only to perhaps the private conversations that may be carried on in the bedrooms of the State, and this itself might be only for a time.

The closing of the two newspapers, The Times and The Workers' Voice, because of the repressive and unconstitutional press laws has denied Antiguans of the right to know, the right to question, and the right to participate intelligently and informatively in the political, social and economic affairs of their country.

Since the existing organs of opinion which are at present functioning, namely the Antigua Star, the Antigua Broadcasting Station and the time which is allocated to Government on the television station are fully and absolutely under Government control; commonsense alone dictates that the citizens of the State will be fed only with the false propaganda, deceit and calumny of which this Government has a virtual monopoly, and that there would be left no effective means of exposing these impostors to the people who have a right to know the truth.

We therefore consider it as our bounden duty to oppose the dictates of the oppressor and come what may, place The Workers' Voice again in the hands of the people, not for sale, but with the hope that our supporters, lovers of freedom will find the means of contributing to this effort and so defeat the objectives of the Government.

It is quite clear to us that the press laws, the agency shop, the formal pronouncement of the Premier of the State to introduce laws to ban peaceful demonstrations and the use of loud speakers, with the remark that he would no longer tolerate such nonsense, are only the beginning of a long trail of abuses to which this State will shortly be subjected.

The long trail of wrongs and the promises and threats to commit more wrongs have cast fear into the hearts of the citizens of this State who now realise that their sacred and fundamental rights have been eroded and that another form of slavery - slavery of the mind, which is more deadly and vicious than the slavery suffered by our forefathers has come upon us. In face of this absolute despotism and cruel usurpation, it becomes necessary for us to marshal all our forces to meet the challenge and to keep the tyrants at bay.

Power corrupts, but absolute power corrupts absolutely, said Lord Acton, and this is so true today in Antigua that if we are not careful the horizon of our vision might be coated only with corruption and all the good things of life would become contaminated and would sink into the cesspool of despair. The Workers' Voice must not and will not die. We must live to tell the tale."

This defiance thwarted the Governments attempt to silence the press, for it could not prevent the Workers Voice from printing free issues, without resorting to further legislation.

The copies of the paper were grabbed up by an eager reading public, and the publishers had difficulty meeting the demands.

The case brought by The Antigua Times against the Government was heard in the High Court before Mr. Justice Alan Louisy, the local Puisne Judge. Judge Louisy in a learned decision found the Newspaper Surety Act and the Newspaper Registration Act unconstitutional and were therefore void, and fined the Government to pay costs. The Government appealed the decision to the Associated States Appeal Court, which also found against them, with the Judges remarking on the number of unconstitutional laws the Government edict upon the people. Not satisfied, the Government appealed to the Privy Council in London for a reversal of the local courts decision. The Lords of the Privy Council in a remarkable judgement in 1975, allowed the appeal, basing their decision on the right of Government to raise revenues for its own use by way of taxation.

Not to be gainsaid in their failure with the press laws, the Government then passed the Public Order Act, which banned peaceful demonstrations by political parties, and public meetings by groups considered opposed to Government and its policies. Such meetings could not be held without the permission of the Chief of Police, who would be entitled to know the meetings agenda and who were the speakers. If speakers at any meeting criticised the Government, the police under provisions of the Public Order Act, were empowered to stop the meeting and could charge the individuals responsible for holding the meeting. The police chief also had full discretion to grant permission to anyone seeking to hold a meeting. Any appeal against the Police would be made to the Minister of Home Affairs, the man responsible for introducing the law. The Chief of Police also banned the use of loud speakers, except for special permission.

It was felt that the law infringed upon the rights of political parties, and was also viewed as unconstitutional. This time, it was the Antigua Labour Party that took the matter to Court, and again the Judge ruled that parts of Sections 3, 4 and 5 of the law were unconstitutional and must therefore be considered null and void. Other sections were left in tact, but before the Public Order Act was tried in the Court, the Antigua Labour Party and supporters demonstrated against the passage of the law in Parliament at the introduction of the Bill, and at its third and final reading. At the first reading, the demonstrators marched outside of Parliament in protest against unconstitutional laws.

Some tourists who had come ashore from a cruise ship that called at St. John's also joined the march in curiosity, some taking pictures. Without notice or reason, Police Riot Squads at the instruction of the Minister of Home Affairs, discharged tear gas upon the unsuspecting demonstrators, resulting with several people receiving severe injuries. Many tourists who were caught up in the Police's assault, swore that they would never return to Antigua again. (See Appendix 2. Privy Council Appeal No.9 of 1974.)

The cases brought against the Government required large expenditure of funds for legal Counsel, which the country could not afford. But the Government's obstinacy and refusal to accept responsible advice, placed undue burden on the taxpayer, who had to face tax increases. In an effort to raise revenue to meet the daily cost of operating the Government and to pay for Ministers' costly trips abroad, the Government made a complete overhaul of the property tax structure of the State.

The Government proposed a general property tax assessment of 10% a properties annual value, calculated not on actual rents received or upon a reasonable assessment of owner-occupied properties, but upon what the Government determined the annual value of these properties should be. In many respects, the assessments of opposition supporters were inflated.

When the new Property Tax Assessments came out in 1973, it was discovered that in some cases, taxes increased by about 1,000% and the minimum increases were in the vicinity of 200%. The indiscriminate tax increases caused a national outcry, and even those who supported the Government saw the unfairness of the restructured tax system.

All sections of the community appealed to the Government to review and reconsider the new taxes, for it was impossible for the majority of people to pay such exorbitant taxes, especially at a time when unemployment in the State was at an all time high, and inflation caused by the high cost of living made the value of the local dollar almost worthless.

Pressure from all sides especially from supporters, caused the Government to reduce the property tax from 10% to 5% of annual value, and to set up a Tax Review Board so that individuals who had genuine grievances could take their complaints before the Board for reduction of their tax.

One serious aspect of this property tax increase was its deterrence to a high standard of housing development in the State. The citizens of the State made much sacrifice over the years to improve their personal development.

CHAPTER 17
SOME EXAMPLES OF VICTIMISATION

Following the pattern adopted by legislatures in the democratic world including the West Indies, the Antigua Parliament made legislative provisions for members who served for a stipulated number of years to receive a pension on their retirement from Parliament, either by resignation or defeat at the polls, or by not contesting elections.

In the majority of Parliaments or assemblies, retired legislators also received substantial pensions, depending on their period of service and size of parliamentary remuneration.

With the defeat of the Antigua Labour Party in the February, 1971 elections, several of the defeated Ministers and Members of Parliament, some of whom had given over 20 years of service and were eligible for pensions applied to the Government for consideration. The Government ignored their applications. It was reported that the Government decided it would not pay pensions to former ALP Legislators.

It was not a matter that by paying the pensions the Government would have created a precedent; the ALP Government had already instituted a retirement fund and paid benefits to a retired Minister. The refusal of PLM Government to honour this legal commitment could only be considered spiteful.

In addition to their refusal to honour pension applications from former ALP Officials, it was stated that the Government threatened certain foreign investors with withdrawal of their business permits to operate in the island if they offered employment to former ALP Ministers and parliamentarians. In light of this threat, companies were reluctant to hire former lawmakers, who were therefore forced to eke out a livelihood from their own resources, as they were prohibited from finding employment in industries they helped to establish.

Continuing their pattern, the PLM Government sought the removal of Novelle H. Richards, Commissioner to Canada for the Associated States.

Four years prior, Richards was approached and requested by the Council of Ministers to assume the position as Commissioner to Canada. He accepted the post, envisioning it as a means of bringing the Associated States together in a federation or another closer association, of which he was a staunch advocate.

The Commissioner served out one three year term and was re-appointed for another term of three years by the Council of Ministers. All the Associated States honoured their financial commitments to the Commission until the change of Government in Antigua, when the PLM Government immediately upon taking office sought the removal of the Commissioner, albeit his contractual agreement with the Associated States and him having worked for a full year with the PLM regime. Premier George Walter and his Ministers made it clear that the Commissioner, an Antiguan by birth, would receive no money from Antigua so long as he remained in office. At the request of the Antigua Government, Mr. Richards was recalled in the middle of his term of appointment without compensation or other financial settlement being made.

CHAPTER 18
HALSTEAD BRIGADE

The unconstitutional measures adopted by the Antigua Government were the cause for the rise of certain cells of underground resistance in the State, chiefly by a group called the Antigua Freedom Fighters.

This group of individuals successfully kept their identity secret, despite strenuous efforts by the Government to uncover individual's identity, purported to be responsible for the publication and distribution of an underground pamphlet. The pamphlet accused the Government and some of its supporters of a number of wrongs and promised retribution for the wrongs. Although the pamphlet was in the realm of yellow journalism and did not hesitate to defame, it kept the Ministers on their toes, for no one knew who would be the next target to be written about.

The Freedom Fighters also claimed responsibility for bomb explosions that did minor damage to a few Government buildings in St. John's.

Another group that created deep concern for the Government was the Afro-Caribbean Liberation Movement, (ACLM), a local black power group, which according to its constitution, had no political ambitions, but were strictly interested in economic and cultural viability. Remarkably, some of the members and leaders of the Movement, including the President, Leonard (Tim) Hector, were once staunch PLM supporters. However, they soon became disenchanted with George Walter and Donald Halstead, as the two gentlemen's character had become questionable. Hector and others felt that the basic objectives of these two men were to secure power for themselves at any price and to wield power without shouldering the responsibility of power within a democratic framework.

On 26th May 1973, the Afro-Caribbean Movement carried out a peaceful Liberation Day March despite the withdrawal of permission to march which was previously granted by the Chief of Police. About 14,000 Antiguans joined the march, including some staunch supporters of the Government. It was reported that the Minister of Home Affairs chastised the Chief of Police for granting the permission, hence his change of mind. The aftermath of this peaceful march resulted in Leonard Hector and others being taken before the Magistrate, charged with contravening the order of the Chief of Police by not receiving permission to march.

***

During 1972, the Minister of Home Affairs, Donald Halstead, with the approval of the Government, established what he called the Special Police Security Unit, comprised of persons of known criminal record and others of doubtful character, recruited to assist the Police Force to maintain order and peace in the island. This Special Unit did not report to the Police Chief, but to the Minister himself. Barrymore Rannie, an Antiguan by birth who lived in the United Stated and had converted to the Black Islam Religion (Five Percenters) and carried a Muslim name directed the unit. This Special Police or Halstead's Brigade as it was dubbed, was intended to mimic the notorious Ton Macoute of Dr. Duvalier (Papa Doc) in Haiti.

Though they did not match the brutality of the Haitians, some of these self-styled protectors of the peace were "trigger happy," and were responsible for certain shooting incidents on the island; unlike the Police Force, the Special Police Unit was well armed.

The Halstead Brigade's main function was to track down the Freedom Fighters - they failed dismally, because this underground group remained at large and perhaps enjoyed themselves at the Government's expense. Some circles were of the opinion that the Freedom Fighters might have been a creation of the Government in an attempt to discredit the opposition, as individuals claimed that certain telephone calls made by the Freedom Fighters were traced to one of the Ministries.

The Antigua Labour Party and the Antigua Trades and Labour Union in a joint statement to the public, emphatically denied any association with violence or with any group that committed acts of violence in the State. The statement further pointed out that violence in the State started in 1967 when the present Government which was then the opposition planned and carried out many violent episodes, which led to a State of Emergency in the State.

Right from that period up to the time of the ALP's defeat, PLM as the opposition, had perpetuated an atmosphere of tension in the State. Upon becoming the Government, the Party through its unconstitutional laws and acts of victimisation and repression, committed many violent acts against the people of Antigua and Barbuda. It was therefore a matter for the Government to put its own house in order. The Government was completely silent on ALP's statement. Whether or not the statement found its mark was another matter.

Large sums of money were spent to retain this private militia, but as it happened, they were not paid sometimes, when the public Treasury was out of money. The unit was disbanded in 1973, when the men became disgruntled at the Government's inability to meet the cost of its upkeep. It was realised then that the unit's loyalty to the Minister did not go beyond receipt of the pay envelope.

CHAPTER 19
UNFULFILLED PROMISES

By early 1974, the economy of the State had taken a sound beating and started a steep decline. With opportunities for employment down to a trickle due to the Government's inability to attract new industries and the closing of the Sugar Industry and other small industries, an atmosphere of gloom and depression prevailed. Young men and women of working age who were leaving school and ready to join the labour force, saw no hope of getting jobs, swelling the ranks of the unemployed. The only hope was to migrate to Canada or the United States in search of better opportunities.

The PLM Government made all manner of promises which never materialised. In 1972, the Government was to secure a loan of $30 million to assist in development programmes. Premier George Walter in a television interview promised a huge land development programme at Five Islands Estate by West German investors, who would erect a 12,000 room hotel among other projects. Hotels were to be built at Corbinson's Point and in the Coconut Hall area. A new airline known as Air Antigua was to begin operating between Antigua and West Germany. A new and first class hospital was to be built at Clark's Hill. All these plans sounded very good at the time, but never materialised.

From a State of booming development and almost full employment in 1967, by 1974, Antigua's economy was in total recession. Although there were no formal surveys of the unemployment status at the time, it was presumed with some degree of certainty that about 40% of the labour force was unemployed.

The commercial sector bore the brunt of the recession as business turn-over dropped steeply. Some well-established businesses went into receivership and many of the businesses that remained open were deeply indebted to the banks, and stayed afloat with hopes for better days to come.

The only projects carried out by the PLM Government during its period of office were projects that were established through external aid from Canada and the United Kingdom, such as a few school buildings, some of which were inherited from the former ALP Government, in particular, the Technical School at Golden Grove.

During 1973, the Government turned over the management and operation of the desalination plant and electricity generating plant to the consulting engineering firm that supervised the installation on behalf of the previous ALP Government, on the understanding that the PLM Government did not have the finances to maintain and operate the services efficiently. Before this arrangement, there were continuous breakdown in these services due to lack of proper maintenance.

In the agricultural sector, the Government concentrated on vegetable production and the expansion of livestock production. While this in itself was commendable, depressed prices which brought very little returns, had peasants and private producers competing with each other for their market share of certain seasonal crops.

In the absence of a bold and vigorous agricultural policy which should have embraced the production of sugar, sea island cotton and other crops for export trade, with livestock development and the processing of locally produced foods, the agricultural potential of the State remained only partially tapped, thereby bringing minimal financial returns.

While the Government appeared to have concentrated on livestock production, which is a necessary feature of development, the policy employed was not in the best interest of the State. Livestock production had low labour content and utilised very large portions of the arable land on the island. Initiating this programme meant that very little arable land would be available for crops of high labour content, if a full-scale agricultural effort was to be advanced.

It would appear that by closing the Sugar Industry, the Government's aim was to turn Antigua into a large cattle ranch without paying attention to the displaced workers in the agricultural sector nor to the best economic use of the land. This must be considered a naive and short-sighted policy that could have serious repercussions in the years to come and especially if this policy was pursued.

The Peasants and farmers are the backbone of a country; every encouragement is given to these people in developed and developing countries to cultivate the land as they play an essential role in the overall economy of their countries. Within West Indian context, the land will always be closely linked to the economy, because despite strong efforts that may be made to broaden the industrial base, it is very difficult for small islands such as Antigua to compete with other larger states in attracting large and heavy manufacturing industries of high labour content that could fully absorb the potential labour force, including those workers who could be employed in the agricultural sector.

The curses of Governments in the modern world are inflation and high unemployment. These are the commodities that topple governments, because they are usually the main sources of unrest and discontent. Every effort is made by all progressive governments to check inflation and ensure that new jobs are created annually to absorb the labour force. The record of PLM Government in this important field varied from nothing to minus, because the State was swept with runaway inflation. Instead of seeking to create new jobs, or providing a climate that would be conducive to attracting investments, the policy was spectacular in closing industries and failing to create new avenues of employment for the people.

The Report on the Sugar Industry survey performed by Peat, Marwick, Mitchell & Co. on behalf of the Government, presented beneficial results that should be heeded by any progressive Government. The survey compared several relevant costs of goods and services in Antigua with their costs in some of the other Commonwealth Caribbean countries; in many respects, Antigua led the way in cost.

One key factor to the high cost of living was the Government's support of the Antigua Worker's Union policy, to chase after higher wages as paid in developed countries, to compensate a select group of workers for their political support. These increases were borne by the ordinary man and woman, who absorbed the raise by paying more for consumer goods and services.

No one could blame workers for benefiting from their privileged position, especially if they had the blessing of the Government. However, with the Government finding itself incapable of handling the sensitive question of inflation, it would appear that a national appeal for reason and commonsense could have been made for a voluntary moratorium on customarily high demands in some sectors, to allow a breathing space for costs of goods and services to level off with some of the other islands.[3]

No one could blame workers for benefiting from their privileged position. However, with the Government finding itself incapable of handling the sensitive matter of inflation, it would appear that a national appeal for reason and commonsense could have been made for a voluntary moratorium on wage increases to allow recovery and to bring the cost of goods and services on Antigua down to the level of other islands.

Calling a moratorium on excessive demands should not be interpreted as suggesting the obstruction of workers rights and their trade unions to negotiate for increases and other conditions of work, these are fundamental rights that must be respected. But it was imperative that a recovery period should have been brought into effect and it would have been more favourable if it were voluntary. Antigua had reached a stagnation point and any effort to woo investment from either local or foreign sources would have had to be accompanied by guarantees of wage control and other concessions.

There are other steps the PLM Government could have taken to curb the chronic inflation and economic decline. However, some measures were not very agreeable to certain sections of the community, especially where Government had to introduce such measures as price and income control. Serious situations call for serious and quick answers, and if a government is to live up to its responsibility, it must find the answers for such situations, no matter how uncomfortable the solution.

Any attempt to negate the question of inflation by imposing stringent and excessive tax measures to meet the growing costs of government services can only place greater burden upon an already over-burdened people, who were taxed beyond their limits through the hidden duties paid on imported commodities they consumed.

The AWU leaders needed to have realised that there was a limit to the country's capacity to meet all of their demands. To have chased after the high wages of industrialised countries within the context of industrial development within the economy of an underdeveloped country, was nonsensical and almost criminal. Foreign investors are attracted to a country because of favourable labour and wage conditions, among other factors. The local investor makes his investment because conditions appear favourable for him to make a return on his investment, he does not invest merely for love of country. It is the hard fact of dollars and cents that is in contention. Remove the favourable conditions for investment and the result is the economic and social stagnation that was evident in Antigua up to 1976.

The key to Antigua's recovery depended upon a concerted effort by all sections of the community to make some sacrifices towards a planned effort of development. What faced Antigua was a complete economic re-construction.

Fortunately, there remained certain services and institutions that could have been incorporated into new efforts at reconstruction, therefore, it was not a question of starting from scratch, but of strengthening what remained, to develop a viable social and industrial base. This could have been done if there was the will and the leadership to do so.

Unfortunately, the world oil crisis with its destructive impact on the economies of oil- importing nations, also added to the gravity of the inflationary situation in Antigua. The various factors combined demonstrated the urgent need for proactive visionary individuals to assume leadership positions within the State.

CHAPTER 20
DISMISSAL OF SELVIN WALTER
AND DONALD HALSTEAD

In December 1973, the island was surprised at the news, but breathed a sigh of relief when it was announced that Selvin Walter, Minister of Trade and Donald Halstead, Minister of Labour and Home Affairs, were relieved of their Ministries by the Premier. No explanation was given. There were numerous rumours as to why the ministers were removed, but one of the most plausible reasons was information that the British Government threatened to cut off aid from the island unless the Ministers were relieved of their post. If there was truth to this rumour, it was definitely an act of interference by the British Government in the State's internal affairs, but a justifiable interference that was not objected to by many, who sought an end to the Ministers' misconduct.

The Ministers dismissal came two years too late, for in that period they caused more embarrassment to their colleagues and the people of Antigua than the country could have afforded. The Ministry of Trade became a ministry of no trade and served as a launching pad for the Minister's peregrinations abroad, at considerable expense to a depleted Treasury.

Instead of introducing new industries, established industries were closed, and triggered a mass exodus of potential investors from the island. The record of Selvin Walter at the Ministry of Trade could be called a disaster to the country.

With respect to Donald Halstead, little more could be expected than what was achieved. Antigua came to the verge of becoming a totalitarian State, saved only by the Court's intervention. His Ministry was accused of setting up pockets of vice and prostitution in the island, by granting permits to adventuresses from Santo

Domingo to carry out illicit trade. It was also alleged that he was engaged in or associated with many activities embracing conflicts of interest, extortion and bribe. If these charges were false, they were not refuted nor investigated to clear his name; so a stigma remained on the Party for condoning such actions without taking steps to rectify the problem.

By 1975, what remained of the PLM Government could only be considered a "lame-duck government". The Government affirmed its impotence by the lack of beneficial activity for the country. The administration lost its credibility very early after taking office and was never able to convince any well-meaning person at home or abroad of its ability to properly govern.

The fact that Antigua and Barbuda had to tolerate such a regime for five years is one of the accidents of democracy. However, no one would have expected such a fantastically poor result from a party who from all accounts, should have been able to build upon the foundations laid by their predecessors, to get the country moving on the road to prosperity. Instead, the country lost its standing and credit worthiness, demonstrated by the Government's inability to obtain small loans or raise other capital.

If the PLM Government was more altruistic instead of holding so steadfastly to power, they should have dissolved parliament and given the electorate a chance to renew or reject its confidence in their leadership. Instead the PLM Government served out its term, while the country's economy fell into greater depression and its citizens lost many of its public services.

Had Antigua and Barbuda's economical growth progressed at or close to the rate of the sixties, it is quite possible that the nation would have enjoyed an annual public sector revenue base close to EC$100 million by 1976. There was every indication of this type of economic and fiscal growth, based on projections from investment prospects in progress and industrial programmes that were already instituted.

Despite this failure, it was essential for planners to concentrate on eliminating unemployment. There was also a need for some measure of rapprochement on the labour front to restrict workers and unions from fighting each other and obstructing industrial peace. Some understanding of peaceful coexistence if not full unity, should have been worked out between workers, perhaps under a temporary or permanent neutral commission entrusted with the task of bringing about harmonious labour relationships.

The fact was, no matter the opportunities for development, if the labour division continued to take on ugly proportions, much of the efforts at development would have been frustrated.

With two unions being a *fait accompli* and little hope of an amalgamation at the time, a remedy should have been sought to keep the unions operating on parallel lines, rather than having them engage in confrontation that brought no lasting benefits to workers, but created tensions that served as a deterrent to economic and social stability.

Thou the Industrial Court established by the previous ALP Government did a good job in settling disputes, the role of conciliator, or harmoniser between unions was outside of its field of competence. There was the possibility of a local labour congress to embrace both unions, but with the political orientation of the unions at sharp division, it was not likely that a congress would become a feasible proposition. It must not be ruled out however.

It was therefore imperative that capable Ministers, who had the ability to bring vision and action into their performance, lead the two key ministries of Trade and Labour.

The severe economic decline of the State, posed a great challenge for anyone appointed as the new Minister of Trade, to attract both foreign and local investment. It would take herculean effort to re-approach investors and change their minds about investing in our State, but it had to be done. In the same vein, the Minister of Labour needed to employ special skills to reduce and keep union tensions at a minimum.

CHAPTER 21
DISASTROUS EARTHQUAKE

On the morning of October 8th, 1974 at approximately 5.51 a.m. local time, an earthquake measuring 7.7 on the Richter Scale struck Antigua and St. Kitts, causing considerable damage estimated at close to EC$100m in Antigua and somewhat less in St. Kitts.

Fortunately, there were neither deaths nor serious injuries, but extensive damage was done to churches and public buildings in both islands.

The earthquake sent tremors as far north as Puerto Rico and was also felt in Martinique. In St. Kitts, extensive damage was done to the Government Treasury Building and to St. George's Church in Basseterre.

In Antigua, the St. John's Cathedral sustained severe damage especially to both steeples; the Roman Catholic Cathedral was also damaged, the All Saints Anglican Church was destroyed and the Lebanon Moravian Church at Sea View Farm was extensively damaged. Other churches throughout the island sustained minor damage.

The Parliament Building and Court House, the Treasury and the old Post Office Building, which housed the Ministry of Labour, were also badly damaged and had to be condemned. Severe damage was also done to the Deep Water Harbour and installations and the West Indies Oil Company experienced heavy damage to the refinery at Friar's Hill.

The roof of the Bank of Nova Scotia in St. John's caved in and private homes and business places experienced varying degrees of damage – shops and stores had to be closed in the wake of the earthquake.

This was the heaviest earthquake to hit Antigua in over 131 years. On the 8th February 1843, a terrible earthquake struck the island causing considerable damage and destruction. The St. John's Cathedral was destroyed and the Court House was seriously damaged. Both structures were rebuilt and repaired on the same sites; the Cathedral was rebuilt at a cost of £40,000.00, (EC$192,000.00) and opened for Divine Worship on 10th October 1847. The Court House was repaired in 1854.

It cost considerably more than the previous 40,000 pounds to restore the Cathedral after the earthquake; rebuilding funds were instituted to raise capital for the repair of the Cathedral and the other churches that were destroyed or damaged.

In 1976, the new ALP Government pledged to repair and restore the Court House and the old Parliament building.

Steps have since been taken by the ALP Government to ensure that future buildings of stone and concrete meet seismic standards of construction, with reinforcement and bracing to minimise damage from earthquakes or other such disasters.

CHAPTER 22
THE ROLE OF THE LABOUR PARTY

From the time of its defeat in February 1971, the Labour Party set about re-organising itself to establish Constituency Branches distinct from the branches of the Antigua Trades and Labour Union. This meant harnessing the youth and other available human potential in the districts and encouraging them to play a more active role in the political affairs of the State. A central youth committee was set up to assist the Executive of the Labour Party in this venture.

V.C. Bird remained in the role of political leader of the Labour Party, while Ernest Williams, the most senior of the four members elected to Parliament (1971 – 76) was given the position of Parliamentary and Opposition Leader of the Party.

In 1972, the Party elected Lester Bird as its Chairman for three consecutive terms; Hugh Marshall, Joseph Myers and Novelle Richards were appointed Vice Chairs, and John St. Luce held the post of Secretary-Treasurer.

On the Trade Union side, after the decision was taken in 1969 to separate the Trade Union and the political party, Joseph Lawrence became President, replacing V.C. Bird. Following PLM's landslide victory in the general elections wherein most of the former Ministers were defeated, Lionel Hurst who was a former General Secretary of the Union, decided he would devote more time to the Union and was elected President from 1971. The combination of Hurst and Freeland did much to improve the strength of the Antigua Trades and Labour Union. Other Senior Officers of the Union included William (Bill) Abbott and Vere Bird, Jr., who were elected Vice Presidents at consecutive conferences.

The Antigua Workers' Union continued with Malcolm Daniel as its President and Keithlyn Smith as General Secretary.

At the end of 1974, the Antigua Workers Union still had virtual control of the Waterfront Workers and of those employed in the petroleum industry and at the Airport. The Antigua Trades and Labour Union concentrated on workers in the clerical and light manufacturing sectors, in the hotel industry and in agriculture.

The economic recession made it financially difficult for the Antigua Trades and Labour Union to operate, as its main sources of income came from workers in industries that were less stable than the Waterfront and the Oil Refinery. The once dependable Government Non-Establishment workers, whose section had become disorganised due to the PLM's policy against the AT & LU collecting dues at Public Works and other Government agencies, paid their dues on a voluntary personal basis. There was therefore no organized mechanism of collecting dues that would have ensured a positive cash flow.

Whether Antigua could maintain two viable unions vying for membership in the same trades and vocations is difficult to surmise at this stage. It is however clear that with the small population, scarcity of jobs and marginal economy, one or both unions will be in serious financial difficulties for some time, unless there is significant economic improvement through industrialisation. Halting industrial development caused the economy to become critically stagnant. This in itself was detrimental to the country's social stability and industrial peace, because both unions staked claims for the bigger slice or all of the small work force.

Such competition created serious problems in labour negotiations, as unions competing with each other for wage increases and conditions of work made unrealistic promises to their members and potentials who were being enticed into membership. Antigua's disproportionately high wage structure relative to its size and economy was clearly evident when compared with similar economies within the commonwealth. Unfortunately, it is not too easy to persuade workers to go slowly on wage increases.

Compounding the union difficulties was the introduction by the PLM of party and union colours, distinguishing the party and its affiliate union.

The Antigua Trades and Labour Union has since its formation, adopted the colour red as a symbol of workers. This colour was only displayed on special occasions such as Labour Day parades. Since the formation of the Antigua Workers' Union and the PLM Party, the colours blue and white became the symbols of these joint institutions and were displayed in daily clothing. This display of colours aggravated tensions among workers, and it was suggested that the show of colours be suspended for appropriate occasions.

***

If Antigua was to survive and become a full-fledged independent member of the international mosaic, the four freedoms declared by President Franklin Delano Roosevelt in his Four Freedoms speech, would have had to be accepted and digested. Particular emphasis would have to be placed on freedom from fear and want and freedom of speech and expression.

Already, these two freedoms were challenged by the PLM Government while in power and with this challenge was an accelerated erosion of freedom from want, for there were more people in want in Antigua, than had been during the previous twenty years. Such conditions, if not arrested, could only result in tensions, misery and poverty.

One fundamental difference between a good and a bad government is, while one might have as its motto – *"I serve"* - and pursue it, the other might adopt the motto, *"I rule"*, and pursue it also. It is not difficult to distinguish the difference between the master and the servant, especially if the master has conditioned his mind to medieval subservience, placing the people's needs secondary to his own. Unfortunately, the administration at the time appeared to adopt this antediluvian policy.

The vindictive destruction of the sugar industry seriously reduced Antigua's trading position. This adversely affected the island's balance of payment position especially at a time when invisible income from tourism and repatriation of funds by migrants abroad was on the decline. In addition, there was no worthwhile investment from overseas into the country between 1971 and 1975 that could have generated the funds to surrogate losses from the decline tourism and the death of sugar.

Instead of promoting trade with vigour, the PLM Government sought aid from every available source – this method of raising capital failed abysmally. Aid is no substitute for trade development; trade has meaning and character. This does not say that aid is not useful, especially for developing and undeveloped countries such as Antigua and the other Associated States. While aid might be an important cog in the development wheel, it is self-defeating to make it the criterion or the key to development. The aid offered can always be withdrawn or might not meet or suit the people's needs.

A government's main objective must always be to create a climate that can attract investment for developing industries, and to relentlessly pursue markets for the goods produced. In Antigua's case, success depended on national involvement by the government, the trade unions and their members.

Individuals must not allow themselves to be manipulated by political opportunists, for in the end, it is the individual who will suffer, when they elect partisan and unscrupulous governments, who are more interested in their grip on power than on alleviating the economic and social ills of the country.

Antigua's electorate began showing signs of political maturity and looked at each party based on their record of accomplishments rather than popularity or promises. They compared the economic decline of the 70s, the burden of higher taxation, the loss of jobs and job opportunities and the deterioration in the social and moral character of the state with its prior condition from 1966 to 1971. The outcome was a body of voters who demanded change and sought an administration that would take the initiative to bring about that change.

For the Labour Party to meet that challenge meant it had to recapture the strong, bold and imaginative leadership of V.C. Bird. Much less would have been accomplished under a different kind of leadership. Any mistakes made were outweighed by the good that was generally done. Mr. Bird did a great job for Antigua and Barbuda and deserves its people's gratitude. However, the immediate and future problems the island faced were more complex than those of the past. The struggle then was workers against the plantocracy and colonial rule, it transitioned into a struggle between labour unions and parties, with the PLM demonstrating that it would go to any length of deception and if necessary destruction to attain and hold on to power.

If the Labour Party was to remain resolute, it had to rally all sections of the community; not as a call for sympathy, but an assertion of its capabilities and a demonstration of its willingness to lead Antigua out of the economic morose in which the state found itself.

The question was, could the Party do it again under the new and changed conditions? Will new ideas be able to emerge and encouraged as the party moved into the future?

The Labour Party had to undergo a complete re-birth and become a new party with a new image, a party of the present and the future, appealing, attractive, and alive, catering to youths and the aged alike, to the rich, the middle class, the underprivileged. It was only within this framework that the Party could undertake the job to be done, by opening its doors without restriction to a cross-section, and enabling leadership to emerge free of petty squabbles and restrictions of vested interests. That has been the downfall of many powerful parties in the past; for where leadership is based upon a small clique of one or two individuals over a prolonged period of time, there is no preparation for a smooth transition. Once that leadership is removed, internal squabbles and factional dissentions develop, which weakens the party and the country. The fact that the Gaullist Party in France could not get a Gaullist elected as President after the death of Pompidou is one such example. The same can be said of the Union Nationale Party in Quebec Canada, which held power under Duplessis for a considerable number of years and was the Government up to 1969, but was unable to elect a single candidate to the National Assembly in 1973.

When the Party can set an example of true democracy within its ranks, then, the people of Antigua and Barbuda can be sure of an organisation that will last and will not disintegrate as soon as its leadership becomes uncertain. There must be participatory democracy from the grass roots up, with ability, acceptability, and tried loyalty given a fair and equal chance to the top. The Party must belong to the people and not merely the people to the Party; only within this context can the party develop itself to play a continuing dominant role in the life of the state, and secure a permanent niche in the hearts of the people.

CHAPTER 23
MERGER OF ALP AND APP

After prolonged negotiation from 1972 to 1974, a decision was made to merge the Antigua Progressive Party (APP) and the Antigua Labour Party. This was the best thing that could have happened in the political life of Antigua, for with this merger, the political base of the Antigua Labour Party had been broadened, thereby bringing in new vitality and fresh ideas to play in the affairs of the country. In the final analysis, both the members of APP and ALP were Antiguans and Barbudans, who had the country's best interest at heart.

Following the merger, Rowan Henry who led APP, became prominently involved in ALP's activities and was slated to contest the elections in the St. John's City South Constituency.

On the 25th of June 1975, Rowan Henry and his wife Gwendolyn, daughter of Dr. Noel Margetson met their tragic deaths together, when they were attacked and killed at their home by their cutlass wielding gardener, Charles Joseph. Antigua lost one of her most distinguished and respected sons, the Labour Party was bereft by this loss. Charles Joseph was convicted of murder and hanged on 19th November 1975.

Rowan Henry served with distinction in the Royal Air Force during the Second World War, after which he embarked on a legal career. He was one of the luminaries of the Antigua Bar with a very successful practice in civil matters. Despite his political involvement and his failure to win an elected seat against the Antigua Labour Party, he was always considered a worthy opponent and was respected for his strong advocacy of the democratic process.

Henry was active in many organisations in Antigua, serving as President of the Antigua Cricket Association, as director of the Society of Friends of English

Harbour and other charitable and voluntary institutions. He was known for his benevolence to many people.

The merger of the APP and ALP eliminated the prospect for a three-cornered election ballot. Although the APP was not strong in numbers, there were certain constituencies in which APP's support was vital to the Antigua Labour Party, if that Party was to win a majority of seats in the ensuing elections. The results of the 1976 election substantiated the import of the coalition with APP on the fortune of the Antigua Labour Party and the people of Antigua and Barbuda.

CHAPTER 24
GENERAL ELECTIONS

In October 1975, the PLM Government introduced a new *Representation of the Peoples* Bill in Parliament, which among several measures called for new registration of all voters in the State and discarded the old electoral list. The time given for the registration of voters was nine days, including a Sunday, starting from 17th to 25th November.

This measure prevented voters who were on the electoral roll for years or might have been abroad for personal reasons from being registered, unless they returned before the deadline. This resulted in the disenfranchisement of a large section of voters who for economic reasons had sought temporary residence in the U.S. Virgin Islands. Voters who were mostly affected were the large numbers of Antiguans who were seasonal workers in the U.S. Virgin Islands, and did not have the means to return home on such short notice to register.

The lowering of the voting age to 18 years by the Parliament brought a large number of new voters onto the electoral roll, and the electoral list jumped from 18,000 to 26,000. Both Parties were very active in getting their supporters to register and the Antigua Labour Party was confident after the registration that they had the edge over the PLM, for the greater majority of the youths were disenchanted with the government and indicated their preference for the Labour Party. There were no changes in the seventeen constituencies.

The Governor, Sir Wilfred Jacobs, upon the advice of the Premier, George Walter, dissolved Parliament on the 1st February 1976, and new elections were set for the 18th February, to take the opposition by surprise. The ALP was well geared for such an eventuality and welcomed the calling of the elections. Intensive campaigns by both Parties were highlighted by huge motor-cades. The Antigua Labour Party campaign slogan was *"Back to work with Labour.*

The Antigua Labour Party brought out its Manifesto several weeks before the elections were called, in which it pledged the re-introduction of sugar production and the gradual abolition of personal income tax, supported by a white paper indicating the means by which elimination of such taxes would be accomplished. The manifesto also promised the establishment of a Youth Parliament and a local Government for Barbuda. The oppressive Press Laws, the Agency Shop and other peremptory measures that were introduced by the PLM Government would be repealed.

The PLM did not present its Manifesto until about five days before the elections, which was a repetition of previous promises.

Election Day, the 18th February 1976, was quiet and peaceful. There were no incidents reported as the voters seemed intent on going about the business of voting for the candidates of their choice.

As the first results of the voting started to trickle in during the night, there were early surprises for both sides. Robert Hall, the incumbent, took the St. Mary's North seat, which was contested by Hugh Marshall, the ALP candidate. This seat was considered a certain win for Marshall. On the other hand, Christopher O'Mard the ALP candidate, defeated Sidney Christian the PLM Deputy Speaker of the House of Representatives, in the St John's City South Constituency. Later results indicated that there was a direct swing of the voters towards the Labour Party, but the results were breathtakingly close in several constituencies, and showed how very well entrenched the PLM had become.

In the early hours of the morning of the 19th February, it was clear that the ALP won the Elections with ten seats against five for the PLM. One independent, Claude Earl Francis, who had broken with the PLM, won against four other candidates in Barbuda and there was a tie between Reuben Harris (ALP) and Edison Lewis (PLM) in St. Phillips North. Upon a Judicial Decision, the seat was awarded to Harris by four votes out of six that were in dispute. These votes were marked in ink instead of pencil and were first considered as spoilt votes by the Returning Officer.

The successful candidates in the elections were:

Antigua Labour Party	Progressive Labour Movement	Independent
V.C. Bird, Sr.	George Walter	Claude Earl Francis
Lester Bird	Robert Hall	
V.C. Bird, Junior	Donald Halstead	
Donald Christian	Victor McKay	
Adolphus Freeland	Charlesworth Samuel	
Reuben Harris		
Joseph Myers		
Christopher O'Mard		
John St. Luce		
Ernest Williams		
Robin Yearwood		

Among the former Ministers or ranking members of the PLM who were defeated were Basil Peters, Gerald Watt, Selvin Walter, Sydney Prince, Geoffrey Scotland and Sidney Christian, the Deputy Speaker of the House of Representatives.

With the Antigua Labour Party winning the elections, the Governor, Sir Wilfred Jacobs called upon V.C. Bird, Sr., the Leader of the Party, to form a government and to advise him on the appointment of Senators.

— V.C. Bird became Premier and Minister of External Affairs

— Lester Bird was appointed Deputy Premier and Minister of Trade, Industry & Economic Development

— Ernest Williams, Minister of Public Works & Tourism

— Joseph Myers, Minister of Education, Health & Culture

— Adolphus Freeland, Minister of Home Affairs & Labour

— Cosmos Phillips was appointed to the Senate and as Attorney General

— John St. Luce, Minister of Agriculture, Lands & Fisheries

— Reuben Harris, after winning his seat, became Minister of Finance

— Lionel Hurst was appointed Minister without portfolio, responsible for Tourism and Leader of the Senate;

— Christopher O'Mard, Minister without portfolio attached to the Premiers Office

— Hugh Marshall was appointed to the Senate and as Parliamentary Secretary to the Minister of Trade, Industry & Economic Development

— Donald Christian, Parliamentary Secretary to the Minister of Agriculture, Lands & Fisheries.

— Upon certain negotiations, Claude Earl Francis, the Barbuda elected independent member, accepted appointment as Minister of Barbuda Affairs.

Apart from the Senators named above, the remaining Senators appointed were:

— Keithly Heath, President

— Bradley T. Carrott, Deputy President

— Donald Sheppard

— William (Bill) Abbott

— W. Walbrook (representing Barbuda)

— Selvin Walter and Keithlyn Smith, representing the PLM Opposition.

— Casford Murray was elected speaker of the House of Representatives from outside the elected members.

Soon after the appointment of Cosmos Phillip as Attorney-General, it was realised that he could not constitutionally serve both in the Senate and the House of Representatives. He resigned from the Senate and Lauriston Jacobs was appointed in his place. In 1977, Jacobs resigned from the Senate for an appointment in the Antigua Trade Office in New York, and Eustace Cochrane was appointed in his place as a Senator.

Following their appointment as Ministers of Government, Lionel Hurst, the President of the Antigua Trades and Labour Union, and Adolphus Freeland, the General Secretary, resigned their posts with the union. They were succeeded by William Robinson as President and Tanny Rose as General Secretary.

Since the change of government in 1976, Antigua took on a new lease on life. The first visible evidence of this change was seen on the faces of the people. Gone were the tensions and hostility that were so visibly pronounced during 1971 to early 1976, almost overnight, the people seemed to have begun smiling again.

There was also visible evidence of the Government's activities to re-vitalize the economic life of the State. Several new small factories came to life, providing new jobs for a job-hungry populace; strong efforts were also exerted to restore the Sugar Industry. The Petroleum Refinery at Friar's Hill which was closed in 1975, reopened under new ownership, with the government retaining a substantial financial interest in the ownership. The government purchased the refinery after the previous owners closed it.

The Tourist Industry was playing a vital role in the economy as the leading industry and its recovery and expansion had a great impact on the people's lives. There was however, an urgent need for several larger hotels to double the existing capacity to meet the growing interest in Antigua as a first-class tourist destination. As a supplement to this expansion, a new airport terminal building with capacity to meet the growth of tourism was constructed at Coolidge Airport through a grant from the Canadian Government. Also, the telephone system was improved and extended to provide an all-island efficient service with overseas connection. During the winter of 1977-1978, Antigua was the host to a greater number of cruise ships with more tourists than ever before, and there were indications that this was a sector of tourism with useful growth.

During 1976, the Antigua Government, under a delegation to Washington, D.C. led by Premier V.C. Bird, successfully negotiated a financial agreement with the Carter Administration in Washington, for the lease of the American Bases, occupied by U.S. service people stationed in Antigua. The U.S. Government agreed to pay a sum, the equivalent of approximately EC$4m to the government, over an eleven year period of the lease. This was the first time since the Bases Agreement was negotiated by Winston Churchill and President Roosevelt during World War II, that Antigua and Barbuda received any direct financial remittance for the properties.

In February 1978, the Government completed its low income housing project at Pigotts, Parham and Potters, where 125 units were built. The project which commenced in April 1977, continued in other areas of the island. Plans were finalised to clear the slums in Fibrey. The PLM Government had started a building programme at Cassada Gardens for middle income families which was put on hold prior to the elections. The ALP Government revived the programme, and built more houses at the Cassada Gardens site.

A new Administration Building, which housed several Government Ministries was constructed on the site of the Bishop Mather Girls' Elementary School adjacent to Country Pond on East Street. The British Government funded the project, which was built with direct labour from the Department of Public Works.

The Government in following through the promises in their Manifesto, abolished personal income tax. Despite the fact that this direct revenue source was removed, the economy's growing buoyancy created other sources of revenue to compensate for any shortfalls.

The Government abolished the Press Laws that imposed financial hardships on the newspapers, and the press was free again to carry out its functions. At the time, there were only two newspapers that were published bi-weekly or weekly, the Workers' Voice bi-weekly and The Leader weekly. The Workers' Voice supported the Government while the Leader supported the Opposition Party. The Afro-Caribbean Liberation Movement in Antigua (ACLM) distributed a fortnightly publication called the Outlet. There were no other independent newspapers.

The Government abolished the Agency Shop and restored legislation, which prevented the deduction of union dues from workers salaries, without their written consent.

The Government also restored the Industrial Court in an effort to bring about a more stable and peaceful labour climate. Mr. Justice Percy Lewis, a former Justice of Appeal and acting Chief Justice of the Associated State Supreme Court, was appointed President of the Industrial Court. Throughout his career, Justice Lewis was noted for his impartiality and sound decisions, however, his appointment came under strong and vitriolic attack by members of the PLM, and in particular, by Halstead and Opposition Leader, George Walter. On the 15th February 1978, Mr. Justice Bishop in the High Court dismissed a motion by Neil Farrel, a member of the Antigua Workers' Union, which challenged the constitutional validity of the Industrial Court.

The Antigua Workers' Union attempted to repeat the disruptive labour tactics it initiated between 1967 and 1971, however, they found a different display of strength by the Government than what was in evidence previously, and in many respects, the Government's approach was effective. Consequently, the leaders of the Opposition began a campaign abroad to enlist sympathy for their efforts.

The AT&LU made a gradual recovery within the means at its disposal. Gone were the days of its full and complete monopoly in the labour field; however, with strong membership support and sound leadership, it continued to play an important role in the life of the State and acted as a stabilising influence among workers.

The Union was 40 years old in January, 1979, and had come a long way. The contribution it made to Antigua and Barbuda over the years was substantial, and now forms an integral part of the country's history.

CHAPTER 25
ARRESTS OF FORMER MINISTERS

Before and during the 1976 general election campaign, the Antigua Labour Party promised the electorate that if it were returned to power, it would be committed to investigating the PLM Government's blatantly shocking behaviour, and the wide-ranging rumours and charges of corruption that was raised against that Government.

The Labour Party Government, upon taking office, hired an impartial firm of chartered accountants from Canada to audit the Government's accounts. The audit revealed a number of irregularities in the accounts, and the new ALP Government decided to set up a Commission of Inquiry to investigate the irregularities involving certain former Government Ministers and civil servants. The Commission began hearings in September, 1976, headed by a Trinidad and Tobago retired Judge, Karl de la Bastide, as Chairman, Mr. S.M. Supersad, a retired Commissioner of Income Tax for Trinidad and Tobago, and Mr. George Thomas, a former warden of Anguilla.

The former Ministers who were under investigation refused to attend the Commission Hearings, by filing writs with the High Court through their lawyers, contesting the legality of the Commission. However, the Commission met and took evidence from numerous witnesses, and as a result of its findings and recommendations, the Attorney-General issued orders for the arrest of former Premier, George Walter, Sidney Prince, a former Minister of Finance, and Donald Halstead of the Antigua Public Utilities Authority. Halstead was charged with fraud among other counts, Walter and Prince with conspiracy to defraud the Government.

After the prolonged preliminary inquiries in which attorneys for the defence to rescind the charges filed several motions, the cases were sent to trial at the assizes. Sir Lionel Luckoo and Mr. Fenton Ramsohoye, two famous criminal lawyers from Guyana, appeared for defendants Walter and Prince at the Commission's Inquiry and the preliminary hearings. Time Kendall assisted by Mr. Conrad Richards appeared for the Crown during the Commission of Inquiry and Mr. Karl Hudson-Phillips, a former Attorney-General of Trinidad and Tobago, assisted by Conrad Richards, appeared for the Crown at the preliminary hearings for Halstead.

The preliminary hearings on the charges of conspiracy to defraud the Government against Sidney Prince and George Walter were heard during January, 1978, and continued to early May, 1978. The presiding Magistrate concluded that a *prima facie* case was made against the two former Government Officials, and ordered them to stand trial at the Assizes.

The three accused, Walter, Prince and Halstead, made appeals to the Privy Council with the hope that the Privy Council would accept arguments to drop the charges that were brought against them. The Privy Council dismissed the appeals.

With all sources of relief exhausted, Donald Halstead who was out on bail and had received authorisation to leave the Island on business to return prior to his preliminary hearings, skipped bail and did not return. He then became a fugitive of the law.

On the 29th January 1979, in the High Court of Justice, George Walter and Sydney Prince appeared to answer charges against them, Case No. 23 of 1978 - The Queen versus George Walter and Sydney Prince.

The case was heard by a jury and presided over by Justice Eric Bishop, the resident puisine Judge. Mr. Karl Hudson-Phillips of Trinidad and Tobago and Mr. Lloyd C. Williams, Director of Public Prosecutions, Antigua, appeared for the Crown. Sir Lionel Luckhoo and Mr. Lloyd Luckhoo of Guyana, assisted by Mr. Sydney Christian and Mr. Gerry Watt appeared for the defendants.

George Walter was charged with two counts of Misbehaviour in Public Office Contrary the Common Law, False Pretense Contrary to Section 25 (a) of the Larceny Act, Cap 44 of the Revised Laws of Antigua (1962); Sydney Prince was charged with Conspiracy to Defraud Contrary to the Common Law.

The case lasted well into three weeks. The jury brought a Not Guilty Verdict on the conspiracy charge and Prince was discharged. The jury, however, found Walter Guilty on all three counts. Mr. Justice Bishop sentenced him to eight years imprisonment to run concurrently, which worked out to three calendar years of imprisonment. The verdict was appealed.

Walter's imprisonment and Halstead's flight left two vacancies in the Parliament which would have called for by-elections in the two constituencies of All Saints and St. John's City North. Robert Hall, the PLM's Deputy Leader assumed the leadership of the Party and the position of Leader of the Opposition in Parliament.

Walter's appeal to the Associated States Court of Appeal was allowed. The Judge found that there were several trial errors during the conduct of the case and Walter was set free.

David Rose was born in British Guiana, now Guyana. He succeeded Ian Turbott who was transferred to Grenada as Administrator. Later Rose was appointed Governor-General of Guyana when that country became independent on 26th May, 1966. He was unfortunately killed in an accident while on an official visit to London, on 10th November, 1969.

Dominica became an Independent Republic on 3rd November, 1978; St Lucia became independent 22nd February 1979; St Vincent became independent 27th October, 1979 and St. Kitts and Nevis became independent 19th September, 1983.

CHAPTER 26
SPORTS AND SOCIAL EVENTS

It would not be fitting to close the history of this period without making reference the rapid strides Antigua made in sports, especially cricket, nor to mention some of the people who had made such contributions.

Credit should go to the PLM Government for the keen interest that was taken during its term of office in employing a sports officer, Danny Livingston, an Antiguan who made a name for himself in County Cricket in England, to coach and promote the Department of Sports in Antigua.

During this period, Antigua made rapid progress in both cricket and football and contributed greatly to the cricket strength of the combined Windward and Leeward Islands team in the Regional Shell Cricket Tournaments.

Two outstanding cricket players emerged in Antigua during this period and became internationally famous as world cricketers. Vivi Richards was hailed as one of the best batsmen in world cricket and Andy Roberts among the best of the fast bowlers. These two athletes became permanent members of the West Indies Test Teams and distinguished themselves in their various fields. Vivi Richards was not only a great batsman, but an outstanding fieldsman and a useful spin bowler.

Cricket is the National Sport of Antigua, and over the years, a number of outstanding cricketers emerged to make names for themselves in Leeward Islands Cricket. Many of the cricketers lacked the opportunities for developing their skills; some could very well have made a West Indian Test side if the opportunities were available to them.

Some of these outstanding cricketers included, Batsmen: Campbell Barrow, H. Willock, Clarence (Joker) Christian, Harold Mannix, Sydney Walling, Patrick Nanton, Arrindel (Babats) Joseph, Derryk Michael, Leonard Gore; Bowlers: Donald

Christian, John Lushington Jeffrey, Steadman Walling, Willie Gore, Gladwyn Bryant, Malcolm Richards (father of Viv), Eustace (Tuss) Matthews, Ralph Christian, Adolphus Freeland. Both Mannix and Joseph were good bowlers and outstanding fieldsmen. Edgar (Dreadnought) Berridge, then living in Antigua, played for St. Kitts, and could have been called up to bowl all day if it were necessary.

The Antigua football team is now a force to be reckoned with in regional football and has chalked up a number of successes.

Netball is a favourite game for Antiguan female athletes, who have been competing with much success against other West Indian teams. Tennis is also becoming another popular sporting activity.

In 1976, Antigua sent a small contingent of athletes to compete in the Summer Olympics Games in Montreal. While the team was not successful in any of the final events, its participation in the Olympics was an indication of Antigua's readiness to advance in international sports.

One social event that has taken roots in Antigua is the Annual Summer Carnival -the last week in July to the first Monday and Tuesday of August. Carnival saw its inception in 1956, and is now a major cultural event, bringing thousands of visitors to the Island each summer.

There is also the Annual Sailing Week which started in 1967 and has grown to tremendous dimensions. This event takes place in April to May and yachts from around the world assemble at Nelson's Dockyard to participate in the various sailing events.

Tennis has also become an international Sport in Antigua with the Annual Tennis Week, in which ranking international tennis players participate.

On 28th October 1977, Her Majesty the Queen and H.R.H. Prince Phillip, Duke of Edinburgh, visited Antigua on the occasion of their *Silver Jubilee Tour* of Commonwealth countries. In Antigua, they met the Premiers and Governors of other Associated States and Montserrat. Her Majesty also presented the accolade of Knighthood to Dr. Sir Luther Reginald Wynter, who was made a Knight Bachelor in her Silver Jubilee Honours List.

Sir Luther Wynter, a Jamaican, lived and served in Antigua for nearly fifty years. He made a sterling contribution to Antigua in medicine and in many social and charitable fields of endeavour. He and his wife, Lady Arah, celebrated their Golden Wedding Anniversary on 26th November 1977.

Antigua lost two of her outstanding Sons during December, 1976, in the death of Dr. Lionel Thomas, then Commissioner in Canada for the Eastern Caribbean Associated States and the Very Rev. Dean Fitzroy Pestaina of the St. John's Anglican Cathedral.

On the 18th February 1978, Claude Earl Francis, the representative for Barbuda, an outstanding criminal lawyer and one time Minister for Barbuda Affairs in the ALP Government, died. This called for a by-election in Barbuda, which was won by Eric Burton, an independent candidate.

CHAPTER 27
A GUIDE TO THE FUTURE

There were many charges and speculations about corruption, nepotism, conflicts of interest and other political sins against politicians, not only in Antigua, but throughout the Commonwealth Caribbean. The time came when effective policies and rules governing those who held and aspired to hold office in Government as Ministers, Parliamentary Secretaries, Legislators and Civil Servants should be addressed and strictly applied.

The professional politician has a right to a respectable living from his efforts as do any other professional, be he doctor, lawyer or otherwise. The politician has a precarious profession, fundamentally based upon the will of the electorate, with a great responsibility to carry if elected to office. In the discharge of this responsibility might hang the tale between progress and decline of a country, between the maintenance of established standards and constitutions, or their destruction.

Democratic developed and developing societies have by trial and error and by long experience, unless they are to drift into fascism, accepted and maintained the institutions of political parties from which may flow the experienced and competent politician, capable of governing the country wisely and efficiently. Politics is not a ticket pulled out of a hat of votes, but a science and an art. Experience has shown that intelligent persons who might be successful in their businesses or professions, made very sorry politicians.

With the realisation of these facts has come the need for proper provisions to be made for those elected, or appointed to office, to enable them to discharge their duties fearlessly, without having to resort to bribes, extortion, kick-backs, nepotism and other corrupt practices, in an effort to maintain themselves and their families. The laws of almost every democratic country in the world are very precise and strict in these matters and any whisper of corruption is investigated thoroughly, and if sufficient evidence is forthcoming, the offender is brought to trial.

In most Commonwealth countries, even a remote connection of a Minister of Government with conflict of interest or corrupt practice, is sufficient to cause his resignation or dismissal from office; or might even bring down his Government. Unfortunately for some of these islands, possible political immaturity of the majority populace and the lack of a responsible, virile and fearless press, some politicians who hold office consider the islands they govern as private estates to deny rights to some and to give more than their rights to others. Some politicians openly abuse their offices and the people's trust for personal wealth or comfort.

No politically alert society can tolerate this type of conduct for too long. Just as the people, the Congress and press of the U.S.A. endeavoured to get to the bottom of the Watergate scandal and brought the offenders to justice, the people of Antigua and the other Caribbean Islands must be prepared to exercise the necessary restraints on their politicians and make them adhere to the proper modes of conduct, or remove them from office.

The Parliament and people of Antigua must therefore, be prepared to face reality, and like other democratic countries, provide reasonable remuneration to their elected and appointed representatives, so as to remove the temptation from those responsible to accept bribes and kick-backs that might come their way. With a good system of remuneration and pension security, there can be no excuse acceptable from the politician that goes astray, and he should be brought to account for any misdeeds he might commit. There are numerous rules and regulations that exist throughout the Commonwealth that apply to the conduct of Ministers and public servants, and every effort should be exerted to enforce similar rules of conduct in Antigua. Any hesitation in this matter can only create serious questions of doubt in the moral integrity of the State. What we need most in these West Indian Islands are leaders imbued with moral and spiritual integrity who have a dedication towards establishing high standards of value, unswayed by expediency, greed and other selfish motives, and who can set the pattern for a just and decent society.

In Christian communities such as Antigua, there are certain ethical and moral codes that strengthen the pillars of the society, chiefly among which is the institution of family life. It is the combined moral fabric of family life that forms the sinews of the nation, thereby providing the resilience and the strength to face fluctuating fortunes and to withstand adversity; the strength of the family unit multiplies and extends through the national family, so breathes new and fresh vitality into the life of the nation.

If the moral fibre of family life is contaminated, the nation is certain to be morally weak. While politicians, like all citizens are entitled to privacy in their private lives, it must be accepted that a greater degree of discretion and restraint is necessary to be displayed in private and public conduct by those who aspire to high positions in the country. Government Ministers and other Parliamentarians and civil servants are continually in the public eye. They come under public scrutiny and they can be an example for good or bad to their admirers and supporters, even to their foes. To them therefore, is a greater obligation, particularly in new societies such as the West Indies , to as far as possible and with due consideration to human frailties, respect the moral standards that form the fabric of society and family life, and do not be contemptuous of them.

To do otherwise would be to sow the seeds of degeneracy from which could spring a crop of moral turpitude and other evils that could be a curse to future generations. Notwithstanding the fact that every ounce of strength must be exerted towards re-building and restoring the prosperity of the country, to concentrate only on this effort and to ignore the influences of corruption and corruptive practices and open immoral conduct, would be inviting calamity on this fair country that needs a chance to survive.

A great deal hinges on the wider political and social education of the people and it is in this area that the Press, as the Fourth Estate, can play an influential and predominant role. Some politicians, for their own selfish interest, seek to have a captive, or servile press, or none at all, for within this framework, their wrongs usually go unchallenged and their governments bear all the hallmarks of dictatorships, be they benevolent or tyrannical.

In a free society however a responsible free and courageous press is a boon to good government because it keeps politicians and others on their toes. The Press is the watchdog of Governments and of wrong-doers and so helps to protect society from destroying itself.

The Press might seem to some people to be a busy-body, but it has its role to play. That is why it is protected within the fundamentals of freedom of speech enshrined in all democratic constitutions. In its role of shaping public opinion, is a great responsibility, and, it should at all times, display fairness and adhere to the truth; criticise constructively without malice, expose wrongs and support what is right. With a vigorous Press in Antigua fulfilling its appointed role, all will be well.

Efforts must also be exerted in improving the quality of life - a healthy mind in a healthy body. Cultural developments together with sports and other social activities, must receive active support by Government and not merely the lip service of the past. It is not sufficient to leave this important segment of national life to the voluntary efforts of a few overworked and willing enthusiasts.

It has come to be realised and accepted by all progressive governments that recreation and the enjoyment of recreation are essential to the happiness and development of a community as the very food consumed by the citizens. Government's contribution to this sector of national life has become greater and greater, and Antigua cannot remain behind in this respect. The efforts of the ALP Government in developing athletic programs have been encouraging and must continue.

One other aspect of development for Antigua must be a greater and more meaningful participation of the people in the political life of the State - termed in some places as Participatory Democracy. That is to say that the people should be able to associate themselves with Government at all levels. The population has become more politically savvy and educated than in the past. The centralising of power and authority that was allowed to develop over the past twenty years or so cannot be suitable to a newly-emerging democratic country, within which people have developed an appetite for politics.

The institution of Local Government in Antigua and Barbuda must be considered and accepted as a necessary measure of social and political development for the State.

During 1976, the ALP Government lived up to its promise by establishing the first local government in Barbuda, which tackled its duties with enthusiasm and vigour. However, local government has not yet been considered for Antigua.

Legally-constituted village districts and town councils enjoying limited powers and authority will bring democracy closer to the people than what they now enjoy and would well serve as a stabilising social finance for the future. Local Councils in Antigua could also present the opportunity to many budding politicians to channel their energies and work off some political steam in useful debates amid activities among their peers. This opportunity is now denied to most, because of the limited openings at the central and national levels.

Democracy is not a cheap commodity. While there might be arguments against additional cost of establishing these councils or against de-centralising certain powers and authority, anything that contributes to improving the quality of life of a people or brings them closer to governing themselves in the real Lincolnian sense of government - for and by the people - is worth paying for. For in essence, it is the people who make the country and provide the tools by which they are governed; it is to them that the real power belongs.

Persistent efforts must be pursued to bringing education at the University level within physical reach of the people of the Island, to reduce the burdens placed on local citizens whose children may not be fortunate to receive any of the limited scholarships available to pay exorbitant tuition.

Consideration should, therefore, be given to locally establishing an intermediate if not fully accredited college or faculty of Arts and Sciences, to accommodate local students who want to pursue university courses in these disciplines, rather than compelling them to go to one of the larger West Indian Islands for this purpose. An agreement could be worked out with the University of the West Indies, for authority to develop higher education in the State.

The effort of the Government to foster the establishment of a medical school in Antigua to train American and other medical students could therefore, be considered a major step in the right direction. This could lead the way to Antigua once again becoming a major centre of education in the Caribbean.

If Antigua can chart a course along the lines mentioned above, there could be reasonable expectations for a future of greater promise. Achieving these objectives will mean sacrifices and hard work by the entire nation, and a national effort with the will to achieve, guided by fearless, inspired and collective leadership.

The locust years took their toll on the lives of all Antiguans and Barbudans - for good or bad – we were all affected. It is hoped that those years are now behind us and may serve as a lesson for the future, rather than the means of social division and partisan feuding.

The two-party State is now firmly established in Antigua and Barbuda and efforts should be made to preserve it as a fundamental pillar of our national life. However, the process of democracy must enshrine our political institutions and there needs to be continuing growth and lessons in tolerance and respect for the other man's point-of-view and honest acceptance that no party or man has all the answers.

Opposition parties in a democratic country are not created to tear down or destroy, but to help to build through constructive criticism, and even at times, by honest agreement. In like manner, democratic governments are not elected to ride roughshod over the will of the people, nor to impose harsh and unconstitutional measures, nor to indulge in sectarian discriminatory rule. This would be raw totalitarianism.

Antigua and Barbuda suffered ten years of social and economic setbacks in her painful growth to full democracy. There might have been material losses as a result, but the society might yet be better for this experience. The answer rests with the people.

In the present state of the country, the words of the late U.S. President, John F. Kennedy, in his Inaugural Address to the people in 1961 seem to have a very significant meaning: *"Ask not what your country can do for you, but what you can do for your country?"* With the full motivation of all Antiguans and Barbudans to this end, Antigua and Barbuda can rise again like the phoenix from the ashes and go on to a greater destiny.

CHAPTER 28
1980 GENERAL ELECTIONS

General Elections were called on the 24th April, 1980, after Parliament was dissolved by His Excellency, the Governor, on the advice of the Premier. Elections were not due before March, 1981, but the move in calling early elections was prompted by the Government's desire to proceed to independence by the end of 1980 and to accordingly secure a mandate for that purpose.

The ALP in their manifesto for the 1976 elections did not declare specifically for independence during the five year period, unless the people decided by way of a referendum. The Party felt that priority had to be given to reviving Antigua's economy, of creating jobs and eliminating the 40% unemployment index, so as to make Independence more meaningful. The Labour Party was also hesitant to support the P.L.M. Government in attaining Independence if that party had won the elections. This was mainly due to its record of misgovernment, corruption and attempts to erode civil liberties.

When the A.L.P. did decide under V.C. Bird that independence was necessary for Antigua's recovery, the P.L.M. Party called foul, and appealed directly to the British Government that independence should not be granted before the Government had a mandate from the people. While the previous Labour Party Government in Britain was willing to grant immediate Independence, the new Tory Government felt that, in as much as the Antigua Labour Party did not seek a full mandate for Independence in 1976, it would be advisable for them to seek such a mandate by way of General Elections.

The 1980 General Elections saw the entry of a new political pressure group into parliamentary politics for the first time. This was the Antigua Caribbean Liberation Movement (A.C.L.M.), formerly the Afro Caribbean Liberation Movement, led by Leonard (Tim) Hector. The Marxist oriented party attracted several dissident young teachers, who were dismissed from Civil Service after a series of teacher's unrest.

The Labour Party contested all 17 seats. The P.L.M. contested 16 seats, omitting Barbuda, where the independent candidate was a P.L.M. supporter. The A.C.L.M. contested 9 seats.

The election results were an overwhelming victory for the ruling Labour Party, which won 13 of the 17 Constituency seats; P.L.M. won 3 seats, while the Barbuda seat was retained by the independent candidate. Newcomers to the House of Representatives were:

- Hugh Marshall, former Minister Without Portfolio in the Senate, who defeated Victor McKay in St. Mary's South.

- Hilroy Humphreys, an A.L.P. newcomer, won the All Saints seat previously held by George Walter, who could not run in the 1980 General Elections, pending a decision in his appeal to the Associated States Court of Appeals, against his conviction of Misbehaviour in Public Office. Hyacinth Walter, George Walter's wife contested the seat and was narrowly defeated by Humphreys.

- George Pigott, a P.L.M. newcomer won St. John's City West seat formerly held by Donald Halstead, who skipped bail and disappeared before his trial. All other seats remained intact for the A.L.P.

Those elected to the ALP were:

Vere C. Bird Sr.	St. John's Rural North
Lester B. Bird	St. John's Rural East
Ernest E. Williams	St. Paul's
Reuben H. Harris	St. Phillip's South
Hilroy R. Humphreys	All Saints
Hugh C. Marshall	St. Mary's South
Joseph A. Myers	St. Peter's
Adolphus E. Freeland	St. George's
Donald D. Christian	St. John's Rural West
Christopher M. O'Marde	St. John's City South

Vere C. Bird, Jr.	St. John's Rural South
John St. Luce	St. John's City East
Robin S. Yearwood	St. Phillips North

For the P.L.M.:

Robert V. Hall	St. Mary's North
George A. Pigott	St. John's City West
Charlesworth T. Samuel	St. Luke's

The A.C.L.M. did not win any seat. The highest number of votes returned by an A.C.L.M. candidate was 69 votes for Leon (Chacku-Wacku) Symester. Leonard (Tim) Hector, Leader of the Party, received only 45 votes. Eric Burton representing the Island constituency of Barbuda was the only independent candidate.

The total votes cast for the Labour Party were 12,742; the P.L.M. secured 8,655; the A.C.L.M. 265; while the lone Independent Candidate polled 251.

V.C. Bird Sr. was invited by the Governor, Sir Wilfred E. Jacobs, to form a Government. In addition to the appointment of the new Cabinet, the following ten senators were recommended for appointment according to the Constitution:

Bradley T. Carrott	President
Donald Sheppard	Vice President
Lionel Hurst	Minister without Portfolio and Leader of Government Business in the Senate
Eustace Cochrane	
William (Bill) Abbott	
Wilbert Sterling	
Robin Bascus	
W. Walbrook	Barbuda
Basil A Peters	Opposition
Geoffrey Scotland	Opposition

The Cabinet Comprised of:

| V.C. Bird | Premier |
| Lester Bird | Deputy Premier and Minister of Economic Development and Tourism |

Ernest Williams	Minister of Public Works & Communications
Keith Forde	Attorney-General
John St. Luce	Minister of Finance
Adolphus Freeland	Minister of Labour and Barbuda Affairs
Reuben Harris	Minister of Education
Joseph Myers	Minister of Public Utilities
Christopher O'Marde	Minister of Health
Robin Yearwood	Minister of Agriculture

Ministers without Portfolio were:

Lionel Hurst, Hugh Marshall and D.E. Christian

Casford S. Murray, a well known St. John's businessman was elected Speaker of the House of Representatives.

V.C. Bird, Jr. was elected Deputy Speaker.

Hilroy Humphreys was appointed Parliamentary Secretary in the Ministry of Economic Development and Tourism.

On the morning of May 12, 1980, the United States Government opened a consulate in St. John's to serve the Leeward Islands and the British Virgin Islands. It was expected that upon the attainment of Independence by Antigua, the Consulate would be upgraded to an Embassy. A British Government office and a Venezuelan Consulate were already in residence in Antigua. It was anticipated that other countries would open offices in Antigua after Independence.

In December 1981, a delegation from Antigua and Barbuda attended a Constitutional Conference in London to negotiate Independence of the Associated State with the British Government.

The delegation comprised members of the Government and a cross section of Labour Party supporters, members of the Official Opposition and a Barbuda delegation to address matters that affected the relationship between Antigua and Barbuda in connection with an Independent Nation.

The Conference, while reserving some Barbuda matters to be settled at a future date, agreed to independence for Antigua and Barbuda for November 1st, 1981.

APPENDIX 3
FEDERATE NOW
1958

A case for a Federation of the West Indies Associated States:
Antigua
Dominica
Grenada
Montserrat
St. Kitts – Nevis – Anguilla
St. Lucia
St. Vincent and the Grenadines

CHAPTER 1
THE NEED FOR FEDERATION

A politically independent Federation of the West Indies Associated States seems to be the only logical step that might be taken by the leaders of Government at this time.

Already, the Regional Council of Ministers provides the nucleus of a loose Federation, and although there is no legal instrument such as a Federal Parliament, the agreements reached by the Council of Ministers are accepted by member States and are in many respects, morally if not legally binding, even though in the present-day context, political morality is feared to be the exception rather than the rule.

Having reached thus far with a temporary workable association, it would seem that the initiative to move to a more permanent arrangement is lacking. The question is, from whom should the initiative come? It is not easy to discard the aura of distrust and frustration that prevails around any federal talk in the West Indies. The present leaders are still too close to the failure of the first Federation (imaginary and real) and the abortive efforts to get the smaller Federation known as The Little Eight started. Therefore, it should not be surprising that the anomalous self-governing status secured from Britain is ardently protected.

On the other hand, it is a well known fact that there are a few leaders who are not satisfied with the present constitutional limitations and would like to go the final stages of self governance as a federation or alone.

It was feared that member nations' relations might erode, if one or more states went to independence individually, while others remained in an indefinite associated position. A potential federal alliance might become non-existent, if individual states sought singular associations or alignments.

The eagerness with which the Governments of the Eastern Caribbean, except

Montserrat, grasped Associated Status with Britain, stemmed from the desire to break from a colonial past, with the sober understanding and reminder that individual independence might be meaningless in their present economic settings. Some leaders even deluded themselves that Statehood was tantamount to Independence.

This perception was short-lived as the real facts began to emerge. Associated Status with Britain was a palliative – a satisfactory arrangement for the less ambitious politician, to bask under the false, non-existent security they felt Britain could provide. Events in the Eastern Caribbean Islands since Associated Status was introduced, proved how ineffective reliance on Britain had become - at least for internal security of individual states. Many countries had to endure the painful experience of diverting needed funds from social services to improving internal security.

The fact too that Associated Status with Britain and the retention of British citizenship by nationals of the Associated States did not give nationals the right of entry into Britain under the British Immigration Act, should have been irksome to Associated States leaders. Further, Associated States' Premiers were denied membership to the Commonwealth Prime Ministers' Club and could not gain admittance to the Prime Ministers' Conference in London. The Independent Commonwealth Territories - including those of the Caribbean - felt they were not qualified to attend, the criterion for membership being full and unqualified independence of each territory.

In Foreign Affairs, Britain still played a strong hand and the States had no alternative but to play an insignificant role, unless they wanted to bring an end to the association.

Was it desirable to continue an associated status with Britain that constituted little more than an appendage without the benefits that such association connotes?

Would Independence of the States - separately or jointly - deny them the right to the limited financial benefits they receive from Britain? This could hardly be the case, unless for some reason, Britain would make a special example to the states for being too ambitious and thus cannot be considered.

There is confirmed evidence of continuing assistance by Britain to a number of her former colonies, which became independent states. It was more than likely that the West Indies Associated States would fall into the category of Assisted Independent States. The fact too that the onus rested on the States themselves to determine their constitutional future, brought the matter within the area of competence. It was hardly likely that Britain could take unkindly to any movement that gave Associated Territories Independence in their own right, bearing in mind that the remainder of former West Indian colonies were already self ruled.

Steps were taken by the Associated States to establish a Common Market This was motivated as a measure of self-protection for Associated States' industries and commerce against the inevitable market saturation by CARITA products from the larger territories without compensatory arrangements, rather than a desire to create a political entity.

That a political association would eventually emerge through economic integration of the Associated States could not be denied. This seemed to be the corollary. Such an association could have been indefinitely delayed or truncated, if the opportunity was allowed to pass, and if individual states went haphazardly on their own to independence, or remained as they were for fear of independence, or of losing the quantum of aid they received from Britain.

The economic development of the states thou of utmost importance, should not over-shadow the need for political integration and independence. It is not absurd as some people might imagine for any one of the Associated States to go to independence alone, but it would be more meaningful and economically profitable for them to achieve it together.

West Indian Jeremiads criticised and condemned the achievement of independence by the West Indian Territories that formed the ill-fated West Indian Federation. Yet in every instance since attaining independence, these territories saw industrial expansion, and their revenue and Gross National Product (GNP) surpassed expectations. This only proved that there was nothing to lose by attaining independence, and everything to gain both psychologically and materially.

No matter how it is diagnosed or dissected, Associated Status is still a far cry from independence. It whets the appetite without appeasing the hunger. When nationals of the Associated States interact with friends and associates in Barbados, Trinidad & Tobago and Guyana who, without exception, acclaim pride in independence, how long can it be expected that the non-independent Associated States will care to remain appendages of Britain?

It is certain that the new generation will not have the patience to wait and will evoke the same spirit that took the other territories to autonomy.

The message is clear. The days of the established and long-tenured politicians will not be as rosy as in the past. Desertion and strife have shaken established political roots in the islands, and in some respects, considerable adjustments had to be made to avert disaster - adjustments that a few years ago would not have been countenanced, much more accommodated. Political vested interest is no longer secure, and this in itself is another factor with which to contend.

Will the present state of politics in some of the islands increase incumbent fears and impede the movement to independence? Will it be the means of drawing the Associated States closer together under an umbrella of Regional Security? Britain already displayed her reluctance in going to the aid of Civil Power in the States unless her interests were challenged. With all due respect to the pros and cons of Britain's motives, at the time of negotiating the self-governing constitution, there was at least one state, which thought it *infra dig* for Britain to contemplate such an adventure.

Notwithstanding that there was an understanding and agreement that upon request, Britain would go to the aid of a Government if the nature of the uprising warranted her intervention. Independence in Association or Associated Status, implies that the self-governing state should be in a position to deal with all internal matters, including armed uprising, without procuring outside help.

Sensing such an eventuality as an armed uprising, Britain proposed a Regional Security Force to be established by the law of the states, which could be used for law enforcement in any member state when needed. This Force did not reach beyond the paper stage.

The cost of maintaining such a Force, while not prohibitive, would have diverted considerable sums of money from the more essential task of developing the States' infrastructure and improving their social and public services; hence the delay in taking action. On the other hand, due to social unrest in some of the States, they were obligated to spend large sums of money to improve their local security forces. With the large recurrent expenditures those states incurred, pooling resources could have provided a Regional Force, perhaps at less cost to the individual states.

The truth is, Associated Status was contemplated as the better of two worlds, that is, independence without bearing the full cost and responsibility. Events proved that this was a misconception, which left the states with no world of their own. Rather than receiving the best, they have had to content themselves with little more than crumbs.

CHAPTER 2
ADVANTAGES OF FEDERATION

Although I was involved in the demise of two Federations, namely the 80-year-old Leeward Islands' Federation, which was dissolved as a pre-requisite for the member Presidencies to enter the larger Federation as Unit Territories of the West Indies' Federation, I never lost hope in the idea of Federation - at least for the smaller Islands of the West Indies. To me, it is still the only reasonable and logical solution.

In 1946, closer union of the Windward and Leewards Islands which formed the Associated States was considered practical at the St. Kitts' Conference; closer Union in 1946 is still not practicable today, and particularly in terms of independence, which was not contemplated in 1946. A Federation of the seven territories is a necessary measure of independence in its true meaning, should it be achieved and be of benefit to the people of the Associated States.

The fact too is, all the States with the possible exception of Montserrat, have comparable economies, similar problems and are nearly of similar size and population; they already enjoy shared common services, making it easier and advisable for them to create a Federal Structure of their own, which would have the full ingredients of equality for each State, without any one or two States having a dominant position, as is characteristic of many federations.

True, it is that exhaustive studies have been made of Federations for the West Indies. Moreover, with the failure of the Little Eight to materialise as a Federal entity, it might seem futile to go over a painful exercise so soon again, particularly in view of the revelations made in the <u>Agony of the Little Eight</u>, by Sir Arthur Lewis, the noted West Indian economist, who was born in St. Lucia, who exposed the frustrations that some who took part in the abortive effort had experienced.

Time and tide are not regulated by man, however, many people had to abandon their stated position or even go so far as to compromise their convictions in an effort to accommodate new situations that were forced upon them. The movement of change has been gathering pace in the West Indies, and one might well be prepared to adjust to making far-reaching decisions for the preservation of our democratic way-of-life, or be swept away in the whirlwind of ideological and disruptive movements that have begun to show their heads in the area.

The relevancy of the argument is dictated by facts and not surmise. It is well known that the failure of the Little Eight Federation was due more to their representatives inability to reach agreements, than in any insuperable difficulties in the agreements themselves. Some of the leaders of Government began to taste greater individual power which was secured after the break-up of the West Indies' Federation, and were reluctant to see their newly-won power reduced and passed on to a strong central government, which some were advocating. They all saw the need for a Federation, but were unable to resolve their differences and come to a workable compromise.

The net result was that the Antigua Delegation, although the foremost advocate of Federation for The Little Eight, became the strongest advocate of a weak Central Government and eventually withdrew from participation in further Federal Talks, when it was realized that there was no desire on the part of the others to go along with that proposal. Mr. Vere Bird Sr., the then Chief Minister of Antigua, had become enchanted with a Western Samoan-type of constitution and advocated it to his supporters. He was eventually persuaded to accept a constitution based on the pattern of the Cook Islands and this became the basis of the Associated States Constitution offered to Antigua and the other Territories, except Montserrat. Barbados knowing fully that Independence was already offered to her, found the Federal Talks a time-wasting exercise and abandoned the whole idea. Thus, the vision of the new Federation perished.

These events are now history, but their roots are in the present uncertainties of the Associated States with respect to the next step that should be taken. No doubt the Governments themselves are prepared to tread with utmost caution, so as not to disturb what may now be considered a tranquil state of affairs, or an innocuous association that is serving a useful purpose.

Despite a self-appointed silence on the issue of Federation among the Associated States' leaders, the matter is not dead. It is sure to pose a challenge to these leaders in the very near future.

The best State Flags and State Anthems do not give one a nationality; it is derives from national sovereignty, a goal that the Associated States had not achieved. Ask a man from Barbados what is his nationality. He looks at you with a glitter in his eyes and with a broad smile of satisfaction on his face says, "a Barbadian of course". Ask a man from Grenada or Antigua the same question, he does not know whether to say 'British' or 'Grenadian' or 'Antiguan'.

This must not be interpreted as an effort to decry British Nationality, for the British has every reason to be proud of their Nationality, their history and achievements. A British Passport is respected all over the world. In West Indian terms however, British Nationality for the West Indies still carries a colonial ring, and from racial conditions in Britain, the West Indian bearing British Nationality is an unwanted person in a country of which he is purported to be a citizen. Therein lies the contradiction.

Population wise, the West Indies' Associated States with over 500,000 people can be compared with a number of small Independent States in the world today. Even considering the Caribbean Commonwealth Territories, the population of the Associated States is twice that of Barbados and very close to that of Guyana, both of which are already Independent.

Economically, the potential of the combined Associated States is far beyond that of Barbados in relation to available land resources, tourism, agriculture and consumer market. With proper development of the infrastructure and the establishment of sound industries and marketing outlets, a viable economy could very well be the outcome within a short period of time.

A sound education system is essential to economic development. While the Associated States have had a long history of elementary education with a sprinkling of secondary education, it is only in recent years that there has been a step-up in the number of student placements provided in the secondary schools. Generally speaking, the standard of education in the islands has improved, but there is still the lack of educational facilities at the technical level to train personnel to meet the demands of a developing country.

Training at the technical level is not an insuperable task. Efforts have already been made by some Governments to establish trade schools. It does not appear that any meaningful development of technical training would be done at a regional level under regional direction and standard, with complementary schools located in some, if not all of the Islands.

Education at university level is already available at the various Campuses of the University of the West Indies, which is subsidised by the States. It might be possible to extend university level training to some of the islands through the development of Extra Mural Centres of the University, or by raising the standard at the existing teacher-training colleges. Codrington College in Barbados has been an example of an Extra Mural College taking the Durham University's Degrees for a number of years. It does appear therefore, that the real advantages of Federation are:

- Giving meaningful national identity to the people of the Associated States;
- Providing a central machinery at constitutional level to expedite and consolidate the overall economic development of the States, to safeguard, improve and expand internal marketing, trade and commerce and to secure external trust;
- Providing adequate safeguards for the internal security of the States and limited defence against external aggression;
- Providing the necessary representation abroad in areas where the external interests of the Associated States can best be served; and
- Pooling resources in the above fields, thereby reducing the costs that would be borne by each State, in undertaking the full responsibility of independence.

Any one of the above advantages could lay sufficient claims for federating. The combination makes the argument for Federation, even stronger and particularly in view of the fact that no valid argument has yet been established against Federation.

It seems that this is the most desirable and only course to be pursued.

CHAPTER 3
A POLITICAL NATIONALITY

Just as the German is a European, a Canadian, a North American, a Nigerian a West African, an Argentinian a South American, a Tanzanian an East African, so also is a Jamaican or St. Lucian as a West Indian. It must not be forgotten that a Cuban, Haitian, Puerto Rican or a Barbadian also has a claim to be West Indians, because the entire Archipelago stretching from Florida in the North to the Orinoco River in the South was named the West Indies, which is divided into the Greater and Lesser Antilles.

For our purpose, it was more because of a political grouping originally known as the British West Indies, the Romance, the use of convenience of the name that the architects of the first Federation decided the name of the Federation should be the West Indies and the Nationals, West Indians. It did not matter to the other independent West Indian countries, because they had already adopted their national names. The Puerto Ricans were American citizens and the people of Guadeloupe and Martinique were French. It can therefore be argued - why not develop your individual nationalities and be an Antiguan, a Grenadian or a Dominican in the same way as there are Barbadians, Jamaicans and Trinidadians. In short, let all of us go on to individual independence which is the right of all peoples. There is nothing at all wrong with that inasmuch as the Islands of the Associated States - with the exception of Montserrat - had the constitutional right to declare their independence.

However, Balkanization of these former West Indian Territories has already done tremendous damage to the area and caused a setback - both economically and socially - despite political independence and Independence in Association with Britain. Albeit the slight progress some individual territories made industrially on their own, West Indians at home and moreover those abroad - had lost faith, and the effect of independence has not psychologically or otherwise restored the feeling of pride and satisfaction that would have been evident if the territories had stayed together. In fact, the individual territorial independence of the West Indian Territories was shallow rather than a worthy device, and the scars of the misadventure remain.

West Indians abroad are considered as under one political hegemony by the people with whom they come into contact. They are not considered as Barbadians, or Kittsians, but as West Indians. Even in matters of External Affairs, Governments of major countries with whom the West Indian Territories have direct interests would much rather deal with a regional authority than ten or eleven individual states having the same problems and seeking to find similar, if not the same solutions for those problems.

There is no doubt that an error has been committed, but there is no reason to quadruplicate the same error. Experience has shown how intertwined the lives and fortunes of the people of the Associated States are. The same reasons that have driven the States into an association to tackle common problems and to deal with common services, are the same reasons that favour a common identity of the people. To sum it up, we are one people with one destiny, who deserve a common nationality. Hence we can change the West Indies' Associated States to a West Indies United States and give our people a West Indian Nationality, leaving the door open for the rest of the West Indian Countries to unite with us at some later date.

CHAPTER 4
TYPE OF FEDERATION

Federation must provide for a central government with adequate powers that enable it to perform its duties. There has been much discussion in the past as to the type of Federation that is best suited to the Islands. Because of the sharp differences of opinion to a strong or weak centre, the first Federation failed, and the second attempt at the smaller Federation did likewise.

It is evident that a compromise must be reached between the advocates of a strong Federation and those who strongly feel that the Units must not be stripped of certain powers, which they think is vital. In most Federations, there has been a continuous power-conflict between the States and the Centre, whereby the States are usually demanding a greater say in National Affairs, while some may want and are trying to see the central power eroded to the benefit of the States. Even in the old Federations such as Canada, steps are being taken to revise the Constitution in favour of the Provinces.

It would be expecting too much to think that a Federation of the West Indies could be set up to meet the full satisfaction of all participants. Now that the States themselves are already enjoying full internal powers and certain designated powers in external matters, it is conceivable that some who had before advocated a strong central government for a Federation, might have second thoughts and would be prepared to see a Federation with only sufficient powers to enable it to fulfil its vital interests, without encroaching on some of the powers the States now enjoy.

The vital interests of the Federal Government could be adequately confined to items (1) to (4) mentioned in Chapter 2 as Advantages in a Federation. To these should be added Immigration and Emigration and the Supreme Courts of the States.

There is adequate scope within these items to enable the Federal Government to expand its activities in domestic affairs and make a vital contribution to the economic, political and social stability of the States and of the Federation as a whole.

The admirable effort in establishing a common market for the Associated States with a common external tariff can only lead to a customs union and to the integration of the economies of the States. This in itself is political in character and could best be served by a central authority with adequate powers to ensure its smooth working and development.

The Common Market will have a greater attraction for investment capital than any single state could provide on its own, and it has greater advantages than a free trade area, which does not provide for a Common External Tariff nor for the free movement of peoples and goods in a common market and in a Federation.

As it is only the fruits of economic development that can provide the means whereby the social institutions and services of a country can be adequately improved and maintained - directly and indirectly - the Federal Government in its overall role in this sphere can be the axis about which the development of the states rotates.

The Regional Development Agency located in Antigua could play an important part in the industrial development of the States, if its role could be strengthened under Federal direction and prodding. As it is, it serves eight individual governments and could easily be exposed to be an impediment in its activities, due to the frustrating indecisions that are associated with the promotion and implementation of schemes that must be agreed upon by all or by a majority of Governments. The delay and uncertainty in setting up the Regional Development Agency is a vivid example of this experience.

The development of external trade is essential to developing countries which internal markets are not large enough to consume all that they produce. While agriculture has been and will continue to be vital to the economies of the Associated States, certain agricultural produce have been facing bad times. Unless the States are in a position to make trading agreements on a reciprocal basis with other countries, developing markets for some basic crops might require skilled salesmanship. The obvious tendency of the states is to go into high manufacturering;

here again, to make investment worthwhile, there must be an available market in which to sell the finished goods.

Whether it be manufactured products, raw materials or fruits and vegetables, the products of the Associated States have to face stiffer market competition in the near future from other producers. The importance of market research and experiments cannot be ignored; superior standards of quality must also be considered a necessary measure in marketing the goods produced. Success in these areas can more easily be achieved on a regional or Federal level with the authority to implement, than if left to individual states, which are occupied with more pressing national concerns.

Population growth is another matter that cannot be ignored. When measured according to current growth rates over the next twenty years, the population of the Associated States - barring any serious calamity - should be in the vicinity of one million people. This population increase is certain to pose economic problems for the Associated States, unless efforts are made to usefully absorb the available manpower.

With the outlet into Britain partially closed to West Indians, and with limited migration to the United States and Canada, the only available labour market to West Indians is the West Indies itself. There are Guyana and the larger Caribbean islands, but migration would depend on the country's immigration laws, its economy and the probability of a Federation with the other West Indian Territories.

Fortunately, the Associated States are not without available land space. Within our midst is Dominica, termed by Robert Bradshaw when he was Finance Minister of the West Indies Federation,as a sleeping giant among its small associates. Dominica has great potentials in its size, its rich alluvial soil and parental waters that are waiting to be tapped by a much larger population than the 250 persons per square mile on that Island.

The effective development of Dominica is far beyond the means of its State's Government; only a combined effort by both a Federal and State Governments with substantial outside help, that would open up the Island to reveal and develop its potentials. With freedom of movement in the Federation and the inevitable attraction of people to developing areas, one could easily see Dominica playing a leading role in economic development.

To a lesser degree is the availability of space in Nevis, Anguilla and Barbuda, three Islands are sparsely populated, but have potential value in their development of tourism and allied services; in the case of Nevis, agricultural potentials. With the prospects of Grenada and St. Vincent overwhelmed with surplus population, these mentioned island could become a haven for people from the Associated States seeking new opportunities and fresh fields. The saying, put down your bucket where you are could prove relevant in this respect.

CHAPTER 5
SECURITY OF THE STATES

The internal security of the Associated States individually or in a Federation, is an obvious necessity. No State or Federation can progress socially or economically if it is exposed to continuous uprisings or threats of uprising, which leads to an unstable Government. The State or Federation must have a strong deterrent against conditions and acts of violence, to safeguard the rights and interests of its citizens who desire a peaceful existence to enjoy the fruits of their labour.

All countries moving into independence have had to make provisions for their internal security, no matter how costly, as national security is a main component of independence. While treaties and guarantees might be arranged with a major friendly country to provide assistance, if the sovereignty or integrity of the State is threatened by outside aggression, it is universally accepted that any government which cannot maintain control within its own borders governs at the mercy of the mob.

There are signs throughout the Caribbean of social disintegration. The youth throughout the Region are restive and are exposed to the thoughts and movements that caused unrest in the United States, Europe and other parts of the world. We seem to be approaching an age of violence and complete anarchy.

The Anguilla insurgency and to a lesser extent, the Antigua situation, are lessons to observe. The Government in St. Kitts did not have the manpower or resources to contain the rebellioin in Anguilla. In Antigua, the Government was forced to come to terms with the instigators who were behind the demonstrations and violence that led to a state of emergency, because the civil power was impotent to deal with the matter. Arsonists and other law-breakers remained at large as a result. The Barbuda situation was saved by a timely move of the Government to increase the strength of the Police in that Island, or it may have resulted in another Anguilla.

The stubbornness of the Anguillan leaders to come to talks with the Government despite persuasion by impartial parties, and their final act of breaking relations with the rest of the State and Britain, as ludicrous as it might appear to some, this act had to be considered with all seriousness. Despite some agreements reached, the Anguillans throughout the unfortunate episode, displayed a marked tendency to ignore agreements.

In terms of independence for an individual state, the prospects of a break-away by one or more parts without the State being fully competent, is not a palatable thought.

It is almost certain that the Anguillan invasion and occupation by British troops is the last episode of the type we will witness in the West Indies. Irrespective of the reasons for the British invasion, it invoked a lot of criticism from various sources - even by some West Indian leaders. Any other state government which finds itself in such a plight, might quite justifiably be told by Britain to deal with it.

If there were a Federation of the Associated States, the Anguilla situation might never have happened, and, if so, it would have been speedily dealt with by the Federal Government, either by persuasion or force. The Federal Government would have adequate deterrent by way of a defence or Regional Police Force under its command, which could be deployed in any area of the Federation where it was needed to restore law and order. The West Indies would then be saved the humiliation of having to implore the former colonial power to maintain peace.

The fact remains that the only safe and sure means of guaranteeing the stability of the Associated States and their individual integrity, is within a Federation which has the power and authority to maintain law and order through its various agencies and institutions and can safeguard its citizens rights of redress and full protection from fear.

With the seeds of anarchy and rebellion reaching West Indian soil, with mounting pressures from activities and other disruptive forces that are apt to pursue the tactics of the revolutionists who seek to overthrow the established order, it is more necessary for the States to unite. In the words of Sir Grantley Adams at the break-up of the West Indies: *"If they cannot take us off together, they will take us off one by one'"*

CHAPTER 6
COST OF FEDERATION

It is conceivable that in the early phases of Federation, additional costs must be faced to establish and administer the Federal Government; but these costs need not be beyond the means of the Associated States. Any additional cost would be offset by the inevitable financial and industrial growth that would accrue to the States as a result of Federation and an integrated economy. There is also the compensatory effect of stability, which a Federal Government would ensure.

The existing combined annual national expenditure of the Associated States financed by true revenue, loans and external aid is in the vicinity of EC$90m, which compares favourably with Guyana and other small independent countries. In terms of finance, although much more money is desirable, the States are not destitute, and there is evidence that they are forging ahead with development programmes.

Most of the affairs the Federal Government would undertake are now financed and operated by the individual States, or contributed to by them on a regional basis. Some subjects could be taken over immediately, while others could be transferred in phases, or if necessary, continue to be operated by the States as agents of the Federal Government, or under Federal Government supervision. The costs of these services need not be more expensive to the Federal Government than they are now to the States, save additional expenses that may be incurred in supervision, with an aim to improve the service. What is entailed therefore, would be a matter of removing the costs of these services from the States to the Federal Government, with the requisite transfer of funds to meet these costs. On the other hand, it is possible that substantial savings could accrue from the reduction of regional meetings which costs have been borne by Individual States as most of the matters now being dealt with by the Regional Council of Ministers would pass into the hands of the Federal Government.

The cost of State Ministers' attendance at the numerous regional meetings has been substantial, but there was alternative, and these costs had to be met. With the establishment of a Federal Government, States' Ministers could devote more time to immediate State concerns that may have been neglected because of their attendance at regional meetings.

The new costs to be faced would be provisions for a Governor-General, a Federal Parliament and Ministers, and establishment of a Regional Defence Force. The Governor-General's Office should not cost substantially more than that of a State Governor, although he should enjoy a higher salary and allowances. The cost of the Federal Parliament would depend upon the size and type of parliamentary representation, such as a Unicameral Legislature, and the number of representatives to each State. Here again, some of the savings from the Regional Meetings could be used to offset the cost of Parliament.

The Ministries would need to be staffed, although in the early stages, the staff may not be sizeable. With the taking over of the subjects such as External Affairs by the Federal Government, it is possible that some of the staff now employed by the State Governments in this Department would become eligible for promotion and transfers, which might not have been available to any marked degree in the States. The Federal Government would also absorb the Regional Secretariat in St. Lucia.

If a bi-cameral legislature would be more suitable for the Federation, the size of the Lower House should not exceed twenty members, with a Speaker appointed from without. This would provide for three representatives each from six states, except Montserrat, which will have two representatives. On the other hand, there could be a Lower House of 13 or 14 members, with six States having two representatives each, and Montserrat one .The same could provide for one or two members each from the States, giving a basis of equality.

At the most therefore, the overall size of the Parliament would be 35 members comprising both Houses, and it could be substantially less if so desired. Dual membership of State and Federal Parliaments should be ruled out.

Not more than four other Ministers would be needed, besides the Prime Minister's and Attorney-General's Departments and the various subjects could quite easily be distributed and accommodated within these Ministries.

An additional sum of EC$400,000.00 annually could adequately take care of the Governor-General, Parliament and Ministers in the early stages, plus the fact that external aid could possibly be tapped for special advisory staff and so on.

The cost of a small Regional Defence Force might be more substantial. I am in no position to say the size of Force or types of equipment and the costs involved, but because this is a necessary expenditure, provisions will have to be made. I presume a sum of EC$600,000.00 annually could suffice.

Other costs that must be considered are the capital costs for setting up the Federal Headquarters, including the Governor-General's Residence. Here again it is believed that the British Government could be expected to meet a substantial portion of the cost, because it was their intention to do so in the proposals for the Little Eight Federation. Consideration would have to be given to renting buildings in the early stages and provision of housing for Ministers and Senior Federal Officials who might be given housing allowances instead. This cost should be allocated to Setting-up Federal Headquarters.

With the Declaration of Independence by the Federation, it might be necessary to have a Mission in Washington with the Ambassador also accredited to the United Nations. The Mission does not have to be large. As a means of economy, the same Ambassador may even be accredited to Ottawa as is done by many small independent countries, or the High Commissioner in Ottawa accredited to Washington and the United Nations.

The establishment of this additional Mission and upgrading of the two missions in London and Montreal could be accommodated within a sum of approximately EC $200,000, depending on what is needed, perhaps a lesser figure would be adequate.

It seems therefore, that the additional recurrent cost to the States for the establishment of a Federation would be in the vicinity of EC$1.2m or less. This sum represents 1.33% of present National Expenditure of the States and Territories.

With the present growth of National Income of over 5%, the States could easily absorb this amount without causing any severe strain on the National Economy, and it would be money well spent for the National purpose.

In the meantime, the host Government in whose Territory the Federal Headquarters would be established (in this case, the likelihood would be St. Lucia), should be prepared to help as much as possible in providing facilities for the temporary use of the Federal Government until a Headquarters is built.

CHAPTER 7
FINANCING THE FEDERATION

Every Government - if it is a Government at all - should have the right to taxing powers. In Federations, these rights may be defined by agreements, limited or over-riding. At any rate, a Federal Government should have the right to exercise an overall Financial control within its territorial and political jurisdiction, whether it be by way of taxation or fiscal policy. This should be a clear understanding from the very outset so as to avoid unnecessary disagreement at some later date if the Federal Government in the exercise of its powers finds itself with surplus funds the States might be envious of, and may feel they are entitled to share.

However, although the Constitution for the Federation must provide for taxing powers, it may not be necessary in the early phases of the Federation to exercise these powers. It is possible a mandatory levy as was done in the Federation of the West Indies could be agreed upon for an interim period, until the Federation is fully established.

This should not by any means prohibit the Federal Government from assuming control in the fields of taxation and fiscal policy by taking measures to unify taxes and duties in the Federation. As a matter of fact, this control should be taken over from the outset and there should be no question of revising the Federal Constitution, an exercise which hastened the demise of the West Indies Federation.

The Constitution should be fully comprehensive and conclusive from the start, providing for full sovereignty and the division of powers between the Federal Government and the States, which is only subject to amendment under its own provisions.

If on the other hand it could be agreed that the Federal Government must raise its own finances from the outset, then customs levies and income tax are the main sources from which the Federal Government should derive its finances. Agreement would have to be reached between the Federal Government and the States, to the re-distribution of surplus amounts not urgently needed by the Federal Government in its operations.

CONCLUSION

I attempted in the foregoing chapters to make a case for Federation. Whether or not I succeeded is a matter for the politicians and the people of the West Indies Associated States to decide.

It is my opinion and of many people with whom I conversed - that we ought to federate, not only for the full unification of the Commonwealth Caribbean Territories, but also for our own self-protection in trade and development and to preserve our political and territorial integrity.

No large country has much respect for very small states, which are more considered a nuisance value than a value to world peace or world economy. An additional six or seven independent states in the Caribbean are not going to add one more iota of prestige to the area, or induce any more substantial help than what is now received.

The people of the West Indies Associated States must begin to think in terms of a National purpose. Is that purpose to be restricted to the little islands that comprise the individual states and their small populations, or directed to what could become a viable Federation with a viable economy?

Where there is a will, there is a way, and it is evident the way is clear for action; it is only the will that is needed. We have wasted a lot of time. The excuse was that external pressures were being exerted by the Colonial power. Now, the matter rests with us - and us alone - and if individuals, or groups, who for their own personal reasons should attempt to place obstacles in the way to the unity of the States, they might well find themselves condemned by their own people as it is certain they will be condemned by posterity. For the fact is, the people of the States are more politically enlightened today and would not be prepared as in the past to leave unnoticed any far-reaching decisions made on their behalf, which might affect their future.

The mechanism for setting up the Federation as an independent country is already provided for in the terms of the agreement reached with the United Kingdom upon termination of the Association, and this is a simple device.

The relevant procedure which *inter alia,* is set out in paragraph 23 of the Report of the St. Kitts-Nevis-Anguilla Constitutional Conference (1966), Command Paper 3031 and which also applies to the other States reads:

> *"One of the main characteristics of the proposed new association is that either side will be free to terminate it (the association) at any time. If the territory arranges it with one or more of the other Associated States to form a federation or to create a new unitary state, it would be open to the territories concerned in view of the terms of paragraphs 15 to 17 above, by a simple resolution of their Legislatures and without recourse to a referendum, to signify their request and consent that the necessary provision to establish the federation or create the new unitary state and to modify or terminate the association with Britain should be made by United Kingdom Legislation."*

Paragraphs 15-17 read as follows:

15.   *The United Kingdom legislation should contain provisions to the effect that no Act of Parliament of the United Kingdom passed after the commencement of the association would extend to St. Kitts-Nevis-Anguilla as part of its law unless it was expressly declared in the Act that St. Kitts-Nevis-Anguilla had requested and consented to the enactment of the Act.*

16.   *Similarly, the United Kingdom legislation providing for the Constitution of St. Kitts-Nevis-Anguilla should reserve to Her Majesty a general power to make laws by Order in Council but no such Order in Council should have effect as part of the law of St. Kitts-Nevis-Anguilla unless it was expressly declared in the Order in Council that St. Kitts-Nevis-Anguilla had requested and consented to the making of the Order in Council.*

17.   *For the purpose of the two preceding paragraphs the request and consent of St. Kitts-Nevis-Anguilla should be signified by resolution of Legislature.*

It is therefore, obvious that the way is clear for the final move without let or hindrance. Britain gave an assurance that she would be prepared to hold a conference to discuss the political and economic implications of termination, and there is no reason to doubt that this would be done in an atmosphere of mutual understanding and satisfaction to all concerned.

As an after-thought, I would like to make a suggestion on the question of Representation. Although it might be convenient to make an *ad hoc* allocation of seats in the Federal Parliament in the early stages, the principle of representation on the basis of population should not be over-looked. Provision should be made in the Federal Constitution for its implementation at some future date, provided that no State would be without representation.

It is conceivable that with the growth of population and with possible movement of peoples due to economic factors, some islands could in due course, out-strip others in population, in which case, the present arrangement for representation would be unsuitable

The painful experience in finding a formula for representation during the Conferences to revise the Federal Constitution of the West Indies should not be repeated, and it would be wise to establish representation per unit of population as a measure that could be introduced whenever the necessity arose.

APPENDIX IV

In the Privy Council

THE ATTORNEY GENERAL

AND THE MINISTER OF HOME AFFAIRS

Appellants

v.

ANTIGUA TIMES LIMITED

Respondent

Delivered by

LORD FRASER OF TULLYBELTON

PRIVY COUNCIL APPEAL NO. 9 OF 1974

The Court of Appeal of the West Indies

Associated States Supreme Court (Antigua)

JUDGMENT OF THE LORDS OF THE

JUDICIAL COMMITTEE OF THE PRIVY COUNCIL

Delivered 19th May 1975

Present at the Hearing　　　　　*Lord Wilberforce :*

Viscount Dilhorne

Lord Edmund-Davies

Lord Fraser of Tullybelton

Sir Thomas McCarthy

(*Delivered by* Lord Fraser of Tullybelton)

The Respondent is a company registered in Antigua. A preliminary objection was taken on behalf of the appellants in both the Courts below, and repeated before this Board, that the Respondent was not entitled to initiate these proceedings under section 15 of the Constitution of Antigua, on the grounds that it was not a person within the meaning of that section. The objection was repelled by Louisy J. in the High Court of Antigua, and his decision on this point was upheld by a majority of the Court of Appeal of the West Indies Associated States. Peterkin, J.A. dissented on this point.

The Respondent was the publisher of a bi-weekly newspaper called the ANTIGUA TIMES. Publication began in December, 1970, and ended in December, 1971, as a consequence of the passing by the Parliament of Antigua of two Acts dealing with newspapers. The Respondent complains that these Acts were unconstitutional and it applied to the High Court of Antigua for redress under section 15 of the Constitution. Section 15(1) provides as follows:

> "If any person alleges that any of the provisions of sections 2 to 14 (inclusive) of this Constitution has been, or is being, contravened in relation to him, then, without prejudice to any other action with respect to the same matter which is lawfully available, that person may apply to the High Court for redress."

The Appellants contend that the word *person* occurring twice in that subsection refers only to a natural person. The respondent contends that the word includes also an artificial or legal person such as itself. The Interpretation Act 1889, which is applied to the Constitution by section 115 (15) of the Constitution provides by section 19 that:

> "The expression *person* shall, unless the contrary intention appears, include any body of persons corporate or unincorporated."

It is therefore necessary to consider the context in which the word person occurs here.

Section 15 is in Chapter 1 of the Constitution, which is headed Protection of Fundamental Rights and Freedoms. The arrangement and working of the chapter evidently owe much to the European Convention for the Protection of Human Rights and Fundamental Freedoms signed by certain members of the Council for Europe in 1950. The European Convention was itself largely based on the Universal Declaration of Human Rights adopted by the United Nations General Assembly in 1948. The Universal Declaration as its title suggests, is concerned mainly, if not exclusively, with human rights, that is with rights of individual human beings, but the European Convention appears to apply also to artificial persons, at least in some of its articles. For example Article 25 provides that the Commission may receive petitions "from any person, non-governmental organisation or group of individuals claiming to be the victim of a violation by one of the High Contracting Parties of the rights set forth in this Convention," and Article 1 of the first protocol to the Convention refers to "every natural or legal person." With that ancestry it would not be surprising if Chapter 1 of the Constitution of Antigua were to apply to artificial as well as to natural persons, and its heading, already quoted, which refers to fundamental and not to human rights and freedoms, gives no indication that it is limited to natural persons.

Before turning to the words of Chapter 1 itself there is one other general matter which Their Lordships consider relevant. The Constitution of Antigua was brought into effect by Order in Council in 1967. Having regard to the important place in the economic life of society occupied by corporate bodies, it would seem natural for such a modern Constitution, dealing with *inter alia,* rights to property, to use the word person to include corporations. As long ago as 1922, a view to that effect was expressed by lsaacs J. in The Austra/Asian Temperance and General Mutual Life Assumnce Society Ltd. v. Howe, 31 C.L.R.290 at 301, and in 1930 in Leske v. S.A. Real Estate Investment Company Ltd. 45 C.L.R. 22 at 25, Rich and Dixon J.J. said this:

> *"The time has passed for supposing that the Legislature would use the word person only to signify a natural person in dealing with a class of business in which the utility of the proprietary company has long been made manifest."*

That statement was made with reference to an Act dealing with contacts for the sale of land but it is also applicable, though with rather less force, to a Constitution such as that of Antigua which includes provisions safeguarding the ownership of property. The attention of Their Lordships was drawn to a number of decisions of the Supreme Court of the United States in which the meaning of the word person in the Fourteenth Amendment to the American Constitution was considered. That Amendment provides *inter alia,* that no state shall 'deprive any person of life, liberty or property without due process of law; nor deny to any person within the jurisdiction the equal protection of the laws.' In Grosjean American Press Co. Inc. (1936) 297 U.S. Reports 233, at 244, Sutherland J. delivering the opinion of the Court said this:

> *"But a Corporation is a person within the meaning of the equal protection and due process of law clauses, which are the clauses involved here.'and he referred to authority for that proposition. In Wheeling Steel Corporation v. Glander (1949) 337 U.S. Reports 562, Douglas and Black JJ. (in a dissenting opinion) said that it had been implicit in all decisions of the Supreme Court since 1886 that a corporation is a person within the meaning of the Equal Protection Clause of the Fourteenth Amendment. These Australian and American decisions, although of course not decisive of the present question, indicate the approach taken to similar questions in those countries in recent times."*

Chapter 1 of the Constitution of Antigua consists of Sections 1-16 inclusive. Section 1 is as follows:

> "Whereas every person in Antigua is entitled to the fundamental rights and freedoms of the individual, that is to say, the right, whatever his race, place of origin, political opinions, colour, creed or sex, but subject to respect for the rights and freedoms of others and for the public interest, to each and all of the following, namely:
>
> > (a) life, liberty, security of the person, the enjoyment of property and the protection of the law;

(b) Freedom of conscience, of expression and of peaceful assembly and association; and

(c) Respect for his private and family life.

The subsequent provisions of this Chapter shall have effect for the purpose of affording protection to the aforesaid rights and freedoms, subject to such limitations of that protection as are contained in those provisions, being limitations designed to ensure that the enjoyment of the said rights and freedoms by any individual does not prejudice the rights and freedoms of others or the public interest."

That section is in very nearly the same words as section 5 of the Constitution of Malta which was considered by this Board in Olivier v. Buttigeg (1967) 1 A.C. 115, and the analysis of the latter section made in the judgment of the Board delivered by Lord Morris of Borth-y-Gest is equally applicable to Section 1 of the Antigua Constitution. The following passage appears at pages 128-9:

> "It is to be noted that the section begins with the word Whereas. Though the section must be given such declaratory force as it independently possesses, it would appear in the main to be of the nature of a preamble. It is an introduction to and in a sense a prefatory or explanatory note in regard to the sections which are to follow, It is a declaration of entitlement. coupled however with a declaration that though every person in Malta is entitled to the fundamental rights and freedoms of the individual as specified, yet such entitlement is subject to respect for the rights and freedoms of others and for the public interest. The section appears to proceed by way of explanation of the scheme of the succeeding sections. The succeeding sections show that the promised scheme was followed."

The reference to race, place of origin, political opinions, colour, creed or sex indicates that the section was referring primarily to human or natural persons, but there is nothing to exclude artificial persons so far as they are capable of enjoying the fundamental rights and freedoms. Counsel for the Appellants argued that section 1 was the master section of the chapter, that the subsequent provisions of the chapter were limited to having effect for protecting 'the aforesaid rights and freedoms,' that is, the rights and freedoms specified in paragraphs (a), (b) and (c) of the section, and that those rights and freedoms belonged only to human persons. Their Lordships cannot agree that the rights and freedoms are limited in that way. The nature and extent of the rights and freedoms protected must depend upon the provisions of the sections respectively protecting them. Some of these sections clearly cannot apply to corporations but others car and, in the opinion of Their Lordships, do. On this matter Their Lordships cannot do better than to quote the following passage from the judgement of Lewis C.J. in the Court below:

> "It is obvious that there are certain rights and freedoms in Chapter 1 of the Constitution which from their very nature cannot be enjoyed by a corporation, e.g. the right to life specified in Section 2, the right to personal liberty specified in Section 3, and the right to be protected from inhuman treatment mentioned in Section 5; but there is nothing in principle which prevents a corporation from enjoying the rights relating to the compulsory acquisition of property (Section 6). the securing of protection of the law (Section 8) and protection from discrimination on various grounds specified in Section 12. It would not be an affront to common sense or reason to contend that if a corporation's property were compulsory acquired (Section 6) the corporation should, in like manner as a natural person, be entitled to compensation. Nor could it be convincingly maintained that a corporation, like a human being , if charged with a criminal offence would not be entitled to the right of a fair hearing in accordance with the fundamental principles of justice as prescribed in Section 8. As regards to the right to protection from discriminatory treatment on grounds of race, place of origin, political opinion, colour or creed (Section 12), this Court delivered a judgement on December 13 1971 which established the principle that a corporation was entitled to enforce the protective provisions of Section 15 of the Constitution in circumstances where it was found to have been treated in a discriminatory manner contrary to Section 12 (2) and (3) by reason of political opinions of its directors. The case in question was Carnacho & Sons Ltd and Others v. Collector of Customs (Antigua Civil Appeal No.6 of

1971) (unreported)."

The Chief Justice went on to explain the facts in Carnacho's case and he concluded as follows:

> "It was contended by Counsel for the Appellants that the point which is here being discussed did not arise and was not argued in Carnacho's case. I agree, but the Court of Appeal assumed (and I consider rightly) that the point could not be successfully contested. It would be a scandalous defect in the law if a company could be treated in the manner in which the company in Camacho's case was treated and the law could not afford it any redress"

Their Lordships agree with the opinion expressed by the Chief Justice and they have no reason to doubt that the decision in Camacho's case was correct. Their Lordships also agree with the opinion of Wooding C.J. in Collymore v. The Attorney-General (1967) 12 W.LR. 5, 20 who said with reference to the Constitution of Trinidad and Tobago that it was intended to protect natural persons primarily but that

> "Some of the particular prohibitions are undoubtedly apt to protect artificial legal entities also."

The section of the Antigua Constitution which in the opinion of Their Lordships is most clearly applicable to corporate bodies is section 6, Protection against compulsory acquisition of property. The opening words of subsection 1 are as follows:

> "No property of any description shall be compulsorily taken possession of, and no interest in or rights over property of any description shall be compulsorily acquired, except..."

The exception refers to payment of compensation. The application of that section to a body corporate could be excluded only by reading into it words such as belonging to a natural person after the words no property of any description, and there appears to be no good reason for doing that. Moreover, subsection (2) (g) of section 6 indicates in Their Lordships' opinion a positive intention to include bodies corporate. Subsection (2) provides that nothing in the section shall be construed as affecting the making or operation of any law insofar as it provides for taking possession or acquisition of property for various purposes there specified, including '(g) by way of the vesting or administration of the property of bodies corporate or un-incorporate in the course of being wound up.' The inference is that, but for this saving clause, the property of a body corporate in the course of being wound up would, or at least might, have been affected by the section. A similar inference arises from subsection (4) which saves any law from the compulsory taking possession or compulsory acquisition in the public interest of any property 'held by a body corporate which is established for public purposes by any law and in which no moneys have been invested other than moneys provided by Parliament Section 10 (the full terms of which are set out hereafter) also deserves special mention. Subsection (1) provides for protection of freedom of expression, which is to include the freedom to receive and impart ideas and information without interference. Subsection (2) provides that nothing in any law shall be held inconsistent with or in contravention of the section to the extent that the law in question makes provision that is reasonably required for (a) (ii) *inter alia* "regulating telephony, telegraphy, posts, wireless broadcasting, television or other means of communication." These are fields of activity in which corporations are commonly engaged and the saving would lose much of its practical value if corporations were not persons who could avail themselves of its protection.

A further consideration is that, if bodies corporate were not entitled to use the machinery of section 15, many anomalies would arise This is a relevant consideration.

National and Grindlays Bank Ltd. v. Kentiles Ltd. (1966) 1 W.L.R. 348. For example a natural person would lose the protection of the Constitution for his business if he formed a company to take it over. An example nearer to the present case is that section 10 (Freedom of expression) would; on the Appellants' construction, draw an unexplained and irrational distinction between newspaper proprietors who were natural persons and those who were bodies corporate. Similarly section 11 (Freedom of assembly and association) which expressly includes the right to "belong to trade unions or other associations for the protection of his interests, would protect the right of a natural person to join a trade association, but not that of a body corporate.

For these reasons Their Lordships are of the opinion that the word person in this Constitution includes artificial legal persons and that the Appellants' preliminary objection fails.

The Respondent in its Statement of claim sought declarations that section 18 of the Newspapers Registration (Amendment) Act, 1971, No.8 of 1971 and section 3(2) of the Newspaper Surety Ordinance (Amendment) Act, 1971, No. 9 of 1971, contravened the provisions of Chapter 1 of the Constitution and, in particular, of section 10 thereof. Its application to the High Court was made, as already explained, under section 15(1) of the Constitution. To succeed, it had to show that one of the provisions of sections 2 to 14 had been, or was being, contravened in relation to it and it does not suffice for it to establish that such a contravention might occur in the future.

Section 118 added by the Newspapers Registration (Amendment Act, 1971, introduced two new requirements with regard to newspapers into the law of Antigua. Anyone who did not print or publish a registered newspaper fifteen days before the Act came into force, could not lawfully publish a newspaper or cause one to be published without a licence signed by the Secretary to the Cabinet, and unless he had paid a licence fee of $600, the equivalent of 125.00 pounds. The licence fee was payable annually.

Persons who printed or published a registered newspaper fifteen days before the commencement of the Act, and who have paid the licence fee of $600, are, the section provides, to be deemed to have been granted a licence. As the Respondent published its newspaper fifteen days before the Act commenced, it would, if it had paid the licence fee of $600, have been deemed to have been granted a licence.

The Newspapers Registration Act of 1883, Chapter 318, required the name of the newspaper, the place where it was to be printed or published and the names and addresses of the editor, printer, publisher and proprietors to be registered before publication. No fee was payable on registration.

Mr. Le Quesne on behalf of the Respondent contended that section 1B was unconstitutional in two respects: first, because it subjected the right to publish to the grant of a licence at the discretion of the Cabinet, and, secondly, because it made the exercise of the right to publish subject to the annual payment of $600. He contended that in these respects section 1B contravened section 10 of the Constitution which is in the following terms:

1) *Except with his own consent, no person shall be hindered in the enjoyment of his freedom of expression and for the purposes of this section the said freedom includes the freedom to hold opinions and to receive and impart ideas and information without interference, and freedom from interference with his correspondence and other means of communication.*

2) *Nothing contained in or done under the authority of any law shall be held to be inconsistent with or in contravention of this section to the extent that the law in question makes provision-*

   a) *that is reasonably required:-*

      i) *in the interests of defence, public safety, public order, public morality or public health; or*

      ii) *for the purpose of protecting the reputations, rights and freedoms of other persons, or the private lives of persons concerned in legal proceedings, preventing the disclosure of information received in confidence, maintaining the authority and independence of the courts, or regulating telephony, telegraphy, posts, wireless broadcasting, television or other means of communication, public exhibitions or public entertainment: or*

   b) *that imposes restrictions upon public officers."*

If the grant of a licence signed by the Secretary to the Cabinet to anyone who wished to publish a newspaper or to cause one to be published was automatic, then it could no more be contended that the requirement of a licence was a hindrance to the enjoyment of the right to freedom of expression than that the requirement to register imposed by the Newspapers Registration Act of 1883 was such a hindrance. The Secretary to the Cabinet when signing or refusing to sign a licence no doubt acts in accordance with instructions he receives from the Cabinet and Section 1B leaves the Cabinet free to discriminate between applicants for a licence as the Cabinet thinks fit, granting a licence to one and refusing it to another without having to give any reason.

Section 12 (1) of the Constitution provides that, save as provided in that section, 'no law shall make any provision which is discriminatory either of itself or in its effect.' This subsection does not apply to any law so far as that law makes provision with respect to persons who do not belong to Antigua. Section 1B, though not discriminatory of itself is so widely drawn that it permits the Cabinet to discriminate not only between persons who belong and persons who do not belong to Antigua but also between persons who belong to Antigua.

The Respondent cannot complain that it was discriminated against as it did not have to apply for a licence, having published its paper fifteen days before the Act came into force. It cannot establish that the imposition of the obligation to obtain a licence before publishing a newspaper constitutes a contravention of the Constitution which either has taken place or is taking place in relation to it. The only part of section 1B which affected it was the requirement to pay $600 as the annual fee for the licence deemed on payment of that sum to have been granted to it.

Their Lordships, while they recognise that the answer to the question whether the requirement to obtain a licence from the Secretary to the Cabinet contravenes the Constitution is not free from difficulty, involving consideration not only of section 10(1) but also of section 10 (2) and other sections of the Constitution, consider that on the facts of this case, the question is hypothetical and does not arise for decision. They therefore express no opinion on it.

In relation to Section 1B it remains to consider whether the requirement of the payment of $600, both by those who are granted licences and by those who are deemed to have been granted licences, amounts to a contravention of the Constitution.

At the trial, Counsel agreed with three propositions of law and that agreement may have influenced the evidence called at the trial. Despite this agreement, it appears from the judgement of Lewis C.J. in the Court of Appeal, that counsel for the Respondent there submitted that it was incompetent for parties by concessions or agreement to tie the hands of the Court in the determination of the question whether there had been an infringement of the Constitution. Lewis C.J. said that he completely agreed with that submission. In Their Lordships' view, a Court which has to decide a question of construction whether it be of a statute or of a Constitution, cannot be fettered in the exercise of its judgement by any agreement between counsel. In their view Louisy J, the Trial Judge, was right to refuse to be bound by the three agreed propositions of law.

The first related to the obtaining of a licence and as the Respondent did not have to obtain one, it is not necessary to refer to it or to comment on it.

The second was that:-
> "Any law is constitutional which provides for a fee for registration of a newspaper, such fee being of a moderate figure in keeping with the established practice in the Caribbean."

Louisy J. rejected this proposition and formulated the following in lieu thereof:-
> "Any law which provides for a licence fee, the nature of which falls within the taxing powers of the legislature is constitutional unless such a law is so arbitrary as to compel the conclusion that it does not involve an exertion of the taxing power but constitutes in substance and effect, the direct execution of a different and forbidden power."

He held that section 1B did not fall within the taxing powers of the legislature and was unconstitutional. He based his conclusion on three American decisions and cited the dictum of Mr. Justice Douglas in Murdoch v. Pennsylvania (City of Jeannette) (1942) 319 U.S. Reports 105, 113 that

> "A state may not impose a charge for the enjoyment of a right granted by the Federal Constitution."

Lewis C.J. in the Court of Appeal also cited this observation. He and St. Bernard J.C. attached importance to the requirements that the licence fees should be paid before publication, Lewis C.J. regarding that as inhibitory 'because in effect they prevent a newspaper from coming into being at all'. Peterkin J.A. dissented.

Section 10(2) of the Constitution of Antigua, however, expressly provides that nothing contained in or done under the authority of certain laws is to be held to be inconsistent with or in contravention of the section. If therefore, section 1B is a law reasonably required for one of the purposes specified in section 10(2)(a), then, though its provisions could otherwise have been regarded as a hindrance to the enjoyment of freedom of expression, it is not to be treated, nor is anything done under it to be treated, as contravening the section.

One argument advanced was that section 1B was reasonably required 'for the purpose of regulating other means of communication', (s. 10(2)(a)(ii)). It was contended that newspapers were other means of communication. Those words also appear in section 10 (1) and there it does not appear likely that they were intended to cover newspapers. It would be unusual if the same set of words appearing in consecutive subsections of a section bore different meanings and, if section (10)(2)(a)(ii) had been intended to include newspapers, it is indeed curious that they were not specifically mentioned. It may be that 'other means of communication' in that subsection was intended to cover only other channels of communication similar to those express, mentioned in the preceding words.

Their Lordships do not, however, find it necessary to come to a conclusion on this for in their opinion the imposition of the licence fee to be paid annually by all publishers of newspapers was correctly regarded by Louisy J. as a tax. Taxation is not referred to in section 10. The only provisions of Chapter 1 of the Constitution that do so are Section 6(2)(a) and section 12(4)(d). (Section 6(2)(a) merely provides that the taking of possession or acquisition of any property, interest or right in satisfaction of any tax or rate due is not to be affected by the provisions of that section which refer to the compulsory, acquisition of property; and section 12(4)(d) enables the Government, any local authority and any body for local purposes to discriminate in the imposition of taxation or appropriation of revenue without contravening the Constitution.

Revenue requires to be raised in the interests of defence and for securing public safety, public order, public morality and public health and if this tax was reasonably required to raise revenue for these purposes or for any of them, then section 1B is not to be treated as contravening the Constitution.

In some cases, it may be possible for a Court to decide from a mere perusal of an Act whether it was or was not reasonably required. In other cases, the Act will not provide the answer to that question. In such cases, evidence has to be brought before the Court on the reasons for the Act and to show that it was reasonably required? Their Lordships think that the proper approach to the question is to presume, until the contrary appears or is shown, that all Acts passed by the Parliament of Antigua were reasonably required. This presumption will be rebutted if the statutory provisions in question are, to use the words of Louisy J, *"so arbitrary as to compel the conclusion that it does not involve an exertion of the taxing power but constitutes in substance and effect, the direct execution of a different and forbidden power."*

If the amount of the licence fee was so manifestly excessive as to lead to the conclusion that the real reason for its imposition was not the raising of revenue but the preventing of the publication of newspapers, then that would justify the conclusion that the law was not reasonably required for the raising of revenue.

In Their Lordships' opinion, the presumption that the Newspapers Registration (Amendment) Act, (1971) was reasonably required has not been rebutted and they do not regard the amount of the licence fee as manifestly excessive and of such a character as to lead to the conclusion that section 1B was not enacted to raise revenue but for some other purpose.

Was the revenue to be raised by the licence fees required in the interests of defence or for securing public safety, public order, public morality or public health? Though there may be some taxing statutes which state the purposes for which the revenue raised will be applied, ordinarily they do not. The purposes stated cover a very wide field of government expenditure and in the absence of any indication to the contrary, Their Lordships think it right to presume that the revenue derived from the licence fees was to be applied to these purposes. That being so, in their opinion, Section 1B, in so far as it requires the payment of a licence fee, is a provision which comes within section 10(2) of the Constitution and which cannot therefore be treated as contravening it, even though it requires the payment of the licence fee in the first place before publication of a newspaper.

Section 3 of the Newspaper Surety Ordinance of 1909, Cap. 319, made it unlawful for anyone to print or public a newspaper unless he had first given a bond for $960.00, the equivalent of 200.00 pounds Sterling, for the payment of any penalty imposed on the printer, publisher or proprietor of the paper in respect of the publication of any blasphemous or seditious libel, and for the payment of any damages and costs awarded for libel.

The Newspaper Surety Ordinance (Amendment) Act, 1971, added a new subsection, which was numbered 3(2), to this section. It made it unlawful to print or publish a newspaper unless in addition to the bond for $960.00, $10,000.00 had first been deposited with the Accountant-General to satisfy any judgement of the Supreme Court for libel, the subsection provided that the deposit should at all times be maintained at that figure and that it should be placed in a deposit account and

335

bear interest at the rate payable at the Government Savings Bank.

This was subject to the following proviso:-

> *"Provided however that the Minister responsible for newspapers on being satisfied with the sufficiency of the security in the form of a Policy of Insurance or on a guarantee of a Bank may waive the requirement of the said deposit. So the printer and publisher of a newspaper can either deposit $10,000 and be paid interest on it, or, if he prefers it, take out a policy of insurance or obtain a bank guarantee. The premium on such a policy will of course cost him far less than the amount of the deposit."*

It was maintained by the Respondent, and accepted by Louisy J., Lewis C.J. and Peterkin J.A., that under the proviso, the Minister had uncontrolled discretion to waive or not to waive the requirement of the deposit. Their Lordships do not agree. In their opinion, the Minister, if satisfied with the sufficiency of the security offered, must waive the payment of the deposit. The word may in the proviso, the context shows, must be construed in that way. The Minister is not given an unregulated and unfettered discretion without guidelines. His discretion is limited to determination of the sufficiency of the security offered.

The third proposition of law agreed between counsel was that:-

> *"Any law is constitutional which provides that no person shall print or publish or cause to be printed or published any newspaper unless he shall have previously deposited with the Accountant-General a sum of $10,000.00 in cash or a bond for the like amount from an established Bank or Insurance Company, to be drawn against in order to satisfy any judgement of the Court for libel against the editor or printer or publisher or proprietor of the newspaper and to be at all times maintained at the sum $10,000."*

This appears to amount to a concession by counsel for the Respondent at the trial that its claim that section 3(2) contravened the Constitution could not be sustained. Louisy J. refused to accept this proposition and he and all the members of the

Court of Appeal held that the requirement of a deposit of $10,000.00 to meet damages for libel was a hindrance to a newspaper's freedom of expression.

It can be argued that any expenditure, required by law from those responsible for the publication of a newspaper, is a hindrance to its freedom of expression in that such expenditure must reduce the resources of the paper which might otherwise be available for increasing its circulation. Such an argument might be advanced in relation to the provision of a bond for $960.00 under the 1909 Ordinance.

In relation to section 3(2), the question to be determined is, In their Lordships' opinion, whether that subsection was reasonably required for the purpose of protecting the reputations and rights of others. If it was, then by virtue of section 10(2) of the Constitution, nothing in or done under its authority is to be treated as contravening the Constitution.

In Their Lordships' opinion section 3(2) clearly had as its purpose the protection of the reputations and rights of others. They do not agree with Lewis C.J. that it is the right of action for libel which gives the true protection to the injured person's reputation. Damages are awarded to a libelled person to compensate him for the injury he has suffered. Unless there is a reasonable prospect of his obtaining the damages awarded to him and of payment of his costs, he may be deterred from instituting proceedings. A mere right of action is not likely to be regarded by him as an adequate protection of his reputation. Further, the fact that the deposit will be used to satisfy a judgement for libel and that, if it is, it must be replenished by them is an inducement to the publishers of a newspaper to take care not to libel and to damage unjustifiably the reputation of others.

The effect of section 3(2) was to increase the amount available for the payment of damages above that fixed by the 1909 Ordinance. Was that increase reasonably required? It is not necessary to repeat what has already been said as to the determination of that question. No valid reason appears for holding that the presumption that this Act of the Legislature of Antigua was reasonably required, is

337

rebutted.

In the circumstances, Section 3(2) of the Newspaper Surety Ordinance of 1909, inserted in that Ordinance by the Newspaper Surety Ordinance (Amendment) Act, 1971, in Their Lordships' opinion comes within and is covered by section 10(2) of the Constitution, and cannot therefore, be treated as contravening the Constitution.

For these reasons, Their Lordships will humbly advise Her Majesty that this appeal should be allowed.

The Respondent must pay the appellants' costs before this Board and in both Courts below.

The Respondents must pay the Appellants' costs before this Board and in both Courts below.

About the Author

Sir Novelle Hamilton Richards, K.C.G.N., was born on 24th November, 1917, in the historic village of Liberta. He attended the Grace Hill Scholl, Antigua Grammar School and the London Polytechnic Institute in England. At the London Polytechnic, Novelle successfully pursued the Diploma Course in Journalism.

On returning home, he was appointed Editor of the Workers' Voice Newspaper, official organ of the Antigua Trades & Labour Union and the Antigua Labour party. In 1951, Novelle was elected to the Antigua Legislative Coucsil, shortly after his entry into the field of politics. It was in 1951 to, that Universal Adult Suffrage was granted to the people of Antigua and Barbuda.

Sir Novelle was re-elected at the next General Elections, but left the Territorial Legislature to become a member of the new West Indies Federal Parliament, after successfully contesting Federal Elections on the West Indies Federal Labour Party slate in 1958. He was thereafter appointed a Minister in the First and only Federal Cabinet of Sir Grantley Adams.

During the brief life of the Federation of the West Indies, Sir Novelle Richards acted as Federal Prime Minister on several occasions. Upon the dissolution of the Federation in 1962, he returned home to Antigua.

Following the attainment of Independence in Association with Great Britain – Associated Statehood in 1967, Sir Novelle Richards was elected the first President of the Antigua and Barbuda Senate. However, later that same year, he was appointed by the Governments of the East Caribbean to be the first Diplomatic Trade Commissioner to Canada.

An author in his own right, Sir Novelle Richards was the composer of the lyrics of the National Anthem of Antigua and Barbuda. He also penned several other publications including **Tropic Gems**, **Twilight Hour** and **Vines of Freedom**.

In the service of his beloved country, Sir Novelle Richards has performed the duties of Trade Commissioner to Canada for Antigua and Barbuda, and on several occasions, Governor-General's Deputy.

Sir Novelle Hamilton Richards dies in Antigua while performing the duties of Governor-General's Deputy in 1986.

Tradition is one of those human traits which runs quite deepin families; it is no surprise therefore, that Gaston A. Browne, an offspring of Sir Novelle, has decided to make politics his vocation.

Gaston Browne successfully contested a seat in the House of Representative of Antigua, and has already began to make his mark on the national political landscape, clearly demonstrating that his family roots are firmly entrenched in the interests and welfare of the working class of the Nation of Antigua and Barbuda. The Hon. Gaston Browne is the Parliamentary Representative for the Constituency of St. Johns City West.

The late Novelle H. Richards was a life member of the International Biographic Association of Cambridge, England. He was married to physician, Dr. Ruby Lake and also fathered several children, one of whom served as the first High Commissioner to Canada for Antigua. Conrad Freeston died in office in Ottawa on 17th July, 1991.